It's Okay,
You Loved Him
. . . and you looked like a fool

Colette D. Orr

Orr Novels Trademark

ISBN-13: 978-0615884844
ISBN-10: 0615884849

Website: http://www.orrnovels.wix.com/colettedorr
Facebook: https://www.facebook.com/orr.novels
Twitter: https://twitter.com/orr_novels
Email: orrnovels@yahoo.com

Giving Thanks

First, I would like to thank God for giving me a love for writing! Lord, thank you for helping me realize my gifts and talents and giving me the courage to follow my dreams.

Next, I would like to thank my awesome parents, Council and Mary Orr. Thank you for your undying love and support. Thank you for always believing in me and never discouraging me to go for the unknown. I definitely couldn't have made it this far without the two of you.

To my amazing friends and the rest of my remarkable family members, thank you for everything! We have great times together and I'm so grateful to have you in my life. To Diane, you're not only my editor, you're also my friend. I couldn't have done this without you. Thank you!

Last, but certainly not least, I must thank my three wonderful children, Janessa, Katlyn, and Chaiden, whom I have dedicated this book to. I pray that your lives be filled with healthy friendships and relationships. You are my motivation and my inspiration! I'm so very thankful that God gave you to me.

Love Always,
XOXOXOXOXO

~INTRODUCTION~

This book mixes humor with everyday situations to reveal how easily anyone, (male or female) can become entrapped in an unhealthy relationship, regardless of their status, good looks, or their intellect.

It depicts the common struggles and temptations people face, especially when trying to live a pure and holy life before God.

This book is not about the vulnerability of falling in love, but the joy and peace that comes when a person discovers what genuine, true, and healthy love is.

~HAPPY READING~

~ O N E ~

Kirsten Denise Jabard was a well-to-do business woman whose smile lit up a room when she walked in.

"Good morning, everybody!"

"Good morning, Ms. Jabard!" everyone responded excitedly, as Kirsten walked through the building and into her office.

Kirsten was very well-respected among her co-workers. She had the tenacity of a bulldog, though, especially when negotiating business deals. Her title was Director, Business Strategy and Development. She was ambitious with street smarts and business smarts. She believed in earning all her promotions the good, old-fashioned way, working for them through blood, sweat, and tears.

Kirsten was a shrewd negotiator and a force to be reckoned with, if crossed. She could easily come off as a giant snob if it wasn't for that infectious smile.

Kirsten was stunningly beautiful. Her skin flawless, cheekbones high, sandy brown hair that gently hung over her shoulders, and hips and curves so graciously passed on by ancestors long gone to glory.

Although Kirsten was gorgeous, she bristled at the thought of men looking at her as a "piece of meat," but the reality was that some of her clients were only going to listen to her because she was beautiful. Kirsten knew this and so did Mr. Wayne, the CEO of her company.

One day Mr. Wayne overheard Kirsten complaining, "I hate when I meet with a client and he stares me up and down like I'm a plate of barbecue chicken fresh off the grill."

Mr. Wayne laughed, but later he decided to stop by Kirsten's office and discuss her concerns.

"Hey, Kirsten, I know you're busy; this'll only take a second of your time. I need to be blunt with you, though, so I apologize in advance if I offend you."

Kirsten looked up at Mr. Wayne as he made himself comfortable on her leather couch; she did a silent sigh.

Yes, I am busy and that one sentence alone just took more than a second, so I hope that's no indication of how long we're going to be here chitchatting.

Mr. Wayne grabbed a piece of chocolate from Kirsten's candy jar. "Oh, I love these, would you like a piece?" he offered, as if the candy belonged to him.

"No, thank you, I had several pieces when I filled the jar this morning," Kirsten responded cynically.

"Okay, well since there will be no small talk here, I suppose I'll go ahead and get to why I came."

Mr. Wayne gave Kirsten a serious look. "Kirsten, let's face it, most of our clients are old farts. They are male-chauvinists who are stuck in their ways and they're not gonna change. You're a very beautiful lady, Kirsten. No one can dispute that, but you're also one of the best negotiators I know. It's up to you to show them that you're not just attractive, but you're also smart. Show them that there's more to you than "meats" the eye.

Mr. Wayne held his fingers in the air and bent them twice to put emphasis on the word meat.

3

"Get it, Kirsten? Meats the eye,"
he chuckled.

"Yeah, I get it," Kirsten said,
giving him an agitated glance.

Mr. Wayne continued. "It's not
all bad though, Kirsten. Sometimes a
pretty face that sits on top of a
barbecue chicken body is the
determining factor that helps us win
these big contracts." Mr. Wayne
slapped his knee while laughing at his
barbecue chicken body joke. Kirsten
didn't crack a smile. Mr. Wayne rolled
his eyes at Kirsten's unwillingness to
appreciate great humor.

"Listen, Kirsten," he said, with a
stern voice. "Getting contract deals
equates to getting big bonuses and we
all like big bonuses. I'm sorry, but
folks like doing business with good-
looking people. It's just a fact. I
don't make the rules, I just tell you
what they are."

Mr. Wayne leaned closer to
Kirsten's desk and said, "Now, as
handsome as I am, do you think any of
these guys will get excited when they
see me walk in a room?" He gave her a
big smile displaying his disgusting,
brownish-yellow, coffee-stained teeth.

In return, Kirsten gave him a blank stare with her arms crossed.

Great! My boss is a professional pimp who obviously doesn't know how to tell time, nor has he been informed that teeth can be whitened, she thought as she glimpsed at Mr. Wayne, then gazed out the window.

He sat there waiting patiently for some kind of response from Kirsten, but there was none. He got up from the couch, waved his finger at Kirsten and said, "I can tell you're thinking bad thoughts about me, Kirsten, but one day you'll see that I only tell you the truth because I care."

Kirsten twisted her mouth. "Thanks for caring, Mr. Wayne," she said, waving goodbye to him as he left her office.

"You're welcome," he responded sarcastically.

Mr. Wayne could tell that Kirsten didn't like his speech, but he didn't care. She was very good at her job, but he knew she needed tougher skin if she was going to survive in this type of business.

On the surface, Mr. Wayne and Kirsten seemed to not like each other at all. Kirsten delighted in being uncooperative with Mr. Wayne and he delighted in pushing her buttons, so most of their interactions were bizarre and awkward to anyone watching. It was obvious that they had their differences, but despite those differences, they understood each other and were great business partners. There was no one Mr. Wayne trusted more with his business than Kirsten and although Kirsten would never admit it, she appreciated Mr. Wayne's honesty and his remarkable business sense.

I started working for Mr. Wayne straight out of college, when I was only twenty-two years old. For as long as I can remember, he's never sugar-coated anything for me. I might not like everything he does, like eating up all of my chocolate, but the one thing I can say is that Mr. Wayne will always tell me the truth, and it doesn't matter if I like it or not, Kirsten thought, as she leaned back in her chair with her arms folded across the top of her head.

Mr. Wayne had been in the construction business for over forty years, so Kirsten knew there was a lot to be learned from him. As much as she hated the male/female biases in the workplace, she knew she would have to keep her emotions out of it and just learn as much as she possibly could.

When Kirsten was first hired for the position, she would give herself pep talks. "Construction is a man's world," she'd say to herself. "Most of my interactions are with men, and not very good-looking ones at that," she grumbled. "But, I will learn to adjust to this business. I will be confident. I will be strong and I will refuse to be anything less than their equal," she'd proclaim every morning before going to work.

These talks eventually paid off for Kirsten, because over time, confidence and strength became natural attributes for her.

Whenever she won big contract bids, she rubbed her hands together, gave a mocking laugh, and yelled, "Oh, how sweet is the victory of conquering poor souls that got distracted by curves and hips. Gentlemen, there will always be more to me than meats the eye."

Kirsten couldn't believe she was repeating something she got from Mr. Wayne, who was the worst joke-teller ever, but his meat joke had rubbed off on her and eventually became an essential part of her victory speech.

Kirsten's attempts at being snobbish always made her laugh, though. She would never say anything like that in front of her mother. Mrs. Jan Jabard would not approve of Kirsten acting arrogant in any shape or form, even if it was just a joke.

Kirsten really wasn't a snob, though, she was just spoiled. Spoiled Rotten! Her dad, Mr. Jacob Jabard could be thanked for that. He worshipped the ground Kirsten walked on. She was an only child, so he did everything he could to give her the world. He taught Kirsten that if things were not the way she wanted them to be, she should just do without them until she could get exactly what she wanted.

"Kirsten, get what you want, how you want it, and don't let anyone tell you that you can't have it," Mr. Jabard would always say. Kirsten applied that logic to every aspect of her life, even if it wasn't realistic to do so.

Despite Kirsten being spoiled by her dad, she was still a down-to-earth country girl from Fountainwater, Georgia; a town probably not even on the map. Kirsten's mother made sure

that she stayed grounded in her country
roots and didn't buy into all that,
"The world is yours, you can have it,
any way you want it," nonsense. She
taught Kirsten to work hard for
whatever she wanted and not to sit
around waiting for some knight in
shining armor to come rescue her.

As Kirsten grew up, a lot of her
mom's time was spent undoing the
fairytale life Kirsten's dad tried to
instill.

"That mess is unrealistic! You're
gonna set this child up for failure
with all that foolishness," Mrs. Jan
would say to Mr. Jabard.

Mrs. Jan was very strict, but she
knew she had to be in order to offset
her husband's unrealistic teachings.
Kirsten had him so wrapped around her
fingers, it was pathetic. Mrs. Jan
wanted to make sure that Kirsten wasn't
just another pretty face in the
workplace, but unfortunately for
Kirsten and Mrs. Jan, in the world of
Business Development, pretty faces
mattered.

One thing Mrs. Jan could be proud
of though was that Kirsten definitely
wasn't looking for anyone to rescue

her. She was quite content being her own heroine. Kirsten was a God-fearing woman. She said she was waiting for a God-fearing man and he had to match all the traits of what she was looking for in her "ideal mate." Kirsten was now twenty-nine years old, and no man had even come close to having any of those traits.

Deep down inside, Kirsten knew she wasn't really waiting for anyone. She hadn't been interested in dating since she graduated college and started working full-time.

Whenever anyone asked her about dating or marriage, she'd defensively say, "I have enough friends and I don't want to get to know anyone new. I'm already heavily involved with church and work and that's enough to keep me busy. I'm happy being single. I go where I want, I do what I want, when I want, and I'm not giving any of that up just to say, 'I have somebody,' so please leave me alone," then she would flash her contagious smile, as she waited for them to kindly oblige her request.

Unfortunately for Kirsten, her best friend, Michelle didn't buy into any of that. She believed Kirsten was just making excuses because she was afraid to fall in love. Michelle knew that Kirsten was a control freak and the thought of losing control over anything always sent Kirsten into panic mode. Michelle believed that everyone should have someone special to share their life with and Kirsten was no exception.

For six months, she badgered Kirsten to go on a blind date with her cousin, Caleb, and for six months Kirsten adamantly said, "NO!"

"Kirsten, how do you expect to know whether a guy is what you want, if you never give any guys a chance?" Michelle asked, angrily.

Kirsten growled. "Okay, Shelly, if it will get you to shut up, I'll go on this stupid date. I don't know why it has to be a blind date though. That's just dumb! Why won't you send me a picture of the guy? That way I'll know if he's what I want before I waste time going out with him?"

"No! You judge people without getting to know them first."

"Hmmm, he must be ugly," Kirsten responded.

"See what I mean? He's not ugly, Kirsten. Just give him a chance. He's a really great guy."

"If he's so great, then why is he still single?"

"Don't be a hypocrite, Kirsten. You're still single and I think you're a great catch."

"Well, I'm single because I want to be and yes, I am a great catch. Thank you for noticing."

"No, you're single because you're a scary cat, Kirsten."

"Blah, blah! If I go out with this guy, you will leave me alone, right?"

Michelle huffed. "Yes, I will, but—"

"Great! Then I'll go. Now, goodbye, Shelly!" Kirsten said, disregarding the fact that Michelle wasn't done talking.

Michelle screamed with excitement, "Yay! Kirsten, you're gonna love him; he's so amazing!"

"Yeah, ok. Bye, Shelly," Kirsten said, while hanging up the phone.

After Kirsten hung up, Michelle immediately called Caleb.

"Hey, Caleb, what are you up to?"

"Hey, cuz, what's going on with ya?"

"Nothing much. Ummm, do you remember my friend Kirsten?"

"Yes, I remember the picture you sent me of the two of you."

"She's very beautiful, isn't she?"

"Yeah, she—"

"Well, the two of you will hit it off great and I would like y'all to meet," Michelle said, cutting Caleb off.

"Sure, I'd love to meet her."

"Caleb, you better treat her good! She's a great girl, so don't mess it up!"

"Dang, you act like I'm a player or something!"

"Well, all men have the tendency to play, so just make sure your tendency has been shut off."

"Michelle, you're my cousin and I love ya, but sometimes you're way too much for folks to handle. Just give me her number."

Michelle decided to ignore Caleb's sarcasm. She gave him Kirsten's number, along with several other relationship dos and don'ts, as if he had never been involved with a woman before. Caleb flipped through the television channels while he waited patiently for Michelle to tire herself out with all that talking she was doing.

The next day he called Kirsten. They chatted for a few minutes and she reluctantly agreed to go out with him on that upcoming Friday.

When Friday came, Kirsten made plans to leave work early so she could get dressed for her date, but instead, she got stuck with the last negotiation of the day.

Lance, her lazy co-worker, went home sick two hours before the negotiation was supposed to start, leaving Kirsten with no choice but to step in.

Kirsten knew Lance faked his sickness because he hadn't prepared for the meeting. Every time she asked him about the negotiation he brushed her off, saying "I got it, I got it!" Now he'd left her with only two hours to put a full negotiation together.

He could have at least told me about his scheme so I would have been prepared to step in. He didn't just get sick, he knew he was going to be "sick" the day Mr. Wayne told him that he'd be doing the negotiation. The little bum!

Kirsten just shook her head. The shameful part was that Lance was a very good negotiator when he decided to show up for work and actually do work while he was there. Kirsten had never met someone so lazy in all her life.

"That boy spends more energy trying to get out of work than he would if he actually just did the work," she'd say.

Kirsten felt her blood starting to boil. The thought of Lance risking such a huge contract deal made her very angry.

"This is a multi-million dollar negotiation, Lance. A MULTI-MILLION DOLLAR NEGOTIATION AND YOU BAILED OUT ON IT LIKE IT WAS NOTHING. NOW, I'VE GOT TO PICK UP THE PIECES!" Kirsten screamed at the walls in her office.

Lena, the receptionist could hear Kirsten yelling, so she decided to stay clear until everything calmed down, and by "everything," she meant Kirsten.

Kirsten tried to calm herself down, but it was kind of hard since she really wanted to go find Lance and choke him.

She took a few deep breaths. *Let me*

go ahead and call Caleb. This meeting will at least get
me out of that stupid date and I'll just never agree to
another one. Where's my cell phone?

Kirsten looked in the side pocket
of her purse where she normally kept
her phone, but it wasn't there.
"Grrrrrrr," she moaned. "Forget it!
I'll call him later. I have too much
on my mind right now anyway. This
negotiation is way too important for me
to be thinking about a phone call or a
stupid date."

Kirsten's negotiation meeting was
with the one and only, Mr. Jason B.
Glaznyte, a man everyone would kill to
do business with. Mr. Glaznyte was
rich and he spared no expenses.
Everything he built was state-of-the-
art. Mirrored-glass windows, beautiful
fountains, classy artwork, fitness
centers, daycare centers, cafeterias;
everything his employees could ask for,
he had it!

For the past ten years, Mr.
Glaznyte had a zero-percent turnover
rate. That was unbelievable to
Kirsten.

No one has left your company in the last ten years?
That is remarkable! We don't know how you do what
you do, Mr. Glaznyte, but my company wants a piece of

the pie.

Kirsten started rocking her head back and forth like she was preparing for a boxing match.

Mr. Glaznyte typically didn't like doing business with small construction companies because he felt small businesses didn't have the resources or the experience to do what he needed and wanted. Kirsten had never met him, nor did she care to. She assumed he was an uppity, old, white man from somewhere up north, like Oregon, who turned his nose up at home-grown southern companies.

She heard that he relocated to the Atlanta area to get another business off the ground. Someone told him about Mr. Wayne's company, so he decided to give them a try. Kirsten knew "give them a try" only meant that he was willing to hear what the company had to offer, so there was only one chance to make a good impression. That was even more of the reason Kirsten didn't understand why Mr. Wayne was so adamant about Lance doing the negotiation. She wasn't jealous that Lance was chosen, but everyone, including Mr. Wayne knew how unreliable Lance was. She didn't

understand why Mr. Wayne would take
that kind of risk with such a
prestigious business owner like Mr.
Glaznyte. She also didn't understand
why he protected Lance so much or why
he gave Lance so many chances. If
Kirsten was queen for a day, Lance
would be the first person she'd fire.

The only good part about the
shenanigans Lance pulled that day was
that it got her out of that dreadful
blind date with Caleb. However, now
she would have to spend her evening
stuck with old geezer Glaznyte, which
she wasn't sure was that much better.

Kirsten loved negotiating, but she
was very nervous about meeting with Mr.
Glaznyte. She heard he was
ridiculously tough on his business
partners. He'd ask millions of
questions just to see if he could
rattle them; he wanted to see how well
his potential partners performed under
pressure.

"I know he's going to be even
tougher on me because I'm a woman,
putting me in the same stereotypical
dumb blonde category as the rest of my
clients. That is until I prove him
wrong with my Power Ranger negotiation

skills," she said, laughing.

Although Kirsten knew she was a top-notch negotiator, she was still more nervous than ever to meet with Mr. Glaznyte.

She decided to stop stressing and try to relax! "Well, there's nothing I can do now, but try to prepare as much as I can and hope for the best," she told herself.

Kirsten started going through previous negotiation briefings.

Maybe I can pull some ideas that match some of the work Glaznyte is used to or maybe even pull some ideas that are totally different from what he's used to. I need to woo him with our company's abilities! If we get this contract, life around here will be beautiful for a very long time and my paycheck will be too.

Kirsten sat there with a huge smile on her face thinking of all the shoes she could buy with her bonus money.

~ T W O ~

"I can do this, I'm a good
negotiator! I can do this, I'm a good
negotiator!" Kirsten said repeatedly,
trying to calm her nerves.

"Yes, well, that's why I hired
you," she heard a voice say, as someone
opened her door. It was Mr. Wayne.

"You got a minute?" he asked. Not
waiting for an answer, he walked in and
sat down.

Mr. Wayne grabbed four pieces of
chocolate from Kirsten's candy jar and
popped all of them into his mouth.
Kirsten stared with disgust at all the
chocolate now caked up on Mr. Wayne's
teeth. She wasn't sure what to make of
his sudden visit, especially since he
knew she was preparing for her meeting
with Mr. Glaznyte.

Typically, Mr. Wayne tried to make
small talk before telling Kirsten why
he really came to see her, but this
time he got right to the point.

"Lance bailed out on ya, huh?" he

asked, disappointedly.

"Ummm, well, I think he was s—"

Mr. Wayne cut her off before she could get the word sick out of her mouth.

"Nah, Kirsten, we both know he wasn't sick. His heart just isn't into the business." Mr. Wayne gazed out of Kirsten's window. "I was really hoping he would prove that he was worth keeping around, ya know?"

Kirsten didn't know what to say. She could tell that this wasn't Mr. Wayne's typical, "shoot the breeze, give a ten minute lecture, make a few lame jokes, then leave" type meeting, so she kept quiet.

He wiped something from his eye and said, "When Lance's dad got hurt and couldn't work anymore, I promised him I'd take care of Lance. I promised I'd teach Lance the value of hard work and do the things his dad just wasn't able to do any more."

Kirsten's eyes looked like they were going to pop out of her head.

"You know Lance's dad?"

"Yep, I know him very well; he's my son and Lance is my grandson."

Kirsten felt like she just

swallowed a bag of sharp rocks.

"Kirsten, I overheard you talking about how lazy Lance was. Well, actually I overheard you yelling about how lazy he was."

"Oh, Mr. Wayne, I'm so sorry, that was so unprofessional of me. I didn't know anyone could hear me."

"No, no, there's no need to apologize. You didn't say anything that wasn't true. It just kind of hurts when you hear someone else say something you already know. I was only trying to groom him like I did you. I was hoping he could one day take over the company."

Kirsten quickly snapped out of her apology mode. *That would surely be the day I quit,* she thought.

"I would never ask you to work for someone like Lance, though," Mr. Wayne said, as if he was reading Kirsten's mind.

Thank God!

"Lance is a good negotiator, though. He has great potential," Mr. Wayne said, reassuringly.

"Yes, sir; yes, sir, he does."

"Kirsten, I know you're busy, so let me just get to the point. I would like you to try to work with Lance and teach him some good work ethics. Try to show him the ropes of this business; give him a chance to succeed, ya know? Then we'll reevaluate him in a couple of months to see if we should keep him on board or not."

Kirsten felt like someone just punched her in the face.

Gosh, Mr. Wayne, your timing really sucks! Why would you spring this on me now when you know I'm already stressed over this last minute negotiation? And what do you mean by "we?" We don't make reevaluation decisions, you do. You know I can't stand Lance, but you want me to show him the ropes! I'd much rather show him the door!

Kirsten took a deep breath and decided to leave those thoughts inside her head where they were best left unheard. She wanted to give Mr. Wayne some sort of response, but when she opened her mouth, nothing came out.

He said, "Now is probably not the best time to discuss this with you, but I know you'll do a great job with Mr. Glaznyte. I already knew Lance would bail, I was just hoping he wouldn't, that's all, but I knew he would. I'll make sure we compensate you for your hard work, Kirsten. It doesn't go unnoticed."

Ummm, what do you mean you already knew Lance would bail? Am I the only one who wasn't in on this little plan?

When Mr. Wayne got up to leave, he grabbed some more chocolate. As he was closing the door he looked back and said, "I really need your help with Lance, Kirsten. You know I don't ask for much, but he's my family legacy. If you could just do this for me, I'd really appreciate it."

Kirsten saw tears in his eyes. Mr. Wayne never showed any kind of emotion, so she knew he must have been heartbroken over the whole Lance situation.

Kirsten always gave Mr. Wayne a hard time, because he never tried to spare her feelings, but he had always been a great boss to her. When Mr. Wayne hired Kirsten, he immediately took her under his wings and within seven years promoted her to Director of Business Development, working directly for him.

Even before Kirsten was assigned to the Business Development Office, Mr. Wayne always gave her pointers on how to market a business successfully. He allowed her to rotate through all the departments, so she could get a feel for what the company had to offer to its clients. People always said that he was grooming her for the Business Development position, but Kirsten blew them off. Before Kirsten came on board, Mr. Wayne took care of all the marketing himself. He never trusted anyone to speak to potential clients about his company, but when Kirsten came along, he knew she was the one he'd been waiting for.

He didn't care that people said he favored Kirsten. "Who cares if folks make a big deal over me showing favoritism? If I see someone with potential, I'm going to invest in them. It doesn't mean I don't like the rest of my employees, but this is about running a successful business, not making friends. Anybody that works hard for me, I will invest in. It's as simple as that," he'd say, nonchalantly.

When Mr. Wayne left Kirsten's office, she knew she would do whatever he needed her to do, even if it was the impossible task of transforming lazy Lance into something useful, except she wasn't sure if Lance could be transformed.

Kirsten let out a huge sigh. She didn't have time to think about any of that now. She had to refocus on her negotiation.

Okay, enough interruptions and please no more surprises. Geez, his Grandson? I never saw that one coming. Things make a whole lot more sense now, but I'll have to finish these thoughts later. I have tons of work to do, so I need to get down to business.

Kirsten asked Lena to hold all of her calls for the rest of the day. "Oh shoot, I've got to call Caleb to cancel our date. Uggghhhh! Well, I'll have to do that after I get this presentation ready," she said, irritably.

Kirsten buckled down to finish preparing her briefing for Mr. Glaznyte. It took her about an hour and a half, but afterwards, Kirsten felt like a huge burden had been lifted off of her shoulders.

Normally, when Kirsten did negotiations, she liked to wear her hair pulled back in a bun, but there was no way she could do a bun this late in the game, so she got a few bobby pins and just pulled her hair out of her face. She did have on her favorite

outfit, though; a navy blue skirt suit.
At least she felt good about that.

*I just need this uppity Northerner to pay attention
long enough for me to give him my award-winning intro
speech, then I can close the deal with him eating out of my
hands,* she thought, laughing out loud.

When Lena heard Kirsten laughing,
she just shook her head. She didn't
know what was going on in Kirsten's
office that day.

Kirsten opened her door. "Lena,
can you please make copies for me while
I get freshened up for the meeting?"

"Sure," Lena replied, "How many?"

"Four, because I also need copies
for his bodyguards."

Lena laughed, "Bodyguards? Mr.
Glaznyte doesn't have any bodyguards."

"Well, from what I hear, he has
three guys that never leave his side,
so what would you call them?"

"BODYGUARDS!" they both yelled at
the same time, chuckling. Lena was
happy that Kirsten was in a good mood
again. Kirsten opened up the
conference room closet door where she
kept her secret mirror and "freshening
up" items. She put on a dab of her
favorite Victoria's Secret perfume,
then reapplied her mascara and lip

gloss.

Kirsten didn't wear much makeup, but whenever she had negotiations she always put on mascara to make her eyes stand out. She convinced herself that if she drew attention to her eyes, her clients would give her good eye contact.

"I need them to be in tune with my words, not my body. Lord knows when men see butts and hips, they lose all sanity. God, I will never understand why you made such simple-minded creatures," Kirsten said, sneeringly.

Lena laughed as she set the negotiation papers on the conference table. "Yes, Ms. Jabard, they do get distracted very easily, don't they?" They both laughed.

Lena went back to her desk to wait for Mr. Glaznyte to arrive and Kirsten decided to do an internet search for him so she could put a name with a face, but she couldn't find one picture of him.

"For a man so well-known, how can I not find a picture of him?"

"Lena, can you come here for a second?"

"Yeah, sure," Lena responded.

"Do you know what Mr. Glaznyte looks like?"

"No, I've never seen him, but I did hear that he was very handsome."

"Please, ain't nobody in this business handsome, Lena!"

Lena laughed. "Well, I don't know. I've never seen him for myself."

"Well, I already know his kind anyway."

Lena laughed some more and walked back to her desk, while Kirsten pictured what Mr. Glaznyte would look like.

He's a typical, old, snooty, Northerner, with a few salt and pepper hair strands combed over to the side to hide his bald spot which is courageously spreading across his shiny head. He's also an obnoxious, rude, know-it-all, who treats people like they're inferior to him, but today, Mr. Glaznyte, you've met your match.

She glanced herself over in the mirror and snickered at her unfounded, judgmental thoughts of a man she'd never met.

Kirsten, you have really got to stop being so judgmental of people. You don't even know this guy. Besides, this is a man who hasn't had any employees to leave his company in over 10 years. There must be something good about him.

Kirsten laughed and vowed to do

better with her judgmental ways. *That really isn't Christian like,* she thought.

Lena buzzed in, interrupting Kirsten's thoughts.

"Ms. Jabard."

"Yes, Lena?"

"Mr. Glaznyte is here, should I send him in?"

"Yes, please. Thank you, Lena."

As Kirsten closed the closet door, Mr. Glaznyte walked in.

"Hi, Ms. Jabard, I'm Jason B. Glaznyte, but please call me Jason."

When Kirsten looked at Mr. Glaznyte, she swore she peed on herself. He was absolutely the most beautiful thing she'd ever seen and not a single bodyguard was there with him.

MY GOODNESS! This man is fine! Those bodyguards might need to be here to protect him…from me!

Kirsten felt like she was standing there for days frozen solid, holding on to the hand of this 6'3" tall, dark, chocolate-covered Hershey's bar. He had light brown eyes that seemed to pierce through her soul.

Lord what a wonderful creation you have made, AMEN!

Kirsten continued to stand there,

seemingly stuck in the grasp of Mr.
Glaznyte's big, strong hands. *You
numbnut, let go of this man's hand before he thinks you're
crazy!*

Kirsten finally gathered her
composure, firmly shook his hand and
prayed that her drooling wasn't
obvious.

All of Kirsten's remarkable
negotiating skills seemed to vanish
into thin air as the presence of Jason
Glaznyte made her weak in the knees.

*Kirsten, what is wrong with you? Ain't nobody in
the world that fine! This is a multi-million dollar
business deal, of which you will get a nice commission, so
if you want to pay your bills and still have money left
over for shopping, I suggest you pull it together quick,
sister!*

The thought of that huge
commission was enough to snap Kirsten
back into reality.

As she walked to the front of the
board room, the clock caught her eyes.
Although her greeting with Mr. Glaznyte
seemed to have lasted for days, it had
not even taken one minute.

*Thank goodness! Maybe he didn't notice my goo-
goo eyes or sweaty palms after all.*

Kirsten couldn't believe all that
heart-pounding interaction happened in

less than one minute and Mr. Glaznyte seemed entirely oblivious to it all.

"I've heard great things about your company, Ms. Jabard. I'm excited to discuss how you will help me get to my next level."

Kirsten was very surprised. This is not at all what she had expected. It seemed as if Mr. Glaznyte had already made his decision before she even gave him her spiel; that gave Kirsten an extra boost of confidence.

She began to go into her award-winning speech, while Mr. Glaznyte listened attentively. He didn't ask any questions, but he did take lots of notes. What was most surprising was that he never looked down at her body; even when she made sudden movements or turns, she didn't catch him staring.

Does he not see all of this fabulousness standing in front of him? Does he not see barbecue chicken? He must be gay. God, he's so fine! Please don't let him be gay!

Kirsten couldn't believe that she actually wanted him to look at her; it was her absolute worse pet peeve, yet she wondered why he wasn't staring. There was something about this man that drove Kirsten insane; she was so

infatuated with him. His demeanor
exuded sexy confidence. Kirsten loved
a man who was confident, but not cocky.
He was everything Kirsten was attracted
to, but he didn't seem the least bit
interested.

Mr. Glaznyte wasn't gay by any
stretch of the imagination, but when it
came to business, he was ALL business.
Pleasure had its own time and place and
he separated the two very well.

"Sir, do you have any questions?"
she asked, as she finished her
briefing.

"No," he replied. "I've been
doing my homework on you guys for a
while. I've also spoken with Mr. Wayne
several times. He's a great man and
very thorough in his business. He
insisted that I receive the full
briefing from his staff. He said his
people are the best in the world, and I
must admit, I'm impressed. Thank you
for your time, Ms. Jabard. It was a
pleasure; I'll give you a call sometime
next week with my decision."

He shook her hand, said goodbye to
Lena and quietly left the building
without any small talk whatsoever.
Kirsten didn't know what to think.

If Mr. Wayne already told him everything he needed to know about the company, why would he set up this meeting? I guess that explains why it wasn't that risky for him to let Lance do the negotiation, though.

Kirsten couldn't help but feel that she had been left out of some secret meeting that everyone knew about but her. She was perplexed about everything that happened that day, so much that she totally forgot to call Caleb to cancel their date.

~ THREE ~

Kirsten and Lena were the last two people left at work.

"It's been one crazy day, Lena. Let's go home," said Kirsten.

"Now, those are the best words I've heard all day," Lena responded. They both grabbed their things and headed for the door.

As the two ladies walked to their cars, Lena asked, "How do you think it went with Mr. Glaznyte?"

Kirsten laughed. "Lena, I have no idea. Matter of fact, this entire day has been nothing but surprises for me. I don't know what to make of any of it."

"You didn't know Lance was Mr. Wayne's grandson, huh?"

Kirsten looked surprised, "You knew?"

"Receptionists know everything!" Lena said. "Did he ask you to mentor Lance?"

Kirsten's mouth dropped open, "You

do know everything!"

"Kirsten, you couldn't see that coming?" You're the best negotiator around. Mr. Wayne really wants to give this company to Lance one day, but Lance doesn't need to be in charge of nobody, you hear me?"

Kirsten laughed, "Yes, I definitely hear you on that!"

Then Lena got very serious. She said, "Mr. Wayne loves Lance like he gave birth to him himself. He'll do anything in the world for that boy, but Lance doesn't appreciate it. I probably shouldn't be telling you this, but Mr. Wayne feels he's the reason Lance's dad got hurt."

Kirsten listened more intensely.

"Lance's dad was in an accident on Mr. Wayne's motorcycle. Lance's mom hated motorcycles and wouldn't let him buy one. Mr. Wayne told him that women would never understand a man's need to be free with the wind, so he told him to take his bike for a spin down their country road. He wasn't even a mile away when two teenagers, who were drag-racing, collided right into him, leaving him severely paralyzed and basically brain dead. He is pretty much a vegetable now."

Kirsten's mouth fell open. "Oh, my gosh, Lena!"

Lena continued, "Lance's mother wanted nothing to do with him. Eventually, she found herself a younger man and started neglecting Lance, leaving him home alone to take care of his dad. Lance was only 12 years old, so Mr. Wayne and his wife, Mrs. Ella moved Lance and his dad in with them and they've been taking care of both of them ever since."

Kirsten stood there with her mouth open. Everything was starting to make sense. "That's why he's so protective of Lance and got so emotional when he asked me to help out."

"Yep," said Lena. "Mr. Wayne is a good man with a heart of gold, Kirsten. When I went through my divorce, I would have lost my mind if it wasn't for Mr. Wayne and Mrs. Ella.

Lena's eyes swelled with tears. Kirsten didn't know what she was about to hear next, but seeing how this day just kept getting stranger, she decided to brace herself for what was coming.

Lena said, "When I was five months pregnant with my fourth child, I came

home one day and found divorce papers
lying on the kitchen table with a note
attached. When I saw what the papers
were, I thought I was going to die
right there. My heart was pounding so
fast, I thought I was gonna have a
heart attack. As I was holding my
chest, I glanced up at the clock. I
knew my kids would be getting off the
bus soon and they would be expecting me
at the bus stop, so I told myself,
'Lena, there is no time for breakdowns
and there is no time for crying either.
You still have kids to raise.'"

Lena paused to try and gather her
composure.

"Every day, when my kids got home,
I made them mommy's special fruit and
cracker snacks and I said to myself,
'Today will be no different.' I washed
my face and hands, took a few deep
breaths, made my kids their snacks, and
headed to the bus stop.

"That night, after the kids were
in bed and asleep, I grabbed the
divorce papers again and I saw the note
in my husband's handwriting. It said,
'The bills are all paid up for six
months; this will free your mind while
you're deciding if you're going to keep

or sell the house. You can have everything, so we don't have to split any profits you make from the sale of the house.'

"Kirsten, I felt like someone had stabbed me. I glanced over at the bill box and saw all the monthly bills neatly lined up. They had six months' worth of money order receipts attached to each of them. I thought, 'How does he even know how much the bills are going to be each month?' I glanced closer at the receipts and saw that each bill was evenly calculated for what it was expected to cost over a six month period. My husband was very good with money, so I knew he worked out the six-month plan with all the billing companies. I looked for some explanation as to why he would do this to us, but there was nothing. I didn't know what to tell the kids. I couldn't bear telling them that their dad just left without a trace and he was never coming back."

Lena's tears began to flood uncontrollably while she was talking. It was evident that Lena was not over her divorce. Kirsten was not the emotional type, but she couldn't help but wipe tears as well, seeing all the pain Lena was obviously still in.

"Kirsten, I just turned off the lights, crawled into bed, and cried myself to sleep.

Around 5:00 the next morning, the phone rang. I thought it was my husband calling to tell me why he did this to us, but it was Mr. Wayne."

Kirsten seemed shocked that Mr. Wayne would be calling so early in the morning, but she dared not interrupt while Lena was talking.

"He said, 'Good morning, Lena. Sorry to call you so early, but we have a power outage at work, so you don't have to come in today.' Kirsten, I knew God had something to do with that because I couldn't bear going into work that day anyway. I tried to thank Mr. Wayne for his call, but instead I just burst into tears over the phone. He was so worried about me. He asked, 'What's wrong Lena?' in his fatherly voice. I tried to apologize to him several times for crying like that, but I just couldn't stop. I told him everything that happened. He told me that his wife was on her way to help me get the kids ready for school and he told me to take two weeks off to clear my head. He said, 'Consider it a paid bonus vacation for being so dedicated to the company all these years.' I tried to thank him again, but his kindness only made me cry more. I really didn't want anyone to come over, but I don't know how I would have done it without Mrs. Ella that morning."

"Wow," was all Kirsten could say.

Lena kept talking.

"About three days later, my husband finally called to tell me he had moved to Los Angeles to pursue his dreams of being in a music band. He said they made him an offer he couldn't refuse. He knew I wouldn't understand, so that's why he handled it the way he did. He assured me there was enough money in the bank for us to carry on our lifestyle without him. I asked, 'How could there be enough money in the bank when we never had any money?' I didn't even give him a chance to respond; I just slammed the phone down. I didn't know how to go on without him, but for the sake of the kids I knew I had to.

"I eventually began to function again. Mrs. Ella came over from time to time to check on me and to give me a break from the kids. I finally came back to work after two and a half weeks because Mr. Wayne thought I needed a little more time. All kinds of rumors were flying around the workplace because I had been gone for so long. Mr. Wayne assured everyone that there would be disciplinary actions for anyone caught discussing my family business. I wasn't sure how he was going to discipline people for gossiping, but at least the threat stopped everyone from talking about me." Lena gave Kirsten a faint smile. "I couldn't have done it without them, Kirsten. They are both angels in disguise."

I've never dislike Mr. Wayne by any means, but I wouldn't exactly describe him as an angel either, Kirsten thought.

Kirsten stood there staring at Lena, who at this point was covered in tears. She wasn't sure what to say or do to help. Kirsten wasn't really the touchy-feely type, but she knew Lena needed a hug, so she decided to give her one, along with some comforting words.

"Lena, I didn't know you had been

through so much. I'm so glad you
survived."

After Kirsten offered her words of
comfort, she felt dumb. *"I'm glad you
survived." I can't believe that was the best I could come
up with.* Lena didn't seem to mind, though.

Lena was a very private person.
She didn't realize how much she had
shared with Kirsten. She liked
Kirsten, but not enough to share her
whole life story with her. Lena's
intentions were only to tell Kirsten
about Mr. Wayne, but there she was,
crying on Kirsten's shoulders like she
had known her forever. Lena quickly
wiped away her tears, gathered her
composure, and told Kirsten she had to
go because her best friend was coming
into town that weekend.

"That is wonderful," Kirsten said.
"Maybe I'll call up my three best
friends and see if they want to get
together this weekend, too."

"Three best friends?" Lena asked,
skeptically. "I don't think I could
trust three women, one is more than
enough for me."

Kirsten laughed and said, "We are
more like sisters. We've been best
friends since elementary school; we

would die for each other."

As Lena walked away, she said, "I couldn't imagine feeling that way about anyone."

Kirsten just smiled, as they waved goodbye to each other and left to plan the upcoming weekend with their friends.

As Kirsten drove home, she couldn't help but think about everything that happened that day. Her heart really hurt for Lena. Lena was a great receptionist and Kirsten knew that Lena had so much untapped potential. She really wanted to help her move up the corporate ladder, but Lena was very content where she was.

Mr. Wayne always made sure she was off work every day by 3:00 pm so she could be home when her kids got off the bus. Although her kids were older now and didn't need her there when they got off the bus anymore, Lena still felt she owed them that stability, since they didn't have it from their father. His leaving them was something Lena would probably never get past. Whenever someone spoke of her ex's budding career as a guitar band leader, Lena's face would glaze over. She didn't think someone should be blessed with a good career if they left their pregnant wife and three kids to achieve it.

The kids' dad eventually came back around. Although he had since married someone else, the kids stayed with him each summer and spring break. He and Lena would alternate Thanksgiving and Christmas holidays. Lena hated when her kids went to stay with their dad; she thought they should hate him as much as she did, but one apology was all it took for the kids to welcome their dad back with open arms.

She tried not to show her bitterness. She knew they needed their dad, but she felt like she still needed him too.

Kirsten didn't understand why Lena hadn't moved on by now. She was smart and beautiful, but Lena avoided any conversations that dealt with men. She didn't even drool over Mr. Glaznyte when he came into the office.

How could she be alive and not drool over that fine piece of chocolate?

Lena's heart just wasn't in a position to bear the pain of being hurt again. Casanova himself could have walked in and she would have shown no interest.

Kirsten was feeling bad for Lena. To keep from crying, she decided to turn on the radio and listen to some music. As she reached for the knob, her phone rang; it was her mother.

"Hey, momma, I'm glad you called, I was going to call you later."

"You were?"

"Yeah, I would like to invite Shelly, Beatriz, and Saidah down to the house tomorrow for a girls' night out."

"Oh, that would just be wonderful, y'all come on!" Mrs. Jan hadn't seen the girls in years.

"Well, I gotta call and ask them first; you know they're married with kids now," Kirsten said.

"Tell them to just bring their kids and their husbands with them, we'll be glad to have everybody."

"Oh, no, no," Kirsten responded.

Mrs. Jan laughed because she knew when those girls got together they forgot about everything else but each other; they all turned back into ten-year-old school girls.

"Okay, well, whatever y'all decide is fine with me."

"Okay, momma, I'll call you back and let you know if we're coming for sure."

"Okay, bye, baby girl," Mrs. Jan said, and then hung up the phone. Her mom was so excited that she forgot she was the one who called Kirsten. Kirsten was so thrilled about seeing everyone that she couldn't even wait until she got home to call the girls. She pulled into a gas station and called Michelle.

"Hey, Shelly, this is Kirsten."

"I know who you are, girl!"

Kirsten laughed, "I need you to call Beatriz and I'll call Saidah, so we can all be on three-way, okay?"

"Okay, sure. Hold on," Michelle responded, as she clicked over to call Beatriz.

Once all the girls were on the phone, Kirsten said, "What do y'all think about doing a girls' night out tomorrow night? We can all meet up at my mom's house and then go to the Charlie Wilson concert in Tallahassee."

They didn't even hesitate. "Yes, I'm in," they all said, simultaneously, like they were identical triplets.

"Awesome," Kirsten said, "I'll see

y'all tomorrow."

All the girls screamed with excitement. Then they hung up and thought about how they were going to tell their husbands that they were leaving for the weekend for a girls' night out.

Kirsten called her mom back and told her that they were coming, then she remembered; "Momma, did you need something when you called earlier?"

"Oh, just to hear your voice, child, and I did that already, so there's nothing else I need. I'll see y'all tomorrow."

"Okay. Bye, momma."

Fountainwater was a perfect meeting spot; it was about a 3-hour drive from where all the girls lived and it was only an hour from where the concert was.

When Kirsten got home, she had planned to pack for her trip, but when she saw her bed, she just crashed. She was so tired that she didn't even turn the lights off or take off her work clothes or remember that she was supposed to be on a date with Caleb.

~FOUR~

The next morning, Michelle called and woke Kirsten up. Michelle was screaming in the phone, so it took Kirsten a minute to understand what she was saying. Michelle screaming was nothing new; everyone knew she had anger issues and any little thing would send her into a fit of rage.

"Shelly, please calm down, you're making my head hurt with all of that screaming," Kirsten said, as she moved the phone away from her ear. That's when she caught a smidgen of Michelle saying, "Caleb is a good man, Kirsten. Why did you stand him up?"

Kirsten dropped the phone. "Oh, my gosh, I forgot to call Caleb." She picked the phone back up and tried to explain to Michelle about her crazy day at work and how she had every intention of calling Caleb to cancel their date, but trying to explain anything to Michelle was useless. She would not let Kirsten get a word in.

Shelly just likes hearing herself fuss, Kirsten thought, but she was the only one who

could deal with Michelle when she would
throw tantrums. Kirsten's coping
mechanism was usually just to hang up
on her, which is exactly what she did.
"I'll call her back later when she's
tired of listening to all that noise
she's making."

Kirsten looked at her phone and
saw several missed calls from Caleb
from the night before. "Oh gosh, I
didn't even hear the phone ringing."
She tried to call him back, but he
didn't answer, so she left a message.
"Hi Caleb, this is Kirsten. I'm so
sorry about yesterday, work got crazy
and—"

As she was trying to explain,
Michelle was beeping in on the other
line. Kirsten hurried and finished her
apology, promised Caleb she'd make it
up to him and clicked over to finish
listening to Michelle fuss. Without
skipping a beat, Michelle kept right on
going as if Kirsten never even hung up
on her.

Kirsten listened for a little
while longer, then she said, "I love
you, Shelly. I have to go get dressed
now. I'll see you in a few hours,
okay?"

Michelle stopped fussing and said, "I love you too, I know things were crazy at work, but you better make it up to my cousin."

"I will, I will. I'm very sorry about that. See you later. Drive safe."

"Okay, you too. Bye," Michelle responded.

With all the badgering Michelle was doing, it was amazing that she was still able to hear Kirsten explaining why she forgot about her date with Caleb.

"Nobody can fuss, while still listening like Shelly," Kirsten said, laughing. "That's what makes Shelly so special, though; I wouldn't trade her for anything in the world." Kirsten smiled, rolled out of bed and started packing for her trip.

The four girls arrived safely at Mrs. Jan's house. Michelle got there before anyone else, probably because she didn't have any kids or pets to slow her down. And her husband was probably very happy to not have to hear her mouth for the weekend.

Kirsten's parents' house was like a second home to Michelle. Actually, all the girls looked at the Jabards' house as their second home and they looked at Mrs. Jan as their second mom.

Michelle and Kirsten had been best friends since first grade; they were kindred spirits and loved each other like blood sisters. Beatriz and Saidah came into the fold around third grade. Beatriz was only nine years old when her family moved to the United States from Puerto Rico. It was her first day of school and the teacher wanted to make her feel welcomed, so she paused her lesson plan and allowed the kids to look up the meaning of their names on her computer. The teacher was pregnant so she frequented the baby-naming websites quite often. The kids were all ecstatic to find out what their names meant. It turned out that Beatriz's and Saidah's names both meant joy and happiness. The teacher noticed how they smiled at each other when they discovered this, so she moved Beatriz to the empty desk next to Saidah. The girls both liked that idea and immediately became the best of friends.

At the end of the school year, the third graders put on a chorus production of Alice in Wonderland.

Alice had a singing part and several
girls auditioned, including Kirsten,
Michelle, Beatriz and Saidah. These
four girls stood out so much that the
chorus teacher rearranged the entire
script so all of them could play the
part of Alice. She thought it would be
good to have such great diversity
within the one main character.

Kirsten was African-American; a
medium shade of brown. Michelle was
Caucasian, Beatriz was Puerto Rican and
Saidah was what one would call the
darkest of African-American chocolate.
Her mom wanted to do away with the
"American" part and just call
themselves full-blooded Africans. She
felt it was a disgrace how African-
Americans forgot where they came from.
She wanted to make sure Saidah
understood her heritage, that's why she
gave her an African name.

The girls worked very well
together in the play and everyone loved
the diversity. From then on, no one
could pull them apart. They became
best friends and were known as the four
rays of the rainbow. That nickname
stuck with them until they graduated
high school.

Michelle and Kirsten was both the
only child, that was until seventh
grade, when Michelle found out that she
had half brothers and sisters living a
few towns over. Michelle's mom was
outraged and kicked her dad out of the
house. Until then, Michelle thought
her parents' marriage was perfect. She
hated her father for cheating, so she
naturally clung to Kirsten's dad, who
was always faithful to Mrs. Jan.

Mrs. Jan would always say to the
girls, "Marriage is about trust and
honesty. You can't worry about what
people say in the streets, as long as
you trust your spouse enough not to
believe it's true."

Mr. Jabard was very handsome and
charming. He could have very well had
another family too, but Mrs. Jan
trusted him to be faithful to her and
he was. He said he didn't have any use
for another woman because God gave him
everything he needed in the one he had.
Michelle would cry every time she heard
him say that. She wished her father
felt the same way about her mom, or
just never finding out otherwise would
have been good enough as well.
Michelle's situation made Kirsten think

of Lena, although their stories were very different.

The girls were all piled up on Kirsten's bed talking about old times. Mrs. Jan yelled for them to come eat dinner, but they didn't hear her. They were too busy laughing like little school girls. Mr. Jabard said they sounded like cackling hens.

Mrs. Jan was walking into Kirsten's room when Beatriz said to Kirsten, "Girl, I can't believe Mr. Jabard still owns this farm." Kirsten responded with a super-Southern accent, "Can't give up these here cows, pigs and chickens now can we, darlin'?"

The girls all chuckled, but through Kirsten's peripheral vision, she could see her mother's eyes piercing through her skin. Mrs. Jan didn't say a word, but the look she gave Kirsten said enough. Kirsten knew her mom did not appreciate that joke.

"I'm sorry momma, you know I would never insult daddy's work," Kirsten said, without Mrs. Jan even having to tell her what she was thinking.

Mrs. Jan replied abruptly, "Now look here, young lady, your daddy is the hardest working man I know. This

farm business helped put you through
college so you could make something out
of yourself. We went without many days
just so you could have, so I suggest
you don't get too big for your
britches."

Kirsten's eyes swelled up with
tears and so did all of her friends'.
Michelle was always ready for a good
cry.

"I'm so sorry, momma," Kirsten
said.

All the girls knew that Kirsten
adored her father and she would never
say anything to disrespect him. Mrs.
Jan knew it too, but she still felt it
was her motherly duty to keep Kirsten
in check.

"If she was grown enough to say
it, she was grown enough to get scolded
for it," was Mrs. Jan's philosophy.

"Now y'all girls come on in here
and get some supper before it gets
cold," Mrs. Jan said, putting forth no
effort to console Kirsten, who was
about to burst into a flood of tears.
Mrs. Jan had tough love with Kirsten,
but when Kirsten needed her momma, she
knew no one could beat Mrs. Jan's
nurturing support.

The cackling hens all gathered around the dinner table. Mr. Jabard was sitting at the head of the table in his King chair.

"Do you feel like a king, Mr. Jabard?" asked Michelle.

"Yes, honey, actually I do. I like it when Mrs. Jan treats me like the king of the house."

Mrs. Jan smiled and said, "You'll always be king at any house I live in."

Kirsten wondered if that was the secret to her parents' successful marriage.

Make your husband feel like a King! Got It, Kirsten thought, as she did an inward chuckle, even though she was still feeling like dirt from what she said about her dad.

Michelle's eyes began to swell with tears because of Mr. and Mrs. Jabard's romantic dialogue, but it was quickly interrupted when Beatriz and Saidah both hit her upside the head.

"Gosh, Shelly, you'd cry if a dog ate a flea!" Saidah said. They all giggled.

Mr. Jabard blessed the food and the cackling hens gobbled down their food like they hadn't eaten in days, giggling at absolutely everything all the way through dinner. The Jabards loved the company, even if all the laughing was a bit silly.

After dinner, the girls helped clean the kitchen then quickly ran off to get dressed for the Charlie Wilson concert. They were all packed in the car and ready to drive off when Kirsten ran back into the house, as if she had forgotten something. She gave her mom a big hug and kiss on the cheek.

Without Kirsten having to say a word, Mrs. Jan smiled and said, "I know you didn't mean it, honey. Just don't let it happen again."

"I won't momma," Kirsten responded, then she gave her dad a big "I'm sorry" hug and kiss too and ran back to the car.

Mr. Jabard was still sitting at the table reading the paper. "What was that about?" he asked, with a puzzled look on his face.

"Oh, nothing. The job of a mother is never done, that's all."

Mr. Jabard took that as an acceptable answer, finished drinking his sweet tea, then got up to watch the news. He left his plate on the table, just as Mrs. Jan wanted him to. She wouldn't have it any other way. She figured as hard as he worked to make sure she had whatever she needed and wanted, the least she could do was take his plate to the sink and wash it for him.

"How a king gonna take his own plate to the sink?" she'd ask jokingly. Mr. Jabard didn't think all that was necessary because he knew Mrs. Jan appreciated everything he did for her, but her sweet-talking always made him blush. After 30 years of marriage, there was still a special glow when the Jabards were around each other. They said their secret was "Keeping folk outcha business."

Kirsten's father had always been a farmer, as far back as Kirsten could remember. Mr. Jabard had a strong but gentle presence about him. Mrs. Jan was a homemaker, a Proverbs 31 woman at her best. During her free time of not tending to the house, Mrs. Jan would ride around the local communities and pick out land for her husband to buy. He was so crazy in love with her, he would have bought the whole United States, while dancing on his head if

she asked him to. She loved him just
as much. Kirsten's dad was truly a
manly man. He paid all the bills,
fixed everything that was broken,
maintained the farm, took care of all
the yard work, kept the cars spotless,
and served the Lord faithfully.

Mr. Jabard truly loved Mrs. Jan;
the kind of love the Bible said a man
should have for his wife. He knew she
could have gone to college on an
academic scholarship and never given
him a second thought. She could have
gotten her degree, married some rich
doctor, lived on a hill with a white
picket fence and have everything she
ever dreamed of, which, he was sure
didn't include cow manure. Mrs. Jan
was smart as a whip. That's why he
bought every piece of land she told him
to buy. Sure enough, the property
value would go up, then someone would
buy the land and build a house. It
never failed; Mrs. Jan had a keen eye
for property. Mr. Jabard called her
his "valued property piece." Most
people gave them a funny look whenever
he'd say that, but Mrs. Jan would
always blush and say, "Oh, stop that,
Jacob."

They were high school sweethearts.
He asked her to marry him at their high
school graduation party, in front of
everybody. He had already gotten the
blessing from her dad. Mrs. Jan's dad
loved Mr. Jabard and knew his baby girl
would be well taken care of. Mr.
Jabard was a hardworking man, with
master negotiating skills. That's why
it was so easy for him to buy up land
at a low price and then resell it for a
nice profit. People would scratch
their heads at how he made such huge
profits on his property.

It really wasn't his passion,
though. He only did it because he knew
it made his wife happy. He could care
less if he never bought or sold another
property a day in his life. His true
love was farming; tilling the soil,
growing crops, and tending to his
animals.

Mrs. Jan sacrificed for him, too.
She loved him, but she didn't want to
get married just yet. She wanted to do
other things with her life, like
establish a career and travel the
world. Then she would get married, to
Mr. Jabard, of course. Back then, her
dad was adamant that she should just be

a wife and bear lots of babies, so
that's what she decided to do. Except
when she had Kirsten, she had a lot of
complications. The doctor told her
that she shouldn't have any more kids
because it might cost her her life.
Mr. Jabard said he didn't know what he
would do if he lost her. The doctor
said it was better for her to have a
hysterectomy, so that's what they did.

Mrs. Jan didn't have any regrets
about how her life turned out. Her
husband let her make all the decisions
on the properties he bought, so she
said that was a good enough career for
her. She would always tell Kirsten,
"Marriage is about sacrifices. You
have to figure out what you can live
with and what you can live without."

Kirsten didn't know what Mrs. Jan
was talking about, but she noticed that
whenever her mom gave her marriage
advice, she'd always lean over like she
was telling her some big secret.

Perhaps they were great words of
wisdom from 30 years of marital bliss,
but Kirsten just blew those types of
conversations off. She didn't care
about all that love stuff. She was
happy with her career and she wasn't

sure if settling down and having kids
was for her. One day, maybe, but
definitely not in her immediate future.

~FIVE~

As the girls headed to the concert, they reminisced about old times. All of them were now married with children, except Kirsten and Michelle. Michelle was married, but she didn't have any kids.

Michelle sat there bragging about how wonderful her husband, Matt was. He was always surprising her with gifts. Matt loved Michelle dearly and desperately wanted to have children, but Michelle refused to get off birth control pills. She was afraid she would find out that Matt had a "secret life" like her father and she couldn't bear for her children to go through what she went through.

Matt would never cheat on her, though. On several occasions Kirsten told Michelle that she needed to get counseling before it caused problems in her marriage, but Michelle would shut down whenever anyone talked about her and Matt having kids. She loved Matt, but she just couldn't bring herself to want to get pregnant.

"Michelle, do you remember how people were so surprised when you married a white guy?" Saidah asked.

"People are stupid. They automatically assumed that I like black guys because my best friend is black. That's ridiculous."

Michelle had never dated a black guy. Not because she was against interracial dating, she just always seemed to be in love with some blonde-haired, blue-eyed dude.

Kirsten chimed in, "But what got me was how folks would call her the angry black woman because she was loud and angry all the time. People thought that joke was funny, but I didn't like it at all. I hate how black women are stereotyped. Michelle is white, loud and angry! I'm black, quiet and conservative, so tell me again how that stereotype makes sense? People need to be judged individually, not collectively. We are not all alike!"

Michelle laughed, "Shut up, Kirsten. I'm not angry all the time; just when people tick me off!"

"Well people sure do tick you off

a lot," Saidah said.

Kirsten started on her rampage again. "It makes me so mad how the world typecasts people without even knowing them." Suddenly, Kirsten realized that's exactly what she did to Mr. Glaznyte. She laughed. *Well, there you have it, I'm no better than anyone else.*

The girls kept talking and Kirsten's mind drifted back to her meeting with Jason. *Lord, I wish you would have told me you were making men that look like that. I would have been back on the dating scene a long time ago. Whew!*

She shook her head and decided to interrupt whatever the girls were talking about.

"You guys will never believe how fine one of my potential clients were today. I totally stereotyped him as an old, white, ugly, bald guy."

"Why the old, ugly man gotta be white?" Michelle asked, "And you should be ashamed of yourself for just giving us that long speech about typecasting and equality, when you judged this man and you had never even met him." Michelle said, as she rolled her eyes. Kirsten couldn't help but laugh.

"She got you on that one,

Kirsten," said Saidah.

Beatriz disputed, "I really don't think it's wrong to identify people by their race as long as they're not trying to be derogatory. I don't care if someone refers to me as 'the Puerto Rican girl over there,' because that's what I am. I just hate when people call me Mexican. I'm not Mexican! I really wish people would get that right."

The girls laughed really loud. Saidah shouted, "Nobody knows the difference, Beatriz!"

Beatriz didn't laugh at all, "Well, nobody knows the difference between African-Americans who pretend they're full blooded Africans, but have never stepped foot in Africa, Saidah."

Saidah gave Beatriz a look that could kill and Beatriz returned the same look right back to her.

The car became totally quiet, then Michelle let out a hearty laughed. "That's why y'all should be white, because white people don't have all these hang ups." Everyone burst into laughter because they knew she was right.

"Diversity is what makes the world

so beautiful," Kirsten responded. "I don't understand why people try to turn it into a bad thing."

"People fear the unknown, Kirsten. 'They are different than me, therefore I don't like them,' is the way some people think. They could just as easily take the time to get to know the person, but instead, they group everyone together and give them all one label. It's really sad," said Beatriz.

All of a sudden Michelle got angry. "Speaking of diversity, why did you stand my cousin up, Kirsten? Was it because he is white?

"Nope, it couldn't have been that because she was drooling over an old, white, ugly, bald guy at work today," Saidah said, giggling.

Everyone knew Michelle was about to go into one of her fits of rage, so Beatriz put her hand over Michelle's mouth and said, "Not this weekend, Michelle, shut it up," then Beatriz turned to Kirsten. "Now, Kirsten, I do want to hear all about this blind date and about this super-fine client that had you drooling at work, but to keep Michelle's mouth closed, you can tell us about her cousin first."

Kirsten started telling them about Caleb, but it only lasted two seconds before Michelle took over.

"Okay, so he's my first cousin on my momma's side and he's in the military on recruiting duty in Atlanta. For six months I've begged Kirsten to give Caleb a chance and all she would say was, 'Michelle, I'm happily single. I work ten hours a day and on the weekends I have dates with my couch, my dog, and my movie flicks. I don't have time for men, so leave me alone.'"

Kirsten interrupted and said, "Well, Shelly that's true, I don't have time to date."

"Hush! You have time to drool over ugly, bald men," Michelle yelled.

"He is bald, but he sho ain't ugly," Kirsten replied.

The girls laughed and Michelle chimed back in. "So why did you agree to go out with Caleb if you didn't want to?"

Beatriz and Saidah both answered, "Because that was the only way she could get you to shut up."

Michelle laughed, "Yes, y'all know that's true, but Kirsten, be honest. Is it because he's white? We know you love dark-skinned men and you won't accept anything different than what's on that crazy list of yours."

"What list?" Saidah asked.

"You know, in high school Kirsten made a list of the things she wanted in a man and if he doesn't have everything on there, she won't even give him a second glance," Michelle explained.

"Yeah, I forgot about that. Kirsten, please tell me you don't still base your life and relationships on that dumb list. You're never gonna get married that way. Those lists are unrealistic. They make you rule out common sense," Saidah responded.

Up until that point, Kirsten pretended to not be a part of the conversation, but Saidah must have hit a nerve because Kirsten responded with an attitude, "No, they do not make you rule out common sense, Saidah, and I will be happily single until I get what's on my list. God knows what I like and He will send him to me."

"No, Kirsten. God knows what you need. He doesn't care about what you like," Michelle said.

"Actually, I believe He can give you both, but you have to be open for

70

change and not have your mind set on "liking" one thing. Allow yourself to think outside the box and you'll see that there are a lot of things and people you will like," Beatriz added.

Michelle jumped in, "And that's why I'm trying to get her to go out with my cousin. I know what Kirsten needs, and Caleb is it. If she gives him a chance, he'll be what she wants too."

"I want what I want and I'm not settling for anything else, but I will go out with Caleb because I gave you and him my word," Kirsten responded.

Michelle rolled her eyes. "Why bother if you're only gonna stay stuck in your stupid ways? You need to get off of your high horse, Kirsten, and stop acting like you're better than everybody else."

"Excuse me! I'm not on any high horse and I don't act like I'm better than anyone. Saidah, do I act like I'm better than other people?"

"Yep," Saidah said, nonchalantly, as she continued to stare out the window.

Kirsten gave Saidah a dirty look and turned to Beatriz. "Beatriz, you are the rational one in our group. Please tell them that I do not act like I'm better than others."

Beatriz looked at the floor, then back at Kirsten with a helpless look on her face. "Kirsten, I love you, but yeah, you can be a bit snobbish," she replied.

Kirsten threw up her hands. "I can't believe y'all! I've never treated y'all like you were beneath me. Why would you say something like that?"

Beatriz answered, "No, Kirsten. Not us, because we're in your circle. Once someone is in your circle, you have unconditional love and patience for them, but if you don't really know someone, then yes, you come off as arrogant. I'm not saying that you are arrogant, but that is the vibe you send."

"That's so not true, Beatriz. I am very approachable," Kirsten responded angrily.

The girls all laughed out loud. "No, Kirsten," Michelle added. "You are not approachable to people you don't know or even to most of the people you do know, but once they've proven that they can be trusted, you

let your guard down. Then you become
as down-to-earth and relaxed as a pig
in a puddle of mud."

They laughed some more, while
Kirsten pouted silently with her arms
crossed. Her mind drifted back to her
encounter with Mr. Glaznyte. *Well, I
definitely wasn't on any high horse with Mr. Hunk of
Lusciousness today.* She smiled and stared
off into space, forgetting all about
her friends, who had now moved on and
were flapping their jaws about
celebrity gossip.

"Kirsten, I think you're afraid to
date," Michelle shouted, trying to pull
Kirsten back into the conversation.
Everything had to be shouted with
Michelle. There was no volume control
on her mouth. "You're afraid that if
you fall in love, you'll no longer have
control over your emotions, and you
don't like to lose control of anything.
You drown yourself in work so you'll
always seem too busy for a man. You're
twenty-nine years old, Kirsten, fastly
approaching thirty. You're gonna be an
old maid if you don't go ahead and find
someone to settle down with."

Michelle kept talking, and
although Kirsten had tuned her out a

while ago, she did hear when Michelle
said she was afraid to fall in love.

"What's wrong with being single?"
Kirsten asked. "I don't understand why
people look at it like it's some sort
of plague. I can buy my own meals, pig
out on my own couch, in my own house,
watching my own TV. I don't need a
man!" Kirsten barked, then she let out
a deep sigh. "I just want the right
one, you guys. I want a God-fearing
man, just like my father. When he
comes, I'll know it; I'll feel it, and
we'll live happily ever after."

"See, that's the problem right
there," Michelle bellowed. "There is
no such thing as happily ever after if
you don't work at it and how will you
know he's the right one if you only
allow yourself to like one type of man?
Get your head out of the clouds,
Kirsten. Marriage is hard. You have
two people trying to head in the same
direction with two different ideas and
agendas. They are trying to get to the
same place, and not necessarily at the
same time. The only way marriage can
work is if couples get rid of their
unrealistic ideologies and get on the
same page about how they're going to

travel their journey together. It's about sacrifice, Kirsten, and compromising your warped way of thinking."

After Michelle finished talking, there was complete silence in the car. All of the girls were disgusted by Michelle's hypocritical speech, knowing she refuses to give her husband a baby because of her own "warped way of thinking."

As soon as Michelle was done, she knew she had just given that speech to herself. In the rearview mirror, Kirsten could see Michelle's eyes watering. Kirsten turned on the radio to try to change the subject. Saidah, who was in the front seat with Kirsten, couldn't resist lashing out. "Is that why you won't give your husband a baby, because you're sacrificing?" she mumbled. Kirsten turned the music up louder hoping that Michelle didn't hear Saidah.

"What did you say?" Michelle screamed, almost jumping out of her seat. Kirsten didn't know whether to try to calm Michelle down or just stop the car and let the girls go at it on the side of the road.

"You went too far, Saidah,"
Kirsten whispered softly. Kirsten knew
Michelle could be a hand full, but
bringing that subject up was just
something Saidah shouldn't have done.
Saidah's personality was very strong
and she didn't back down from anyone.
She wasn't intentionally trying to hurt
Michelle, but she knew Michelle needed
to hear the truth. Saidah saw the hurt
in Michelle's eyes and said calmly,
"I'm sorry Michelle, but you are
ruining a marriage with one of the best
husbands in the world because you won't
forgive your dad for what he did to
your mom. Matt is not your dad. He
did not cheat on you. He deserves to
have kids of his own."

The girls could tell that Saidah
was trying to diffuse the situation.
Kirsten and Beatriz braced themselves
for what Michelle was going to say
next, but she didn't say anything. She
just sat there staring out the window,
totally quiet, which made them even
more nervous.

Beatriz tried to change the
subject by asking Kirsten about Mr.
"super fine" Glaznyte, but Kirsten
couldn't be excited knowing that her

sister was in so much pain in the back
seat. She nonchalantly responded,
"Beatriz, let me just say, he was
nothing like I thought he would be."

Kirsten turned the music up
louder. Beatriz laughed, then they all
started singing along to one of
Prince's songs that had just come on
the radio.

♬ ♪ ♬ Until the end of time, I'll
be there for you. You own my heart and
mind, I truly adore you ♬ ♪ ♬

The girls sang as loudly as they
could. Michelle eventually joined in;
Beatriz squeezed her hand. They were
all glad that Michelle had rejoined the
group. They sang every song that came
on the radio all the way to the concert
and then they sang every song along
with Charlie Wilson during the concert.

The girls had a great time. It
seemed as if they had forgotten all
about the tense moments during the ride
down to Tallahassee. It was just like
old times. After the concert was over
they jumped back in the car and sang
all the way back to Kirsten's parents'
house.

Kirsten still had a key to the
house so the girls let themselves in

and did their best not to wake
Kirsten's parents, but Mrs. Jan didn't
sleep through anything. "You girls had
a good time?" she asked, as they were
tiptoeing down the hallway. "Yes,
Ma'am," they all yelled back, giggling
like second graders. They couldn't
sleep so they stayed up for the rest of
the night catching up on each other's
lives.

Beatriz and Saidah talked about
the funny stuff their kids does, while
Michelle talked about the exciting
trips she and Matt take around the
world, and Kirsten talked about Mr.
Glaznyte.

Michelle looked at Kirsten and
whispered, "I've never heard you talk
this much about any man, ever! Let me
guess; he's dark-skinned, muscular,
with beautiful eyes and pretty teeth,
isn't he?" Kirsten just blushed.
Beatriz and Saidah both laughed and
shook their heads.

Michelle said, "That sounds like
everything on your stupid list,
Kirsten."

"I know, I know," Kirsten
responded, still blushing.

"That's so superficial, Kirsten.

Don't be fooled by someone's outward appearance. Find out what's in his heart because that's what matters," Michelle said, still whispering.

"Oh, you know how to whisper?" Kirsten asked.

"Yes, I do," Michelle said, not wanting to wake Kirsten's parents.

"Is he a Christian?" Beatriz asked. "I know that's on your list too, right?"

"Of course it is Beatriz, I'm not that superficial," Kirsten said, sounding aggravated.

"But you are unrealistic, Kirsten," Saidah mentioned.

"Oh gosh, let's not start this again," Kirsten responded. "I just want what I want. What's so bad about that?" she asked.

"And it sure does sound like Mr. Glaznyte is what you want," Saidah said, with a smirk on her face.

"Shut up and go to bed," Kirsten said, turning off the lights.

The girls didn't go to sleep, though. They kept talking about everything they could think of until the sun came up. They finally dozed off around 6:30 am and at 8:30, Mrs.

Jan was knocking at the door.

"Girls, come get some breakfast so y'all can get ready for church."

"Church," Saidah said, pulling the covers over her head. "But I just went to sleep. I'll just stay here and have pillow worship today."

She didn't know Mrs. Jan was still at the door. "There is no such thing as pillow worship, Saidah, now y'all get up and come eat."

Saidah jumped up, embarrassed that Mrs. Jan overheard her. Kirsten shook her head. "You know my mom don't miss anything, Saidah." They all laughed at how humiliated Saidah was, but they managed to drag themselves out of bed, ate breakfast, then got dressed for church.

The sermon was about taking God out of the box and allowing him to give you above and beyond what you could ask or even think. All the girls looked over at Kirsten, but she just kept looking at the Pastor, nodding her head in agreement.

After church, they all went back to Kirsten's parents' house, ate lunch and packed up their bags to go home. As they were heading out of the house,

they gave Mrs. Jan and Mr. Jabard big
hugs. Michelle looked like she was
about to cry. "I just love you guys,"
she said. She hugged Saidah tighter
than anyone else. She didn't seem to
want to let her go. Kirsten's parents
didn't know what that was all about,
but they figured it had something to do
with their trip to Tallahassee.
Kirsten and Beatriz smiled. They were
glad Michelle didn't hold a grudge
against Saidah for what she said.
Michelle finally let Saidah go and they
both wiped away tears. Everyone else
exchanged hugs, said goodbyes and went
back to their lives as adults, mothers,
and wives.

~SIX~

The next morning Kirsten woke up excited for work. For some reason she felt it was going to be a good day. Compared to Friday, any day would be good.

When she got to work, Lena handed her a note saying Mr. Glaznyte had called. She and Lena smiled at each other, hoping he was calling to say they got the bid. Lena crossed her fingers, while Kirsten went into her office to return Mr. Glaznyte's call.

"Glaznyte's Electrical Trades and Appliances," Mr. Glaznyte answered.

Doesn't he have a secretary to do that for him? Kirsten thought.

"Hi, Mr. Glaznyte, this is Kirsten Jabard from—"

"Hey, Ms. Jabard, I was waiting for your call. We've decided to give you guys the bid."

Kirsten almost dropped the phone. She knew this was big, really big. No, this was bigger than big.

"I'm very delighted to hear that, sir. We won't let you down," she said.

"I've done my homework on you guys; y'all do excellent work, so I'm looking forward to doing business with you."

Y'all? This man just said y'all; there's no way he's from Oregon.

"We look forward to doing business with you as well, sir."

"Please tell Mr. Wayne that I'll be in touch."

"Yes, I sure will," Kirsten said before hanging up.

She ran out to Lena's desk and yelled excitedly, "We got the contract bid, we got the contract bid!"

Lena gave her a big hug. "I'm so happy for you, Ms. Jabard."

"For us!" Kirsten said. "Let's go celebrate."

Lena forwarded her work phone to her cell, put a sign on her desk, and rushed out the door with Kirsten.

Mr. Wayne was out of town, so they decided to take their time coming back to work. Kirsten knew he wouldn't mind since they just landed a deal with the biggest businessman in the Atlanta

area. She and Lena went to a small
coffee shop around the corner. They
laughed and talked about their weekend
with their friends. Kirsten told her
all about the concert.

"I love Charlie Wilson," Lena
said.

"Well, next time I'll make sure
you come with us. You'll love my
friends."

"I'm too old to hang out with your
friends, Ms. Jabard. I ain't no spring
chicken, ya know."

Kirsten chuckled. "Will you
please stop calling me Ms. Jabard? And
it'll probably do you some good to hang
out with us young folk."

They laughed and chatted some
more. After a few hours, they
eventually made it back to the office.
Everyone gave them funny looks because
they had been gone for so long. It was
obvious they hadn't been working
because Kirsten had coffee and cookies
in her hand.

"We got the bid with "Glaznyte's
Electrical Trades and Appliances!" she
screamed. Everyone clapped and
cheered, except for Lance. He knew he
forfeited some big money by going home

sick that day.

"Thank yooooou," Kirsten mouthed
to Lance. She knew she was taunting
him, but he deserved it.

"Yeah, yeah," Lance said with a
half-smile that quickly turned into a
frown.

Kirsten went back to her office
and did nothing for the rest of the
day. "Hmmm, Lance may be on to
something here. Being lazy really
isn't so bad."

The day past slowly with neither
Kirsten nor Lena doing much work, then
3:00 came and Lena went home. Just as
Kirsten was getting ready to walk out
around 4:30, her phone rang. It was
Mr. Glaznyte.

"Hi, Ms. Jabard, this is Jason
Glaznyte." Kirsten's heart dropped.
She thought he was calling to say he
changed his mind about the business
deal.

"Hi, Mr. Glaznyte, what can I do
for you, sir?"

"I have one quick question for
you."

"Sure, please ask," Kirsten said,
nervously.

"Once my company gives you guys

the bid, will you and I have any more professional dealings with each other?"

That's a strange question, Kirsten thought.

"No sir, not really. Once we do the paperwork for the bid, you will basically be working with our contractors from then on. I only do initial marketing and negotiations. You may meet with Mr. Wayne occasionally, but you and I shouldn't have a need to interact at all after this. Why do you ask?" Kirsten inquired, with a puzzled look on her face.

"Well, I would really like to take you to dinner sometime, but I can't have my work interfering with my personal life. I just need to make sure that all conflicts of interest are eliminated."

Kirsten wanted to scream. She thought she'd die right there in her office chair. *Oh, I will make sure ALL conflicts of interest are eliminated, Mr. Hotness.*

Kirsten took a deep breath before responding; she didn't want to sound too happy or too desperate.

"Sure, we can do that," she said, nonchalantly.

"Great! I have to go out of town

for a few days to take care of some
stuff for my son, but I'll get back
Friday morning, so how does Friday
night sound?"

"That sounds good, Mr. Glaznyte."

"Ms. Jabard, if I'm asking you
out, I think you should call me Jason."

Kirsten giggled. "Yes, and please
call me Kirsten."

"That's a deal," he said, and they
both hung up.

*I didn't know he had a son. Hmmm, so he must
be divorced and clearly not as perfect as I thought. He
definitely isn't an old, white, bald guy from up North
either.*

Kirsten burst out laughing at how
wrong she was about him. "Never judge
a book before you see the cover,"
Kirsten said, and she laughed some
more.

When Kirsten got home she thought
about Caleb. She felt really bad for
standing him up. He never called her
back, so she figured he must have been
pretty upset.

As far as Kirsten was concerned,
it all worked out, because there was no
way she was going out with Caleb now.
Jason was everything on her list; well,
outwardly anyway. She still had to

find out if he had good values and morals, if he was a Christian and things of that nature, but at the moment, he seemed perfect. Kirsten couldn't believe she was so head-over-heels for this man already.

The week went by fast for Kirsten because all she could think of was her date with Jason on Friday. When Friday finally came, Kirsten didn't know what to do with herself. It wasn't time for her alarm clock to go off yet, but there was no way she could go back to sleep either.

Who can I call at 5:30 in the morning that loves me enough to not curse me out? Hmmm, that would be my mom or Shelly!

She decided to call Michelle since she knew Michelle got up every morning at 5:00 to make her coffee and watch her favorite show.

"Hey, Shelly, I didn't wake you, did I?"

"Girl, you know I'm not asleep."

"Good, I can't sleep, so I need to chat."

Michelle laughed. "Well, you called the right place."

Kirsten told Michelle about Jason asking her out. Kirsten was acting

like a little school girl, all giggly
and silly.

"Pull it together, girl. He's
just a man," Michelle said, sounding
aggravated. "For someone who wasn't
interested in dating anyone, you sure
are excited about going on this date."

Kirsten took a deep breath.

"You're right, Shelly. He is just
a man, but he is just the finest man
I've ever laid eyes on." Kirsten said,
laughing some more. "He's everything I
love looking at, Shelly!"

"Oh gosh, please don't be one of
those desperate women, who's just
excited to have a good-looking man on
her arm. A relationship is so much
more than good looks, Kirsten."

"I know, I know, but it sure is a
great place to start," she responded.
Kirsten laughed and Michelle shook her
head.

"I can't believe how this guy has
your head so far in the clouds and he
hasn't even touched you yet."

"He's the one, Shelly! I can feel
it."

"Kirsten, the only thing you know
about him is that he's your type,
physically. Everything that glitters

isn't gold, ya know."

Kirsten let out a loud laugh, "That's something my grandma would say. Are you turning into an old woman, Shelly?"

Michelle laughed. Then she became serious, "I have something to tell you."

"What is it, Shelly? Is everything okay?"

"Yeah, everything is great. What Saidah said to me on our trip really hurt, ya know?"

"Yeah, I know. I'm really sorry she said that."

"I'm not," Michelle responded.

"Huh? What do you mean by that?"

"Kirsten, you've said the same thing to me many times, but for some reason when Saidah said it, it really hurt, but it also made me think. It made me think about how good Matt is to me and how devastated I would be if I lost him."

Kirsten eyes filled with water. *Gosh, I'm crying about everything these days. I have never been this emotional! What is wrong with me?*

Michelle kept talking. "When I got home from our trip I threw my birth control pills in the trash and I made

90

love to my husband like I have never
made love to him before."

Kirsten gasped, "Oh wow, Shelly!
That is wonderful!"

"Kirsten, I've deprived him of
having children for five years and he
has stood by my side, trying to be
understanding of all the pain I was in
from my dad. He's never tried to force
me to get pregnant and I knew he wanted
a baby so bad. I could see it in his
eyes whenever we passed by someone
else's baby or when we passed by the
baby section of a store. I refused to
deal with my hurt, and it caused me to
hurt him," Michelle said, crying.

"I'm so proud of you, Shel—"

"I also called my dad," Michelle
said, abruptly.

"You did what?" exclaimed Kirsten.

"I called my dad. We talked for
three hours, Kirsten. He cried and of
course you know I cried. He begged for
my forgiveness and I begged for his.
It was so beautiful. It was long
overdue."

"Yeah, it was, Shelly. I'm glad
you finally did it, though. So what
now?"

"Well, now I'm gonna just wait to

see if my eggs are alive and well enough to let my baby daddy fertilize them."

They both laughed. Michelle didn't even sound like the same person. She was so calm and peaceful. "I'm still scared, though. I've been praying a lot lately, just asking God to help me through my fears."

Kirsten smiled. "I can't think of a better person to ask for help than Him. He will get you through this."

"Yeah, I think you're right about that, Kirsten," Michelle responded. "Well, hun, I have to get ready for work. Call me tomorrow and tell me all about your date with the ugly, bald, white guy."

Kirsten laughed and said, "I sure will! I love you."

"I love you too," Michelle responded.

When they hung up, Kirsten realized she had been talking to Michelle for an hour and a half. If she didn't hurry she was going to be late for work. She quickly showered, got dressed and rushed out the door. She managed to make it to work on time and even managed to get some work done, despite being nervous about her date with Jason that evening.

Three O'clock came and she hadn't heard from Jason. She wondered if he had made it back home safely, but she dared not call to check. Kirsten wasn't the type of woman to check up on a man. Her life was normally too busy to check on anybody, but she sure did want to call Jason. She didn't know why this man had her in such a daze. She didn't even know him, but was already feeling a connection with him.

As she daydreamed of what their date would be like, the phone rang; it was Jason. He asked if they were still on for the night and said he wanted to take her to a place that was special to him. He asked if he could pick her up around 6:30. She agreed and told him how to get to her house. The rest of Kirsten's time at the office was a blur. All she could think about was Jason. She couldn't wait to get to know him because everything she thought about him so far was pleasantly wrong.

Kirsten rushed home after work and got dressed. She was so nervous that she ended up bumping her hand into the dresser and chipping a nail.

"AAAAAHHHHHHHH!" Kirsten screamed. I do not have time to fix a chipped nail. "He's just a man, he's seen chipped nails before," Kirsten said, trying to sound like Michelle. "I've got to calm down. This man is going to think I'm a nutcase, and it's true. I am a nutcase, over him. I don't know why, but I am truly a nutcase over this guy."

Kirsten decided to watch TV to help calm her nerves before Jason arrived. She took a deep breath, grabbed the remote and said, "Okay, Kirsten. Relax. Calm down. He is just a man, remember? He is just a man."

~SEVEN~

Kirsten heard a car outside, so she peeped out of the window. It was 6:25 and Jason was there to pick her up. "I love a man who's on time," Kirsten said, when she saw him pulling into the driveway in his black Mercedes-Benz E350 Coupe. "Would I expect him to be driving anything else?" she mumbled.

She rushed back to her room to pretend she wasn't ready yet; she didn't want to seem too anxious.

Jason rang the doorbell. Kirsten counted to 20 before answering. When she opened the door, Jason gave her a purple, silk flower.

Ummm, that's weird, Kirsten thought, but she graciously accepted the flower and even placed it in a vase as if she'd convinced herself it was real.

"Go ahead," said Jason, with a smirk on his face.

"Go ahead, what?" Kirsten

responded.

"Ask me why I gave you a fake flower."

"Because you're fake?" Kirsten asked, bursting out into laughter like she was ready to quit her day job and become a comedian.

"Ha, Ha, Ha," Jason responded. "Nope, that's not it. This is our first date, so I'm giving you one flower. I'll give you a different colored flower every time we go out, provided that you'll want to go out with me again. Hopefully we will end up with a whole bouquet of colorful flowers that represents our special times together."

Now, that's a James Brown pimp line if ever there was one. Surely he must be after sex to pull that one out of his hat.

Kirsten smiled and decided, *pimp line or not, I love the idea.* **She told him how sweet his gesture was and said she couldn't wait to see the beautiful bouquet they're going to make together.**

So far, Jason seemed like a gentleman and she was trying not to prejudge him, especially since her last prejudgment didn't go so well. He told her how beautiful she was and asked if

she was ready to go. She locked up the house and they walked to his car. Jason opened the door for her, made sure the temperature in the car was just right, and put on some soft jazz music for the ride. Kirsten was very happy that he had class and didn't entertain her with any "flip it, pop it, drop it, turn it around, bop it, don't stop it," songs.

To Kirsten, Jason seemed perfect, but she was still very nervous about being on a date and it didn't help that it was taking Jason forever to get to this "special place" of his.

She glanced over at Jason. *This man smells so good. I hope he's not just after sex. If he mentions one thing about sex, I'm going to bolt right in the middle of the conversation. I really don't know where we're going, though, and I really wouldn't know how to get back to my house from here. It will probably be very inconvenient for me to leave, so I sure hope he knows how to act tonight.* Kirsten sat there doing inward giggles, trying to calm her crazy thoughts.

"Are you okay?" Jason asked.

"Yeah, I'm good," she said, giving him a smile.

He gave her a weird glance and said, "We should be getting there

97

shortly."

"No worries. I'm enjoying the ride," she responded, in hopes that her apprehensions weren't too noticeable.

They finally pulled up to a tall building that said, "Ryan's Blues and Jazz." It was an upscale Jazz restaurant in Atlanta, which was not what Kirsten expected for a first date, but she decided not to complain. Jason parked the car in the lot across the street.

No valet parking? Well, this is not exactly what I envisioned, but okay. Whatever.

They walked in and of course everyone knew Jason.

"Hi, Mr. Glaznyte! Right this way; we have your special table waiting for you," the waitress said, as she led them to the elevators.

The elevator? Why are we going to the elevator?

At this point Kirsten just threw all expectations out the window. She knew she had to be open-minded if she wanted to have a good time. The elevator took them to the 4th floor.

"Have a great night, sir/ma'am," said the waitress when the elevator doors opened.

"Thank you," they both responded,

but Kirsten said it with much hesitation. *She's not going to walk us to our table?*

"Kirsten, relax. There are no bogeymen up here."

"Is it that obvious?" Kirsten asked, laughing.

"Yes, now come on," Jason replied, grabbing her hand and pulling her off the elevator.

She loved the feel of Jason's hand holding hers. It had been a long time since any man even came close to touching her. When they walked off the elevator, she realized that they were on the rooftop. There were several tables up there, but Jason led her to the one in the far corner. Kirsten still wondered why the waitress didn't walk them to their table, but the setting was just too beautiful to worry about that. The night had already been everything she didn't expect, so she decided to just go with the flow for the rest of the night.

The moon was glowing brightly, and they were playing her favorite classical piece, "Moonlight Sonata," by Beethoven.

"That's one of my favorites,"

Jason said, rocking his head to the music.

"Moonlight Sonata?" Kirsten screamed.

"Yes, I love it. It's a great masterpiece," Jason said, wondering why she screamed.

"It's my favorite too! Wow, that's a funny coincidence," Kirsten responded.

"Is it really your favorite? Yeah, that is a funny coincidence," Jason said, shrugging his shoulders.

Kirsten was starting to love this place and her date with Jason. He pulled out the chair for her and told her to order whatever she liked. The outside of the menu said, "The Best of New Orleans in Georgia."

That's a unique title, Kirsten thought. She couldn't wait to see what was on the inside. She opened the menu and it was nothing but good old-fashioned New Orleans cuisine. Jambalaya, Crawfish Shrimp Etouffee, Gumbo, Red Beans and Rice, and every other kind of seafood you could think of. Kirsten's mouth began to water.

"Ah, I seem to have found something you're comfortable with,"

Jason said, laughing.

Kirsten was so embarrassed. She knew Jason could see how she was staring at all the pictures. "Yes, food is my weakness, I cannot tell a lie," she responded, with a shy grin.

"Well, order whatever you want," Jason replied.

Kirsten quickly tried to change the subject. "I see why this place is special to you."

"Yeah, I come here whenever I'm stressed about something. The atmosphere immediately calms me. I come a couple times a week and sit at this same table. I think they save it for me, because it's never taken."

Kirsten smiled at Jason's humbleness. *Of course they save it for you! Just look at how scrumpchalicious you are? I'd save a table for you too.*

Jason continued, "This place helps me think and put my life in perspective. It's the first time I've had company with me though," he said, looking back at his menu.

"Really?" Kirsten asked. She wasn't sure whether to believe him or not. *This guy seems to have some hidden Casanova skills. Only a Rico Suave could get away with that silk flower mastermind, but I must admit, I liked it, so way to go, Rico!*

"Yes, really! I don't have many associates," he responded.

So far, Kirsten liked everything she was seeing. Jason was great company and she could feel the chemistry between them. Kirsten didn't want to believe in love at first sight, but she was definitely seeing Jason as someone she wanted to keep around and he was feeling the same way about her. He even mentioned the connection they seemed to have. Jason was a true gentleman and the night was simply beautiful. They stayed there five hours, eating, dancing, laughing, and talking. Everything was perfect.

Kirsten finally looked at her watch. She couldn't believe it was 12:30 pm. "Oh goodness, I have to go. I've got to get up early in the morning." Jason looked at his watch.

"Wow! I didn't realize that we had been here for so long. I'm surprised they didn't kick us out."

Kirsten knew better than that, just by the way Jason was greeted when he walked through the door. "I doubt very seriously that they will kick you out, Jason."

He smiled. "Maybe, maybe not, but I don't want to find out," he said.

When they got ready to leave, Jason left a nice tip, but Kirsten didn't remember seeing him pay for the meal. She didn't even remember the waitress bringing him a check.

Maybe I was just too busy enjoying his company, but surely this man paid for our food.

As Jason and Kirsten were walking out, the waitresses were just as nice to him as they were when he first arrived.

"I can't believe they're not giving us dirty looks," Kirsten said.

Jason gave her a stern expression. "I wouldn't come here if they gave me or my guest a dirty look. They are always friendly. Not just to me, but to everyone. That's why it's my favorite," Jason responded.

During the ride home, Kirsten was much more relaxed than she was on the way there. When they got to her house, Jason walked her to the door. He gave her a hug, told her what a great time he had, and asked to see her again soon. Kirsten happily accepted his invitation.

"I'd like that," she said.

"I'd like that too," he replied, with a smile. Then they both said goodnight.

Kirsten hadn't been on a date since she left college. *That was eight years ago!* She gasped at the thought of that. Right after graduating from college, Kirsten became a devout Christian; she was really trying to keep herself pure before God. She wasn't a virgin, but she really wanted to wait until she got married before she had sex again. She wondered how Jason would react to that decision. *Waiting is really important to me, so I hope it doesn't cause any issues between us.*

When Kirsten got inside the house, she really wanted to call the girls and tell them all about her awesome date with Jason. She knew they would be very happy that she did something else with her life besides negotiate business deals with old grumps. *I can't call them now. If I do, they will keep me on the phone all night and their husbands will be very ticked off.* She decided to just postpone that call until later.

The next week, things were pretty busy at work for both Kirsten and Jason. The construction guys were out viewing the site where Jason was going to build his new business and Jason was busy with them. Kirsten and Lance were out of town attending a conference, trying to network for future business deals. Lance didn't like it, but he knew his job was on the line. He was doing whatever Kirsten told him to do. Of course, Kirsten got a kick out of it, but she didn't hold her breath. She knew it was only a matter of time before Lance would revert back to his old ways.

Mr. Wayne must have had a talk with Lance and told him that he was on thin ice for all the shenanigans he pulls, because Lance is following me around like a lost puppy.

It was only about an hour and a half before the conference would be over. *Thank goodness,* Kirsten thought, as she and Lance tried hard not to fall asleep; the speaker was boring them to tears.

"Can you please just shoot me and take me out of my misery?" Lance asked, desperately. Kirsten laughed. This was the first time she noticed that Lance had a sense of humor.

Just then, Kirsten's phone lit up; it was Jason calling. *Oooooh! What a pleasant surprise. Thank you for rescuing me from this convention for the dead and buried!*

Kirsten quickly excused herself.

"Take me with you," Lance mouthed to her as she was leaving. Kirsten was too happy to hear from Jason to be bothered with Lance, but she was very proud of the effort Lance was making. For that, she gave him a B plus.

"Hello, this is Kirsten Jabard, how can I help you?" she answered, trying to sound professional.

"Hi, Kirsten. This is Jason."

"Hi, Jason," she said, trying hard not to reveal how happy she was to hear from him.

"I was calling to see if you wanna do something after work?"

"Well, I'm out of town right now. I'll be back this evening, but I have a date with my dog. She expects me to walk her in the park and I can't be late," Kirsten laughed.

"Well can you walk me, too?" Jason asked, panting and growling like a dog.

Kirsten wasn't sure if she should laugh or call the cops. Jason noticed that the phone got quiet. "That was a bit too much, huh?"

"Yes, no more dog noises, please."

They both laughed. "But you are more than welcome to join us," Kirsten said.

"Aw, thank you. Would you like me to pick you ladies up?"

Kirsten was very impressed that Jason was willing to let her dog ride in his E350 Coupe.

"That's very sweet, but we'll meet you there."

"Okay, just give me a buzz when you're on your way."

"Okay, sure will, bye," she said.

Before walking back into the conference, Kirsten said a prayer, *Lord, I might need some help with this one. This man makes everything in me move and jump.*

She took a deep breath and went back into the mortuary that they were calling a conference. She tried hard to pay attention. Lance, on the other hand, was asleep when she came back to her seat. She didn't bother to wake him. They were sitting in the back and as long as he wasn't snoring she figured, *hey, he's only doing what I've wanted to do all day!*

When the conference was over, she tapped Lance on the head and said, "Wake up! You can drive us back to Atlanta since you're well-rested now."

Lance was embarrassed; he wasn't sure how long he'd been asleep, but it was long enough for him to have slobber in the corner of his mouth.

When they got to Atlanta, Kirsten rushed home, threw on some sweats, then she and her dog, Poodles hopped in the car. Kirsten named her Poodles because she is a Poodle. It was no secret that Kirsten lacked in dog-naming creativity.

Jason's car was already at the park when she and Poodles arrived. Jason got out of his car and gave Kirsten a hug, then grabbed Poodles' paw and pretended to kiss it.

"Nice to meet you, my lady," Jason said to Poodles. Poodles licked Jason's forehead. "Whoa there, let's not come off too strong on our first encounter. I like my women conservative," Jason said, laughing at Poodles.

Kirsten let out a huge laugh. She knew she and Poodles had both fallen for Jason. She looked down at Poodles, who was wildly wagging her tail. *Love at first sight for you too, huh, Poodles? I know, he's just so darn handsome!*

Kirsten and Jason walked Poodles

around the park several times. She and
Poodles were huffing and puffing the
entire time. Kirsten couldn't help but
notice how Jason didn't even seem to be
breathing hard. She looked at his
biceps and triceps bulging through his
shirt. *Lawdy, please help me not to lust.* Kirsten
wasn't sure how she was going to keep
herself focused on her no-sex
commitment with all that fineness
around her.

After they were done walking, she
and Jason sat on the bench and made
small talk. He asked about her
hobbies, her dreams and goals, and he
told her about his. She figured he had
already accomplished all of his dreams
and goals, but he said he was far from
it. He talked a lot about his son,
whose name was Ryan.

He told her that he and Ryan's
mom, Lacey got divorced a few years
ago, but they shared joint custody. He
also told her how happy he was that
Ryan and his mom had just moved from
Vermont to Alabama.

"I miss that lil boy so much; I'd
love for him to come live with me,"
Jason said.

"Aw, that's wonderful, Jason. Do

you think his mom will ever agree to let him stay with you?"

"Not as long as she's alive," he said, laughing.

Kirsten wasn't sure how to respond to that.

"It worked out great when we lived in Vermont, because I got to see Ryan every day, but when I moved to Atlanta, I figured I'd just have to fly to Vermont a lot. Then one day his mom called and told me they were moving to Alabama. Now, I just have to drive about two and a half hours on the weekends to go see him; that's not bad."

Kirsten really admired how dedicated he was to being a father. She wondered how Lacey was able to relocate so quickly after Jason moved to Atlanta, but she still thought it was wonderful that they were closer to him. She definitely wanted to know more about this Lacey. Kirsten was not getting a good vibe concerning her, but for now, she would just relax and enjoy Jason's company. Other than having an ex-wife, he still seemed wonderful.

"Where are you from originally?" Kirsten asked.

"A little country town in Mississippi; if you blink you might miss it."

Kirsten laughed. "That sounds like my home town."

"Oh, you're a country girl, huh? Well, you look all citified, now."

"Ha! I'm far from citified."

Jason smiled like he wanted to say something that he shouldn't. "Most of my family lives in Louisiana, though. We moved from Louisiana to Mississippi when I was around eight or nine."

Kirsten and Jason chatted a little while longer, then she decided it was time to go. He walked her to her car and gave her another hug. *He sure loves to give hugs and I sure love to receive them.* She didn't want to let go and Poodles was jumping up and down waiting for Jason to acknowledge her as well. *Look, little missy, he's mine! Go find your own man,* Kirsten thought, while giving Poodles a dirty look.

Over the next few months Jason and Kirsten's friendship developed into a magnificent relationship. Kirsten decided to tell Jason about her commitment to not have sex until marriage.

Jason's eyes got big. "Huh? Are you serious?"

"Yeah. Are you going to be okay with that?"

Jason raised his eyebrows, "Ummm, yeah, it's cool."

"Okay, because it's very important to me that I wait."

"Then, we will wait," Jason said, reassuringly.

Although Jason was new to the area, he had already become very active in a local church. Kirsten was very committed and active in her church as well. She and Jason eventually started visiting each other's churches. Everyone at Jason's church seemed to love Kirsten and everyone at Kirsten's church seemed to love Jason, except the Pastor's wife. Kirsten felt that she always acted weird whenever Jason was around. She'd whisper stuff in Kirsten's ear like, "Be led by God" or "Always seek God's will." Kirsten didn't know why she did that or what she meant by it, but it was thoroughly annoying, if Kirsten could be honest.

Jason was everything she told God she wanted.

"He's so perfect and beautiful.

That is, if men can be perfect and
beautiful," Kirsten would say,
mockingly. It was clear that Jason was
the good, God-fearing man Kirsten had
been waiting for; what more was there
to pray about? As far as she was
concerned, he was definitely the one
she was meant to be with.

Kirsten and Jason couldn't stay
away from each other. There was so
much magnetic chemistry between them.
There was a lot of sexual tension
between them as well. Jason never
pressured Kirsten into sleeping with
him, but it had been three months since
they started dating and they could both
feel the sexual tension building up
whenever they touched each other and
Jason touched Kirsten a lot.

Everyone could see their
attraction for each other. They talked
several times a day, and they met up
several times a week for lunch. Things
were wonderful between them, and she'd
never been happier.

~ EIGHT ~

One day, Kirsten and Jason met for their usual lunch date, but when Jason saw her, he was looking her up and down like one of her perverted clients.

"You look so amazing," he said, as he was still gawking.

"Thank you baby, but I've had this dress forever; it's very old. I think I got it from—"

"Hey, I have a surprise for you. Get in the car," he said abruptly.

"Jason, we haven't even eaten lunch yet, and I'm starving!"

"I'll feed you later, I promise. Come on."

What has gotten into this man?

They jumped into his car and headed towards the side of town where Jason lived. When he turned down the road to go to his house, Kirsten said, "Why are we going to your house?"

He smiled, "I need to show you something. I'm not completely done with it yet, but I'm ready to show it to you."

Kirsten was excited about her surprise. When they pulled into his driveway, she noticed that he had fenced in his back yard.

"Oh, that's nice," she said. "When did you do that?"

"There's more, come on," Jason replied.

Kirsten didn't understand why Jason seemed to be in such a hurry. He put his hands over her eyes and told her to follow his lead.

"Jason, what are you up to?"

"You'll see. Just trust me, and no peeking."

"How can I peek when you have your fingers pressed against my eyes?"

"Good, now stop asking questions and come on."

He walked her through his house and into his back yard.

When he took his hands off of her face, she saw two small play areas. It looked like a playground for infants. Kirsten gave Jason a weird frown. She didn't know what to think or how to react, but she was sure this surprise wasn't for her. She stood there with a puzzled look on her face, then she looked up at Jason's huge, prideful grin. She really wanted to be happy, but she was never good at façades, so she decided not to say anything.

"Kirsten, it's for Poodles!" Jason said, with excitement. I'm not done with it, but I wanted to go ahead and show it to you today.

"Oh, this is for Poodles? I love it, Jason!"

Kirsten was ecstatic that Poodles had some play toys at Jason's house. She was also glad that she didn't have to stand there any longer with that dumb look on her face, trying to figure out why Jason built a baby playground in his back yard.

Jason grabbed her hand. "I like having you here with me, Kirsten, but I know you have to leave early so you can take care of Poodles. This way, Poodles can come with you and you can stay as long as you'd like; y'all can even spend the night if you want."

Kirsten let out a small gasp, as she pictured herself wrapped up in Jason's biceps and triceps all night. *Hmmmm, that would be—*

No, Kirsten! Bad thoughts! Shake it off! Shake

it off!

"Jason, this is the sweetest thing anyone has ever done for me, but I don't think it's a good idea that I spend the night at your house. I'm really trying to live a righteous life before God, ya know? I know some people think it's old-fashioned, but it's important to me that God is happy with my lifestyle," she explained.

"I know, baby, and I respect that. I just really love your company and I don't want you to have to rush home to feed, walk, or take care of Poodles. She can get all the exercise she needs right here in the back yard," he responded. "Come on, I have one more thing in the house to show you."

They went inside. "I have a bed for her too, see," Jason said, pointing to a pink and white polka dot doggie bed, with the word "Poodles" engraved on the side.

Kirsten laughed. "A Bed? It sounds like you want Poodles to move in."

Jason looked deeply into Kirsten's eyes and slowly kissed her lips. "I want Poodles' momma to move in."

Kirsten's eyes grew so large, that

she thought they were going to pop out of their sockets. Jason leaned over and kissed her again, but this time more passionately. Kirsten knew there was something different about the way Jason was kissing her. She knew she needed to stop him before things went too far, but she somehow felt lost for words. Inside she was obstinately saying, *No! Kirsten, don't do this,* but nothing was coming out of her mouth. Jason picked her up and carried her into his bedroom. Kirsten knew what Jason wanted, but she just couldn't bring herself to tell him no. The passion between them was so strong, that she soon became overwhelmed with desire for him as well. She sighed, as she faintly told herself, *No,* one last time.

Jason's body was unexplainably breathtaking. He was like a beautiful mountain lion viciously claiming his territory. His amazingly intense expressions of intimacy made Kirsten's head spin! It was more than she had ever hoped for and better than she ever dreamed it could be. She didn't know Jason would be that wonderful. She didn't know lovemaking could feel that wonderful. She laid in Jason's arms,

Colette D. Orr

contently helpless, forgetting all about how hungry she once were and all about the pile of work waiting for her back at the office.

Kirsten was typically out of the office with clients most of the time anyway, so no one would suspect that she wasn't actually working. At that point, she wasn't sure if she was going to make it back to the office at all. She cuddled tighter with Jason like she was a damsel in distress and he had just come to rescue her. Kirsten was truly at a loss for words and apparently so was Jason. They both laid there, quietly soaking up the elation of their first experience together.

As time went on and weeks passed, Jason and Kirsten grew closer. She felt bad that she was no longer waiting until marriage before having sex, but every time she saw Jason, he was all over her and she was all over him. They both seemed to lose their minds around each other. Their animal magnetism led them to have many rendezvous, whenever they could, wherever they could. Kirsten didn't know what had gotten into her, but she

119

loved how young and wild Jason made her feel.

Eventually she and Poodles started spending the night at Jason's place, but Kirsten refused to leave any of her things there. She told herself that leaving clothes would be giving in to the "shack-devil," and she was determined not to "shack up" with Jason.

Kirsten continued to go to church, but she felt very guilty about her life. Whenever she saw the Pastor and his wife, Kirsten did her best to avoid them, always acting like she was in a hurry to go somewhere. Jason said he felt guilty too, but as soon as church was over, all of his guilt seemed to vanish. Eventually, the guilt became too much for Kirsten and she stopped going to church as regularly as she once did. The Pastor and his wife would call to check on her, but she eventually stopped answering because she had run out of excuses.

Six months passed and Kirsten and Jason were head over heels for each other. Kirsten was still adamant about not leaving any clothes at Jason's house, but she had a small backpack of

essential items she did keep there.
She went to her house every day after
work to get clothes and to make sure
everything was okay with the house.
Her lawn guy, Everett, was there every
week and he was pretty good about
checking on things for her, so she
didn't worry too much.

Jason went to Alabama almost every
weekend to visit Ryan and since he
never offered to take Kirsten with him,
she used that time to stay at her house
and get caught up on laundry, or
reading, or whatever else she couldn't
do when she was at Jason's. Jason not
inviting Kirsten on any of his Alabama
trips eventually began to bother her,
but she never made a big deal about it.

Kirsten felt that she didn't have
the right to ask to meet Ryan because
Jason hadn't met any of her family or
friends either. However, unlike Jason,
Kirsten hadn't been home to see any of
her family since she and Jason started
dating; Jason went to see Ryan every
weekend. Kirsten also thought it was
strange that Jason never brought Ryan
back to Georgia with him. She really
wanted to be a part of everything in
Jason's life. She knew how much he

loved Ryan and she really wanted to meet him. Jason was so good to her, though, so she didn't want to seem petty. Aside from that, she and Jason's relationship was wonderful. It was more than Kirsten ever imagined it would be, so she decided to just push aside those uneasy feelings and try to not overreact.

"Kirsten, don't make a big deal out of this. What you and Jason have is strong. Don't go ruining it with insecurities. It's only been seven months; you'll meet Ryan in due time," she would tell herself.

As time went on, and things became more serious between her and Jason, Kirsten decided that it was dumb to keep driving to her house every day for clothes. Jason was more than happy to make room in his closet for her things. He told her so several times a week. She started keeping a few outfits at his house and Jason kept Poodles a supply of dog food there as well.

"You are so wonderful to me, Jason." Kirsten said.

"I love having you here. I don't ever want you to leave."

"Aw! I don't ever want to leave."

Three more months passed and Kirsten couldn't believe that she was practically living with Jason. Before she knew it, she was doing everything a wife would do, but without the papers. Shacking up was not something she believed in, but there she was, staying at her boyfriend's house at least five nights out of the week and the only reason she wasn't there on the weekends was because Jason was in Alabama.

Kirsten thought about everything that had transpired over the last ten months and it really bothered her. She didn't know how she had gotten to this point. In the beginning she was very adamant about not having sex before marriage, and not living together without being married, but now she was doing both. She was so far gone; she needed to clear her head and get a reality check. There were only two people she could count on for good reality checks-her mom and Michelle, but she couldn't tell either of them that she was living with Jason, so that left Beatriz and Saidah. Neither of them were judgmental, but they would definitely give her a good perspective on her situation, which she could use, since everything was starting to get hazy.

She decided to call both of them and put them on a three-way call. She hadn't talked to either of them since their trip to Fountainwater, so it was time to catch up anyway.

Beatriz was obviously busy when Kirsten called because she answered the phone yelling in Spanish.

"Beatriz, you know we can't understand you, so please calm all that down!" Saidah said. Beatriz laughed and said, "Well I tried to teach you several times but you were unteachable, Saidah."

"I learned," Kirsten said, proudly.

"Yes, you did, Kirsten. It was just Saidah and Michelle that I could never get to shut up long enough to learn anything."

"Goodie two shoes!" Saidah said to Kirsten and they all laughed.

"Hey, I need some advice," Kirsten said, interrupting the laughter. She told them everything that was going on with her and Jason, how bad she felt for sleeping with him, and even worse for living with him. She told them how strong their sexual chemistry was and how they had sex all the time.

"You guys we have sex before work, after work, before dinner, after dinner, before we go to bed, after we go to bed, before—"

"That's RI-DI-CU-LOUS!" Saidah said, interrupting. "Y'all need help."

Beatriz laughed, "Sometimes it's just good like that, Saidah."

"It ain't ever gonna be that good!" Saidah responded.

Kirsten didn't laugh. She felt helpless when it came to Jason. She said, "I love him, you guys. I love him so much, but I know I shouldn't be sleeping with him and I know I shouldn't be living with him either. I just can't ever seem to tell him no; I feel like it's my duty to satisfy him."

"Ummmm, not if you ain't his wife!" Saidah said, with an attitude, sounding like Michelle.

"I love being with him, Saidah. I'm not complaining; trust me, it's just that—"

"Whatever! It's still ridiculous," Saidah said, interrupting again. "But hey, you're a grown woman. If you want to sleep with him all day, every day, that's your business. You guys are in a committed relationship and at least it means something to both of you," she said, trying to be supportive.

"Kirsten, you really wanted to wait until you got married, though; I thought he was a Christian. Doesn't he care about waiting too?" asked Beatriz.

"He is a Christian, Beatriz! He's an usher at his church. He is very involved and committed to the church, but he says, 'a man has needs and humans weren't meant to go without sex.' He just may be right, ya know? But he's so wonderful to me you guys, he really is."

"HORSE PUCKEY!" Sadiah shouted.

"Well, if he's so wonderful, why won't y'all just get married?" Beatriz asked.

"Married?" Kirsten squealed, like it was a dirty word. "I don't know about that. Y'all know how I feel about getting married. I love my career too much to settle down. Besides, I haven't even met his son yet; there's no way I'm going to marry him without meeting his son."

"He has a son?" Saidah asked.

"Yeah, he's two years old. His name is Ryan Glaznyte and he looks just like Jason. Well, at least in the pictures he does. He lives in Alabama with his mother and Jason goes to see him practically every weekend," Kirsten said, grudgingly.

"So why haven't you gone with him?" Beatriz asked.

Kirsten got quiet. "He's never asked me to go and Ryan has never come here," she mumbled.

Beatriz raised one of her eyebrows. "What? Are you sure this guy isn't already married, Kirsten?"

"No, No! He's not married!" Kirsten said, angrily. "I have to go. I'll talk to y'all later."

"Wait, Kirsten," said Beatriz. "It just seems a little strange that you all have been dating for ten months, you're living together, he goes to see his son almost every weekend, but he's never asked you to go with him, nor has he brought his son to see you. You don't think that's kind of strange?"

Saidah chimed in. "Ryan Glaznyte, Ryan Glaznyte, isn't there a restaurant; some high scaled jazz place

in Atlanta that's named after a Ryan
Glaznyte?"

"No," Kirsten said. "Jason
doesn't own that place." She laughed
at the thought of that.

"Are you sure, Kirsten? I went
there once and somebody said it was
named after the owner's son, Ryan
Glaznyte. I thought the son was a
grown man, not a two-year-old," Saidah
said, laughing.

"Hush, Saidah, you're talking
crazy. That is not Jason's
restaurant!" Kirsten said, raising her
voice. "We go there all the time! If
he owned that place, I would know it."

"But, Kirsten, Glaznyte is not a
common name," Saidah said.

Beatriz asked Kirsten the same
question again, "Are you sure this guy
isn't already married? Are you sure he
doesn't have another life going on that
you don't know about? You know that
happens all the time."

Kirsten didn't want to hear any
more. She hated she had even called
them. "I love Jason and I totally
trust him. He would not keep secrets
from me and he would not betray me with
some secret life. I'm hanging up now,"

Kirsten said, as she hung up the phone.

Kirsten let out a huge, "Grrrrr" sound. She was very aggravated at the accusations Beatriz and Saidah had made about Jason. "Jason loves me. He would never lie to me or have some secret life."

They have given me a headache with all that craziness!

She decided that she was going to just stay at her place that night so she could clear her head.

On her way home, she called Jason and told him that she and Poodles weren't coming over. He asked if something was wrong, but she said no, she just needed to take care of some stuff at the house. Right before they hung up she asked, "Jason, you know that jazz restaurant that we go to all the time?"

"Yeah, what about it?"

"You don't own that place, do you?"

"Ummmm, yeah, I'm part-owner."

"Part-owner? Who owns the other part?"

"Well, it's kinda complicated."

"I work million-dollar negotiation deals on a daily basis, Jason; nothing is that complicated."

"Okay, well Lacey owns part of the restaurant."

"Lacey!" Kirsten said, sounding upset.

"Yeah, I bought it for Ryan, but her name is on the license and deed. When Ryan turns eighteen, it will be completely his, but until then, Lacey and I own it together."

Hearing the word "together," pertaining to Jason and Lacey kind of stung a little for Kirsten. She didn't see Jason being "together" with anyone but her.

"But, you're divorced," she said, raising her tone. "Wasn't that negotiated during the divorce proceedings?"

"Well, we were already divorced when I bought the business, that's why I said it's complicated."

"What? Why did you make her part-owner if y'all were already divorced?"

"I really didn't want to, but one day Lacey called me, acting all crazy, saying she was going to take me back to court for more child support unless I made her part-owner of the business. I wasn't even sure if the business was going to do well, so I agreed to make her thirty percent part-owner, Ryan twenty percent and me fifty percent, but when Ryan turns eighteen, she would have to turn her thirty percent over to him. Lacey said she just wanted to make sure she was taken care of if anything ever happened to me. I didn't want to hear her mouth and thirty percent didn't sound unreasonable, so I agreed."

"Jason, why couldn't you just say no? Is it that hard to just tell her no?"

"It's harder than it seems, Kirsten. Trust me. With Lacey, it's just easier to say yes."

"I really don't understand what you mean by that, Jason. If you don't want to do something, you don't do it. That's not complicated! You're one of the most prestigious business owners in Atlanta. You have a reputation for walking out of meetings if potential business partner doesn't seem prepared, but now you're telling me that you don't know how to say no to someone? That doesn't make any sense, Jason! So why didn't you tell me you own that place? I thought we shared stuff like that with each other."

"We do, baby, we do. I didn't expect you to understand and to me it was just an unnecessary argument waiting to happen. I hate arguing, so I decided it was best if I just didn't mention it."

"So how long were you going to keep it from me? Until Ryan turned 18, after the business is all his? I don't like secrets, Jason. I need to know that what we have is special. I need to know that I can trust you. I need to know that what we have is real."

"Baby, I've never felt more real with anyone in my life. What we have is real; it is special. Can I come over so we can talk about this in person?"

"I have a terrible headache, Jason, and I'm too upset to talk. I'm not sure that there's really too much more to say concerning this subject anyway."

"Come on, baby. Try not to worry about that stuff, okay? We don't need to let business rubbish get in the way of what we have. I made a mistake and I'm really sorry. I should have told you. I promise to share stuff like that with you from now on. I just didn't see it as a big deal. Like I said, it's all going to Ryan as soon as he turns eighteen anyway, so who cares that she's on the deed for a few years? To me, this is temporary, so there was really no need to bring it up. Try to get some rest, and I'll call you in the morning to check on you."

"Bye, Jason," Kirsten said, with an attitude.

"Bye, babe."

Kirsten didn't know what to think. She couldn't believe that all this time Jason hadn't told her he owned "Ryan's Blues and Jazz."

Well, I guess I do understand why he would make Lacey part-owner of the restaurant, she thought, then quickly changed her mind. "No, that's not true! I don't understand! I don't understand it at all. If they were divorced why would he give her thirty percent of his company and what does he mean by, 'With Lacey it's just easier to say yes?' That's bull, Jason," she said, furiously.

Kirsten let out a big sigh. She tried to just think of all the good in her and Jason's relationship. "I do trust Jason. I know he would not lie to me. Besides, we're not married. He has his own life and his own business matters and I have mine. It's really not my concern who owns part of his business, although none of my business matters include any of my exes. I really don't think I like this Lacey chic," Kirsten said.

Kirsten was glad she was almost home because her head was starting to pound; she really needed to get some rest.

When she got home, her lawn guy was outside cutting the yard. He stopped the mower.

"Hi, Ms. Jabard, I haven't seen you in a month of Sundays. How are you?"

"A month of Sundays? What does that mean, Everett?"

He laughed. "That's what my grandma says when she hasn't seen someone in a while."

Kirsten smiled, "Oh, well I've

never heard that one before. You've been getting your checks, right? I recently signed up for online bill pay, so they should be mailed directly to your house now."

"Yes, yes! I'm getting your checks; that's never a problem. Oh, I cut those tree limbs down that were hanging over the back of your house and I got some of those leaves off the roof as well."

"Oh, thank you! You're the best!" Kirsten said, as she headed inside the house. "Have a good evening, Everett."

"You too, Ms. Jabard."

Everett sure can talk, but I wouldn't trade him for any other lawn guy in the universe.

Everett had been Kirsten's lawn guy for two years; he came every week like clockwork. If he saw something that needed to be done, he did it. If he didn't get it all done that day, he came back the next day until it was finished. Everett's work ethics were superb.

Perhaps I could ask Everett to mentor Lance, but I like Everett way too much to do that to him.

When Kirsten went in the house, she took care of Poodles, then took a bath and got in the bed. Poodles stood by the front door as if she was waiting for something. When Kirsten turned out the lights, Poodles began to make whimpering noises. Kirsten came back to see what was wrong. "Poodles, I already fed you and let you go potty, so why are you standing at the door whining?" That's when she realized that Poodles was expecting to go to Jason's.

Kirsten gave Poodles a puppy dog look. "I know, Poodles, I know, but mommy needs to clear her head tonight." As Kirsten walked back towards her bedroom, Poodles stared at her with her head turned sideways. Poodles looked around, then dragged her doggie bed into Kirsten's room and laid down as well.

Kirsten laid in the bed thinking about her relationship with Jason. She knew things had gotten out of hand. Her parents would kill her if they knew she was shacking up, *but is it really shacking up if I still have my own house? I only leave a few outfits and other small items at his place, so it's only partial shacking, that doesn't count.*

Jason often expressed to Kirsten how much he wanted her with him every night and she really wanted to make him happy. She really wanted him to be the one that God had for her. Their chemistry was so strong and their bond was unbreakable. To her, he was perfect. They just needed to work out a few minor hiccups, especially this restaurant thing, which Kirsten still wasn't happy about.

"I know we're not married, but I am so bothered by it; I don't know why I'm bothered, but I am. I just can't believe he never mentioned it. We go to that restaurant all the time, ALL THE TIME! Not once did he fix his mouth to say, 'Oh, by the way, I own this place, that's why they treat me so good here' or 'Oh, by the way, I bought this restaurant for Ryan, that's why it's named after him.' It wasn't that hard to say, and I don't understand why he couldn't say it. Instead I had to find out from my friends and now, I'm way too embarrassed to go back and tell them that they were right. They're going to think Jason is a jerk and he's not. I just don't want to have to defend him again."

Poodles laid there, staring at Kirsten fussing to herself in the dark. Kirsten's head pounded even more from all the venting she was doing. *I really need to take something for this headache and I really need to calm down.* Kirsten took a deep breath. She decided to give herself a pep talk.

"Jason and I have something really special. He's a grown man and he doesn't have to tell me everything. Besides, anybody that makes my body scream the way he does, have got to be from Heaven, and made just for me. No man has ever made me feel this way and I love him. I'm not going to waste time on petty stuff. It's not like he's cheating. It's a restaurant for his son for Pete's sake."

Kirsten tried to disregard how she was feeling. She loved Jason dearly and did not want things to go downhill for them.

God, help me sort through all of this!

Kirsten knew God wasn't pleased with her lifestyle. "I really need to start back going to church. Jason goes to church every Sunday, but I feel so guilty whenever I step foot through that door. I really do love Jason, but I don't know if he wants to get married and I don't want sex to be the only reason I'm rushing to get married."

Kirsten and Jason had never talked

about marriage before. She didn't know how he felt about it and now she was starting to even question how he felt about her. "If he cared about me as much as he acts like he does, he would have told me about the restaurant. Even if he didn't tell me that Lacey was part-owner, he should have at least told me the business belonged to him! I really don't get his logic behind all of that. Why does love have to be so complicated?"

Kirsten felt so confused. She was starting to realize that there was so much she didn't know about Jason.

Do I even know who this Jason Glaznyte is?

The next day, Jason called and asked how she slept. He told her that he missed her like crazy and wanted her to come over. Kirsten explained how she was feeling about the restaurant, not meeting Ryan, the sex before marriage, and all the shacking up. Jason said he understood. He asked her to forgive him for not mentioning the restaurant, he assured her that she would meet Ryan and told her that he would never pressure her to have sex if she didn't want to. Then he told her how lonely he was without her and how much he missed her. He asked if he could stop by so he could see her.

Kirsten missed him too, and she wanted to try and patch things up with him. Besides, she knew she could never tell him no, anyway. He said he would grab dinner for them if she was hungry.

"I'm always hungry," she responded.

Jason laughed, "Well, in that case, I'll hurry," he said. Jason stopped and picked up dinner for them and even brought a toy for Poodles.

Poodles and Kirsten were both very happy to see Jason. They ate dinner and Poodles played with her new toy until she tired herself out. Then she went to take a nap. Jason got up to leave and Kirsten walked him to the door. She felt her body jump when she brushed up against his arm. Jason gently touched her waist and leaned over to give her a kiss goodnight. Kirsten tried to fight the temptation, but Jason looked and smelled so good. The next thing she knew, they were in her bed. She doesn't even remember how they got there. *"What kind of stronghold does this man have on me?* She thought, as she lay in his arms.

The next morning, the alarm clock went off at six o'clock. Jason got up, showered, gave Kirsten a kiss on the forehead, then went home to get dressed for work. That night he came over again, and again the next night, and again until he had pretty much moved in with Kirsten. Their relationship had seemingly grown into a very solid union.

Soon, Kirsten and Jason's one year anniversary came and Jason wined and dined her like never before. They had built a beautiful bouquet of silk flowers, just as Jason promised on their first date. He reminded Kirsten of all the wonderful memories the bouquet represented. He told her that he knew she'd been frustrated lately, but he didn't want those memories to ever end and he would do everything he could to make sure he had her in his life forever. Kirsten thought Jason was about to propose. She didn't know what she would say. She wasn't sure if they were ready for marriage, but if there was anyone she wanted to be with forever, it was Jason.

He didn't propose, which was fine, but it left Kirsten wondering why he was saying all those sentimental things like he wanted her in his life forever and he didn't want their memories to ever end.

I'm already sleeping with him, cleaning for him and cooking for him. He doesn't have to throw out commitment words if he doesn't plan to commit. I'm fine not being married and it's obvious that I'm not going anywhere, so he could have kept all that mushy stuff to himself.

Kirsten was starting to see that Jason just liked saying sweet nothings and that's exactly what they were-sweet nothings. She tried not to let all that empty romantic talk bother her, but it did.

Kirsten was in the prime of her career and she wasn't quite ready to settle down and have kids yet, but even if they did get married, she wasn't sure if Jason even wanted to have kids. Jason just didn't seem interested in all that "family" stuff.

He already has one child. Maybe we could have one more, and that would give us two, but I haven't even met the first one yet and IT'S ONLY BEEN A YEAR, she said, sarcastically. *But I'll just try to be patient and see how things unfold.*

~**TEN**~

Eight more months passed and
Kirsten and Jason had been dating for
about a year and a half.   Their
relationship was still great, but
meeting Ryan was just not something
Kirsten gave much thought to anymore.
Not because it wasn't still important,
but she had accepted the fact that she
may never go on any trips with Jason
and it may be a long time before she
ever met his son.   *It's fine! Jason loves me and
that's what matters most,* she said, trying to
make herself feel better.

A couple of months later, on one
Friday evening, Jason called and asked
Kirsten to come over because he had a
surprise for her.   He told her to bring
Poodles with her.

"I thought you were out of town
this weekend?"

"No, I'll be here all weekend, so
come on."

Kirsten wondered what he had up

his sleeve. She remembered the last
"surprise" he had for her ended with
her naked and in his bed.

She and Poodles hurried over to
his house and rang the doorbell. The
surprise was more than she ever
imagined it to be. Ryan, who was now
almost four years old, answered the
door.

"Hi, my daddy told me to let you
in, but who are you?"

Kirsten gave Ryan the biggest hug.

"I'm so happy to meet you Ryan, my
name is Kirsten."

"Ms. Kirsten, Ryan. This is Ms.
Kirsten." Jason said. Kirsten smiled
at Jason's respect for her.

Ryan and Kirsten got along great,
just as Jason knew they would. Ryan
was there for the whole weekend and
Jason wanted Kirsten and Poodles to
stay there as well. Of course Kirsten
was ecstatic about spending the weekend
with them.

Everything was wonderful. They
had a great time together. Ryan was
the perfect addition to Jason and
Kirsten's relationship and Kirsten felt
that what she and Jason had was finally
solidified.

Later on that evening, Jason and Kirsten were lying in bed. Jason grabbed her hand and said, "Kirsten, you belong here with me. I want my home to be your home." then he gave her a key to his house. Kirsten didn't know what to make of Jason giving her a key, but she liked the thought of it.

On Sunday afternoon, Jason packed Ryan up to take him back to Alabama. As usual, he didn't ask Kirsten if she wanted to go, but this time she asked him.

"Do you mind if I ride with you, baby?"

"Of course you can, you could have always gone with me."

"Really? Aw, that's sweet, baby. I wish I had asked sooner."

"That's okay, we will both work on our communication. Go pack some things in an overnight bag and we'll be waiting for you in the garage."

"Why do I need to pack a bag?"

"Because we're staying overnight."

"Jason it's only two and a half hours away, we can drive that with no problem and still be back by nine o'clock."

"Kirsten, that's not how I drive.

Besides, we will lose an hour coming back from Alabama because of the time difference."

"You know I have to go to work in the morning. I can't stay overnight."

"Well, just sit this trip out then, babe. You can ride with me on the next one, okay?"

"Okay," Kirsten said, disappointedly. She didn't seem to mind as much this time, though, because she had finally met Ryan and on top of that, Jason had given her a key to his house. Kirsten couldn't be happier.

As Jason and Ryan were walking towards the door, they both stopped and gave Kirsten a kiss, then Ryan said he had to go back to his room because he left his favorite toy.

"Oh, baby, I forgot to mention to you that I'm going to a VIP party for work while I'm in Alabama, so I probably won't be back until Tuesday," Jason calmly mentioned.

"A VIP party? How long have you been planning to go to this VIP party, Jason?"

"Well, invitations came out a few weeks ago, but I wasn't sure if I was going. Since I have to take Ryan back,

I think I'll just go while I'm there."

"So, you just decided that?"

"Yeah, a few minutes ago while I was packing."

"But didn't you have to RSVP for the party?"

"Yeah, I did that a few weeks ago, but I always RSVP, it doesn't mean I'll actually go. It's just business. Sometimes you make it and sometimes you don't. You know how it is."

"No, I don't think I do. If I RSVP for an event, I'm pretty sure I'm going to make it and I'm also pretty sure that I'll take my boyfriend with me."

"Come on, baby, why are you acting like that? Those parties are full of people hee-heeing and haw-hawing in your face just to get something from you. It's not a real party; you wouldn't be interested in that."

"You don't know what I would be interested in because you didn't bother to ask. Just say you didn't want me to go."

Jason put his arm around Kirsten's waist. "Why would I not want you to go? I don't understand why you're making such a big deal about this.

Baby, I would love for you to go everywhere I go. You know that, but sometimes it just doesn't work out that way. Just stay here and veg out on the couch all weekend and when I get back we'll do something special, alright?"

"I'm going to my house, Jason; I'll see you when you get back."

"Baby, you know you mean the world to me. If I really thought you were interested in going to this dumb party, I would have been honored to take you as my date. I honestly didn't think you would be interested. From now on, I'll take you to every party I'm invited to, okay?"

"You promise, Jason?"

"Pinky Promise, so please don't be mad, alright?" he said, giving her a kiss.

Just then Ryan came out of the bedroom with his bag of toys. "Ewwww, kissing is yucky! Look, Ms. Kirsten, I have all of my favorite toys!"

"Yes, I see that Ryan. Looks like some pretty cool toys you've got there."

"I have Spiderman, Incredible Hulk, Batman, Super—"

"Let's go Ryan," Jason

interrupted. "You'll have plenty of time later to tell Ms. Kirsten about your toys."

"Okay. Ms. Kirsten, if you're here next time I come, I'll tell you all about my super heroes and all the super powers they have! POW, WOW, KA CHOW!" Ryan said, doing his karate moves and sound effects as he went out the door.

"Oh, don't worry! She'll be right here with big papa when you come back," Jason said, winking at Kirsten. Kirsten couldn't help but smile.

Geesh, I should at least be able to stay mad at him for a day, but no, as soon as he comes near me with that body, and those lips, and eyes, and biceps, and triceps, and all his fineness, I just melt away like the Wicked Witch of the West. "I'm melting, I'm melting. What a world, what a world," Kirsten thought as she waved bye to Jason and Ryan. *I'm so pathetic!*

It was four months later Jason and Kirsten were celebrating their two-year anniversary. Jason decided that he wouldn't go to Alabama. He was going to stay and spend the weekend doing whatever Kirsten wanted to do. He gave her a diamond necklace and made several more promises of memorable moments. They had a wonderful evening together;

he always knew how to make Kirsten feel special. There was still no sign of a ring, but this time Kirsten wasn't expecting one. She had settled into the idea that Jason didn't want to get married and them living together really wasn't so bad.

"If it ain't broke, don't try to fix it," is what she would say to herself whenever she became frustrated with their situation.

The next day, Kirsten and Jason were just hanging out at his house watching television when the doorbell rang.

"Who could that be?" Jason asked. He looked out the peephole and all he could see was Ryan smiling. When he opened the door, he saw Lacey standing there. Lacey didn't bother to greet him, or Kirsten for that matter.

"Since you couldn't come see your son this weekend, I decided to bring him to you. You obviously have lots of free time on your hands these days," Lacey said, looking over at Kirsten. "I'll just leave Ryan in Georgia with you; maybe you can use some of that time to bond with him instead of whatever else has peaked your interest."

Kirsten's mouth fell open and so did Jason's. This was Kirsten's first time seeing Lacey, so she made sure she got a good look. Lacey was indeed beautiful, but she dressed like a hooker. She had on a very short zebra jumper with red stilettos, red polish on her fingers and toes, and red lipstick to match. Her booty looked like it had been stuffed with two basketballs. Kirsten didn't think she'd ever seen a butt that big. She was surprised that all of it could fit into that kiddie jumper she obviously just purchased from the zoo's gift shop.

Jason didn't know what to say about Lacey's surprise visit. There was no doubt that he was angry. His eyes were fire red, but he managed to put on a happy face for Ryan. He bent down and hugged Ryan.

"Hey buddy, go sit with Ms. Kirsten while I talk to your mom outside."

"Yeah, go sit with your stepmom Ryan, while me and ya daddy talk," Lacey said, sounding loud and ghetto like Michelle, *but even Michelle isn't this bad.*

Whomever it was that stereotyped black women as being loud and angry had probably just met Lacey. Michelle was Mother Teresa, compared to this chic!

Kirsten's hands were shaking. She didn't know what was about to happen next, but she managed to sit Ryan on her lap and read him a story while Jason and Lacey argued outside. The door didn't close all the way so Kirsten could hear everything they were saying.

"Lacey, what are you doing?" Jason screamed from the top of his lungs. Kirsten had never heard Jason raise his voice before. She hoped he'd quiet down for Ryan's sake, and the neighbor's sake too.

"Ryan told me about your lil girlfriend. He said you had to do something really important with Ms. Kirsten this weekend, that's why you couldn't come to Alabama. I figured you lost your priority list so I decided to find it and bring it to you. From what I hear, she is very good with Ryan, so I'm sure she won't have any problems being a stepmom."

"Are you serious, Lacey?" Jason screamed.

"Very!" Lacey responded, pointing

to the big black trash bags of Ryan's clothes and toys she had unloaded in Jason's driveway and all over his lawn.

Jason peeped in his driveway. "OH MY GOD, LACEY! REALLY?"

"Oh, yes, really! Enjoy your life, Mr. Glaznyte," she said, as she got in her car and drove off. Jason felt sick to his stomach as he watched Lacey's car disappear down the street.

Kirsten went to the side window so she could see the bags of clothes and toys. Big, black trash bags were everywhere; she didn't know what to think. Jason just stood there as if he was waiting for the bags to magically disappear or for someone to wake him up from this nightmare.

Kirsten told Ryan that they were going to play a game to see who could put his toys in his room the fastest. Ryan was all for the game. She opened the door and looked at Jason who was still standing there dumbfounded.

"Come on baby, pull it together for Ryan," Kirsten whispered.

Jason started taking bags of clothes to Ryan's room and then loaded the rest in the garage until he could figure out what to do with all that stuff. He wondered if any of his neighbors were looking out the window shaking their heads at the ghetto début Lacey just performed for them.

"She never ceases to amaze me with her shenanigans," Jason said to Kirsten.

She'd be perfect for Lance, because he never ceases to amaze me with his shenanigans either. **Kirsten wanted to laugh.** *This is no time for jokes! Besides, Lance has gone from ninety percent shenanigans to about thirty percent, so even he is too good for Lacey now.*

Kirsten decided to stop with her silly thoughts. Jason was obviously distraught and Kirsten knew their lives were about to change, but she was very happy that Ryan would be living with them.

"It'll be okay, baby," Kirsten said to Jason.

After they got all of Ryan's stuff off the lawn, Jason went straight to bed.

"Daddy's not feeling well, Ms. Kirsten."

"No he's not. Do you think we can go to bed early, too?"

"Yes, because I am so tired from lifting all those heavy bags. I have

too many clothes and toys, Ms.
Kirsten."

"You do have a lot, Ryan."

"I could donate some."

"Yeah, I guess you could, we'll
see."

"Can you sleep in my room with me
tonight? Daddy won't even know you're
gone."

"Sure can, let's go buddy."

They all slept very well that
night. The next morning, Jason acted
like nothing had happened. It was just
like Ryan was visiting for the weekend,
except every day had become the
weekend.

A few months went by and Jason
picked up on full-time fatherhood. He
enrolled Ryan in one of the finest
daycare centers in the city and
everything was good. Kirsten settled
into her role as stepmom. She and
Poodles pretty much moved back in with
Jason and they were living happily as a
family, even though there was still no
sign of a proposal.

Jason's birthday was coming up so
Kirsten decided to throw him a BBQ in
Fountainwater with all of her family
and friends so he could finally meet

everyone. *It's been two and a half years and my friends and family have never met Jason. Well, he was the one gone every weekend, so it's his fault that they've never met.* **Now that Ryan was living with Jason, he was home every weekend and Kirsten loved it.**

She called everyone to see if they could come to the BBQ. They were very eager to meet Jason and Ryan so they all came down for the day.

Everyone loved Jason, and Ryan played with Beatriz and Saidah's kids as if he'd known them all his life. The guys brought Jason into the "man-fold" and told him everything they knew about Kirsten, and Jason enjoyed every bit of it.

Mrs. Jan baked cakes and pies and Mr. Jabard worked his magic on the grill; he wouldn't let any of the guys touch his chicken and ribs.

"You young bucks don't know how to grill," he said.

That was fine with them because all they wanted to do was sit around and play cards, anyway.

Kirsten never knew Jason was so good at playing cards. Beatriz and Saidah didn't seem to remember the conversation they had about "Ryan's

Blues and Jazz" and Kirsten wouldn't
dare tell them that Jason did in fact
own the restaurant and had
intentionally kept it from her to avoid
an "unnecessary" argument.

Although Kirsten thought Jason's
excuse was pitiful, she decided that it
was in the past. The weekend was
perfect and she didn't see any reason
to mess it up. *Lord knows if Michelle got wind
of it, the entire barbecue would be ruined,* **but**
Michelle was changing and she always
did act like she had sense around
Kirsten's parents. The girls would
laugh at her attempts to be calm and
cordial when Mrs. Jan and Mr. Jabard
were around.

While Jason and the guys were
playing cards they asked him if
marriage was in the plans for him and
Kirsten.

"Nooooo way," Jason said quickly,
then he softened up his response and
said, "I don't think Kirsten wants to
get married; she's never even hinted
about it. I know she doesn't wanna
shack up though. She's made that very
clear," he said sarcastically. The
guys laughed.

Saidah's husband said, "Don't be

naïve man, all women want to be
married. They just want it to be
right. If you make them feel safe and
protected, they'll marry you without
questions."

Jason responded abruptly, "What
woman's gonna make a man feel safe?
With my ex-wife, I always had to sleep
with one eye open."

"Oh, you had a crazy one, huh?"
Saidah's husband asked.

"Man, she was a roller coaster. I
never knew what I was going to get from
one day to the next. I still don't
know!"

Michelle's husband, Matt chimed
in, "Well, don't make Kirsten pay for
your ex's crazy ways. Kirsten is a
great girl, man. I've known her all my
life. When you find a good one, you
need to make sure all your old wounds
are healed because you'll end up making
the good pay for the mistakes of the
bad. I love Michelle, but it got rough
for a minute. She was always punishing
me for what her dad did to her mom, but
then one day she came home, threw me on
the bed and she's been dropping it like
it's hot ever since. Life is better,
man, let me just tell you, life is

better."

The guys chuckled. Jason thought about what Matt said, "Nah, I'm good, that was the past, and I'm long over that. I couldn't find a better woman than the one I have right now."

The men talked about their wives for a few minutes longer, then they went back to talking trash about the card game that Jason was winning. They told Jason they were letting him win because it was his birthday.

The "cackling hens," as Mr. Jabard called them, were in the house eating up Mrs. Jan's pies and catching up on old times.

As far as Kirsten's family and friends were concerned, Jason seemed to care a lot about her and she seemed to be very happy with him. Mrs. Jan knew that everything wasn't as wonderful as they made it seem, but every relationship has its ups and downs, so as long as Jason treated her baby good, he was alright with her.

~ELEVEN~

Jason and Kirsten got back to Atlanta pretty late, so when the alarm went off the next morning, neither of them wanted to get up. Jason kept leaning over Kirsten and hitting the snooze button.

"We're gonna have to get up eventually, ya know," she said.

"Yeah, I know."

"By the way, Happy Birthday, sweetheart."

"Thank you, baby."

"So, what do you want to do today?"

"Babe, you just threw me the best barbecue birthday get-together I've ever had; I don't want anything else. I have a lot going on at work today, so when I get home I just want to wrap up with the love of my life. That will be the icing on the cake for a fabulous birthday weekend."

"Ok then, I'll cook your favorite

Colette D. Orr

meal, and we'll wrap up."

"That sounds good; what's my favorite meal?"

"Baked fish with lemon juice, mashed potatoes, and broccoli," Kirsten said, smiling.

"Very good, mamma! I can't wait to taste. What time do you need me home?"

"No later than 7:00, please. Ryan needs to be in bed by 8:30 and I don't want him to miss your par-tay."

"Par-tay, huh? I can't wait."

Jason and Kirsten continued to lay there wasting time chatting. Before long, thirty minutes had passed. Kirsten yelled, "Oh, gosh, I've got to get outta here. I have a big negotiation today."

"Well, I'm sure they will be just as smitten by you as I was when I first met you."

"Aw, you're so wonderful, Jason. I was smitten by you as well, but I have to run before you try to distract me and keep me here another hour."

"Oh, how I would love to get you distracted right now."

"Down, boy! I have to go," Kirsten said, jumping out of the bed and running towards the bathroom. "I swear that's all he thinks about," she mumbled as she closed the bathroom door.

"No, I also think about sports," Jason said, swinging the bathroom door open. "It's not my fault that you're so enticing."

"Jason, get out! I'm going to be late for work."

"No you won't, ten minutes is all I need, I promise."

"Yeah right!" she responded with a haughty laugh. "Jason, you wouldn't know what ten minutes was if it hit you in the neck."

After a few more seconds of trying to coax Jason out of the bathroom, his irresistibility finally got the best of Kirsten.

She was eventually able to get dressed for work, but it definitely wasn't within the ten minutes Jason had promised. She rushed out the door and left Jason there lousing around the house. She wouldn't be surprised if he called in, but she knew Jason would never call in.

"Jason could be dying, hopping on one leg, no arms, half a face, and one eye and he would still manage to find a way to get to work," Kirsten said, laughing.

During lunch she picked up an ice cream cake for Jason. She rushed back to work, put it in the office freezer, and hurried to her desk to finish her project.

"Mmmmmm, ice cream cake. My name is Lance by birth, but it can be Jason by choice."

Kirsten shouted from her office. "Lance, if you touch Jason's cake, I'll cut your ankles off!"

Everyone in the office laughed. "Oh, Ms. Goodie two shoes got a violent streak in her; who would've thunkit?" Lance said, laughing.

"Thunkit is not a word, Lance, now keep your fingers off my cake."

Lance closed the refrigerator door and walked away with his head down as if he actually thought he had a chance of getting a piece of the cake. He and Kirsten had been spending a lot of time together since she started mentoring him. Kirsten still didn't think he was ready for a lot of responsibility, but she had to admit that he was trying much harder than she thought he would.

For that, she developed a small liking towards him; very small, but still a liking nevertheless.

After work Kirsten rushed to Ryan's daycare to pick him up. Ryan was so excited when he saw all the party stuff in the car.

"Yay, it's my party!" he said, throwing his arms up in the air.

Kirsten laughed, "No, sweetie, it's daddy's party. Today is his birthday and we're gonna help him celebrate."

"It's still daddy's birthday? But, we already celebrated for him. It's time for my party now, Ms. Kirsten," Ryan said as he put his hands down in disappointment.

"Well, when your birthday comes, we will have a big celebration for you too, but I would really love it if you would help me celebrate daddy's birthday today."

"Yay, it's daddy's party," Ryan said, throwing his hands back up in the air. Kirsten let out a loud laugh.

"When is your birthday, Ms. Kirsten?" Ryan asked.

"It's December twenty-third."

"Is that close to Christmas?"

Kirsten smiled, "Yes, it sure is."

"Do you get extra presents from Santa?"

"No, not really, but when I was a little girl, my parents made sure that I had birthday parties. They told me that my birthday should always be celebrated even if it was close to Christmas, and not to let anyone cheat me out of my extra gifts," Kirsten said laughing.

"Does daddy cheat you out of extra gifts?"

Kirsten hadn't thought about it that way, because Jason was always out of town on her birthday and when he came home, he brought back really nice gifts for her, but now that Ryan mentioned it, Jason had definitely cheated her out of celebrating.

"No, he doesn't cheat me out of extra gifts," she said, hoping Ryan wouldn't pry too much farther.

"Ms. Kirsten, I'm gonna get you an extra, very special gift for your birthday."

"Ryan, that's so sweet. Thank you!"

"I'm gonna get you a stuffed Poodle to go with your real Poodle. It can sleep with you and daddy."

Kirsten gave Ryan a blank stare. "Thank you, Ryan. I would love to have a stuffed Poodle to go with my real Poodle. I know your dad would love it too," she said, smiling.

When they got home, Kirsten let Poodles out of the kennel. Poodles ran straight to the back door without giving Kirsten or Ryan any kind of greeting. Kirsten opened the door and let Poodles play in the back yard while she and Ryan put up all the decorations. Ryan was a perfect little helper, even though he got distracted several times with all the balloons floating around the room. They managed to get everything decorated and Kirsten started on dinner, while Ryan sat on the floor drawing pictures.

"Daddy!" Ryan said, running to the front door.

"Jason, what are you doing home so early? You're ruining everything!" Kirsten said, in an aggravated tone.

"Because I'm the boss and it's my birthday. I told myself that I could leave early today. I love the decorations," Jason said, as he kissed Kirsten.

"Where's my kiss, daddy? I helped put up decorations too," Ryan said with his lips puckered up. Jason leaned his cheek over so Ryan could give him a kiss. Then he hi-fived him and said, "Thank you, lil man. I appreciate you using all those big muscles of yours to help out." Ryan balled up his fist and showed off his scrawny muscles. "Wow, I just don't think I've ever seen muscles so big," Jason said to Ryan. Ryan was so impressed with his newly discovered muscles that he had to go stare at them in the bathroom mirror. Jason laughed, then turned to go into the kitchen with Kirsten.

"Don't come in the kitchen, I want dinner to be a surprise."

"Ummm, so would you like me to pretend that I don't know what you're cooking?" Jason asked, teasingly. Kirsten gave him an ugly look and continued to cook.

"Where's Poodles?" Jason asked.

"She's in the backyard playing," Kirsten answered. Jason went to the window and tapped it. When Poodles saw him, she ran up to the window and started barking, then she ran over to the door, and back to the window. Jason laughed.

"Poodles is very excited to see me, baby. I think she loves me more than you do."

Kirsten laughed and said, "Well, if you built me my very own castle in the backyard, I'd be happy too."

"So you're not happy?" Jason asked, turning around to look at Kirsten

"Yes, of course I'm happy," she responded.

"Good, because now I need to go let my other woman in so she can give me kisses," Jason said as he opened the door for Poodles to come in. Poodles jumped up on Jason like she hadn't seen him in years.

"Poodles, don't forget that I'm your owner," Kirsten said, as if she was jealous.

"Don't hate, baby! You know me and Poodles got a special bond."

Kirsten laughed. "Whatever!" she said, as she checked on the fish in the oven.

Once dinner was done, Kirsten and Ryan sang "Happy Birthday" to Jason.

"I love sitting at the table together for dinner, baby. Do you know Ryan and I never did this before you came along?"

"Really?" Kirsten asked.

"Yeah, me and Ryan normally veg-out in front of the TV when we eat dinner, don't we Ryan?"

"That's horrible," Kirsten said.

"Yes, that's horrible, Daddy," Ryan said, shaking his head with mashed potatoes all over his mouth. They all laughed.

"Oh, hush up and wipe your mouth, son," Jason said to Ryan.

"Eating together was a must for my family," said Kirsten.

"And so it will be for ours," Jason responded.

"Yay, daddy won't be horrible anymore!" Ryan chimed in. Jason and Kirsten laughed some more.

"This food is delicious, baby. I'm so surprised that you cooked my favorite meal. How did you know that's what I wanted?" Jason asked with a serious look on his face.

"You're not funny, Jason, but I'm glad you like it."

After dinner, Kirsten and Ryan gave Jason his gifts. Kirsten's gift was a very nice Rolex watch and Ryan's gift was a stick figure picture he drew while he was sitting on the floor waiting for Kirsten to finish dinner. Jason loved both of his gifts. "They are perfect," he said. "I'll hang both of them up in my office. One on my wall and the other will hang on my wrist." Jason laughed at his poor attempt at humor. Humor was not Jason's strong suit, but Kirsten appreciated his efforts.

She fixed Jason and Ryan a bowl of ice cream cake; they gobbled it up like they had never eaten ice cream before. She shook her head at both of them. "I see where Ryan gets it from," Kirsten said, staring at Jason who had ice cream cake and cookie crumbs stuck in his thin mustache.

"Jason, can you not feel those cookie crumbs in your mustache?"

He licked the crumbs off with his lips. "Yes, of course I felt them, but can't you see I'm too busy eating to worry about that right now?"

"And what's your excuse Ryan?" Kirsten said, looking at the mess Ryan made.

"I'm just a little piggy, Ms. Kirsten," Ryan responded.

Jason and Kirsten laughed. "Yes, you are Ryan, but you're my little piggy," Kirsten said.

"Mine too, but now our little piggy needs to take his bath and go to bed," Jason said to Ryan. Ryan finished gobbling down his ice cream and went to gather his bed clothes. He came back two minutes later.

"All ready for bed," Ryan said with dried up ice cream all over his hands and face.

"Ryan, you haven't even taken a bath, let's go run your water," said Jason. He grabbed Ryan's hand and they walked down the hallway to run the water for Ryan's bath. Ryan continued to try and convince his dad that he was already clean. Kirsten stayed in the kitchen and tried not to laugh.

"Bye, Ms. Kirsten, I'm going to take my bath, although I told my dad I was clean."

"Bye, Ryan. I think you'll feel much better after you soak in the tub a little, then I won't have to taste ice cream when I give you a goodnight kiss."

Ryan made an abrupt stop in the hallway and turned to Kirsten. "Ms. Kirsten, can you be my mom? I don't have one anymore."

Kirsten thought she was going to burst into tears. "Oh, Ryan, honey, you do have a mother."

"Well, I don't see her anymore."

"Yeah, I know, but you should pray for her. Maybe God will help her realize what a wonderful time she is missing, because you are just bushels of fun."

"What's a bushel? Is that like a shovel or a rake of fun?"

Kirsten laughed. She didn't know where Ryan got a shovel and a rake from, but Jason used that as an opportunity to turn Ryan's attention back to his bath before he asked Kirsten to be his mom again.

"Come on Mr. Rake, shovel, and bushel of fun, into the bath we go."

Kirsten loved having a child in the house. Ryan was so philosophical for someone who was not even in Kindergarten yet. She would love to be

Ryan's mother, but she wasn't sure that she and Jason would ever get married. Jason's mind always seemed to go somewhere else whenever someone mentioned marriage. Kirsten wasn't sure if it was the getting married part that bothered him or the having more kids part. He'd experienced both, so it was baffling why he became so disconnected whenever the subject came up. Kirsten hadn't experienced either and she wasn't sure if Jason would ever ask her to marry him or if he wanted to have a family with her. She wasn't even sure what Jason thought of his relationship with her. Jason was a good man, though, and she didn't want to pressure him into committing. Kirsten wasn't in a hurry to get married either, but she hated not knowing where their relationship was going. She also hated that they were living together without being married.

To make herself feel better, Kirsten said, "In my mind and heart, we're already married. We're living together and we're already raising two children; one is human and the other one is fur." Kirsten erupted in a laugh and looked down at Poodles. She began explaining to Poodles.

"Poodles, a lot of people live together before they get married. It's good to know what you're getting into; it's really not a terrible idea. I need to stop making such a big deal out of it. Jason is very good to me! I need to relax and just go with the flow."

Kirsten looked at Poodles who was diligently listening.

"Why am I talking to a dog? I must be going crazy," Kirsten said, shaking her head.

She finished cleaning the kitchen, then sat on the couch to read her Bible before she went to bed. When she opened the Bible it landed on Romans, Chapter Twelve.

"Brothers and sisters, in view of all we have just shared about God's compassion, I encourage you to offer your bodies as living sacrifices, dedicated to God and pleasing to him. This kind of worship is appropriate for you. Don't become like the people of this world. Instead, change the way you think. Then you will always be able to determine what God really wants—what is good, pleasing, and perfect."

Kirsten sat there and stared at the wall.

Of all the scriptures in the Bible, this is the one I turn to? Wow! Okay Lord, I hear you, you're right and there is no justification for doing wrong. I'll get it right, I promise.

Kirsten felt bad that she had turned so far away from God. Although she continued to read her Bible, she knew her relationship with God had changed drastically since she met Jason. She wasn't reading the Bible as much, nor was she praying like she once did. She felt guilty for how she was living. *God never intended for people to live together without being married. I don't care how I try to justify it.*

Just then Jason walked in the room. "The little fellow is all clean and tucked into bed," he said.

Kirsten laughed. Jason sat down by Kirsten. She laid the Bible on the coffee table and they started watching a movie. It was 10:15 when Jason's phone rang. He and Kirsten both looked to see who was calling that late. Lacey's name came up on caller ID.

"She knows Ryan goes to bed at
8:30, so why is she calling so late?"
Jason asked as he got up and went into
the kitchen to get more ice cream.

"Hello," he answered. "Hi Lacey,
you just missed Ryan, he's gone to
bed," Jason said like he was in a hurry
to get Lacey off the phone.

Kirsten huffed, then grumbled,
"She didn't just miss Ryan. He went to
bed two hours ago."

Kirsten heard Jason laugh and say
to Lacey, "Thank you, but I can't do
that."

Do what? Kirsten wondered.

"Lacey, sorry to cut you off, but
Kirsten and I are watching a movie so I
have to go. I'll tell Ryan you
called."

Kirsten heard Lacey still talking
as Jason was hanging up the phone.

"What did she want?" Kirsten
asked Jason before he was able to even
make it back to his seat.

"Just to talk to Ryan and wish me
a happy birthday," he responded.

Jason obviously thinks I'm stupid, Kirsten
thought to herself. "What did she ask
you to do?" Kirsten asked, trying not
to sound too upset.

177

"Huh? What do you mean?"

"You told her that you couldn't do something. What was she asking you to do?"

"Oh, nothing. You know Lacey. I never know where her head is," Jason said as he sat down and started back watching the movie. He tried hard to concentrate on the movie, but he could feel Kirsten staring at him.

"Kirsten, she asked me to bring Ryan to Alabama to see her next weekend, okay? But I'm not, so don't get all worked up."

"No, you should go. I'll pack up some things for me and Poodles and we'll make a family trip to go see the woman who dropped her kid off with all his clothes and toys in black trash bags."

Kirsten got up and walked out of the room. Jason followed her down the hallway. "Don't let Lacey get to you, baby. She knows I'm not coming to Alabama. Ryan is here with us, so if she wants to see him, she can come here."

Kirsten wasn't sure if she liked that idea either; she was very uneasy about Lacey. Kirsten didn't know what

Lacey's motives were. Lacey hadn't talked to Ryan since she dropped him off, now all of a sudden she wanted Jason to bring him to see her?

What kind of person is this? **Kirsten** thought. She also thought it was quite the coincidence how Lacey chose Jason's birthday to want to talk about seeing a child she gave up parental rights to. On top of that, she called after she knew Ryan had already gone to bed.

"It's 10:30, Jason, she had to know Ryan was asleep."

"It's only 9:30 in Alabama, Kirsten."

Kirsten looked at Jason like he was crazy. "Ryan goes to bed at 8:30, Eastern Standard Time. Tell Lacey to figure out what time that is for her."

Kirsten did not like Lacey one bit! She thought they had gotten rid of her when she agreed to give Jason full custody of Ryan, but now Kirsten knew that Lacey wasn't going anywhere, ever!

Kirsten took a bath and got in the bed. Jason was lying on the bed waiting on her.

"Dang, baby! I thought you got lost in there."

"I had a lot on my mind; I needed to de-stress."

Jason was hoping that Kirsten would be ready to give him his final birthday present, but Kirsten was not in the mood. Jason knew he had an effect on Kirsten, though, and she really couldn't resist him for long. He snuggled up beside her and told her how beautiful she was and gave her kisses until he felt her caving in.

Being upset seemed so silly when being with Jason made her feel so wonderful.

"Forget Lacey," Kirsten said laughing as she returned Jason's kisses.

"That's right baby, forget her," he whispered, while turning out the lights.

~ TWELVE ~

Several months passed without any more interruptions from Lacey. Jason and Kirsten's relationship was going very well. They had been dating about three years now and Jason decided that it was time to make things a little more official.

"Hey, babe, why won't you sell your house and move your things in here? You know I have more than enough room. It makes no sense for you to keep paying a mortgage on a house you don't live in."

Kirsten liked the thought of not having a mortgage payment anymore, especially since she was only stopping by her house once or twice a week now. She knew shacking up was something she couldn't do forever, though, not if she wanted to please God and she really did want to live a holy life before God. This was not what she envisioned life to be like when she met Jason. She kind of felt trapped in this

undesirable situation and didn't know
how to get things back on the right
track without losing Jason altogether.
Losing him would be unbearable. She
loved him so much. In a weird kind of
way, she actually felt addicted to him.

She contemplated on ways to add
more spirituality to their
relationship. That way, she would at
least not feel as guilty about what was
going on. For them to both profess to
be Christians, they had very few
discussions about God. They didn't
pray together, nor did they read their
Bibles together. Kirsten didn't
understand how it had gotten to this
point.

Jason still went to church every
Sunday and Kirsten periodically went
with him. She couldn't bear going back
to her church and risk running into the
Pastor's wife, who she was sure would
tell her that she and Jason were both
heathens.

With Jason's regular church
attendance, Kirsten was surprised that
he didn't seem bothered at all by their
living together without being married.
Kirsten loved Jason dearly, but she
knew something had to change. She used

to read her Bible and pray every single day, but she felt too guilty to do any of that anymore. She didn't see the point in asking God for forgiveness if she knew she was just going to go right back and do the same thing over and over again.

She knew she and Jason needed to get married to make things right, but because Jason was so wonderful to her, she didn't want to make a big deal out of it.

"Minus Lacey's drama, Jason and I have a remarkable relationship," she would say. "I just don't want to ruin it. I know I need to get things right with God, though. I just don't know how."

That night, before Kirsten went to bed, she decided it was time to pray. *"God already knows what I'm doing anyway, so there really is no need to keep avoiding Him."*

Jason and Ryan were both in the living room, so Kirsten figured that was a great time to spend some alone time with God. She went into the bedroom and got on her knees.

"God, please forgive me for all the things I've done wrong and give me wisdom on how to handle what's going on between Jason and I. I don't want to continue living in sin. Will you please help me work this out? Thank you for being so good to me and blessing me the way you have, even though I don't feel worthy and thank you for being so forgiving and merciful towards me. I put it all in your hands. Amen!"

After her prayer, Kirsten got in the bed and began to read her Bible. It seemed to be a little dusty and that made Kirsten feel really bad. Jason came in and saw her reading.

"We need to do more of that around here," he said, then he kissed her forehead.

"Yes we do, babe," Kirsten responded with a smile.

Jason got in the bed and waited for Kirsten to finish reading. Then he said, "I'm gonna make things right with you, Kirsten." She smiled and thought, *Wow! God, that was fast!*

She gave Jason a quick kiss on the forehead, then turned her back towards him and went to sleep. Jason knew something was different with Kirsten, so he just rolled over and went to sleep as well. This would be the first night that Jason and Kirsten slept in the same bed without him touching her.

The next day was Kirsten's birthday. Jason asked if she thought anymore about selling her house.

"Yes, I have," was all Kirsten said. Jason didn't know what to make of Kirsten's vague response, so he thought it was best not to push the issue.

Kirsten figured Jason was planning something special for her birthday, because he had been unusually quiet the past few days. She waited for him to tell her what he had planned for the evening, but instead he got straight out of bed and got dressed for work, then he got Ryan up and ready for school.

Kirsten giggled.

I don't know why he's trying to pretend he doesn't remember my birthday. I know he's up to something.

Kirsten decided to just play along.

She yelled to Ryan, "Hey, buddy, it's Friday, do you know what that means?"

"Ice cream!" Ryan yelled back.

Every Friday after school, Kirsten took Ryan to the park and then out for

ice cream. Kirsten thought for sure
that would get Jason to confess
whatever he had planned, but he didn't
say a word. Just as Kirsten was about
to say something to Jason, her phone
rang; it was Michelle.

"Hey, Shelly."

"Hey, birthday girl!

"Aw! You remembered, thank you!"

"Of course I remembered. You're
my best friend. So what are y'all
doing today?"

"Well, I don't know. No one has
mentioned anything yet."

"Are you serious? He hasn't said
anything? Do you think he's planning a
surprise dinner or something?"

"That's what I thought, but now
I'm not so sure. I take Ryan to the
park every Friday. When I mentioned
going to the park, I was sure Jason
would tell Ryan that he couldn't go
today, because they were taking me out,
but he didn't say anything."

"Well, Kirsten, he didn't do
anything for your past two birthdays
either, so—"

"Shelly, he was on business trips,
he couldn't help that. This year, he's
actually in town. There's no way he's

not going to do anything for me,"
Kirsten said, sounding upset.

"I'm sorry, Kirsten. I wasn't
trying to get you upset."

"I'm sorry too. I guess I'm just
a little aggravated that he barely even
said good morning. He just rushed out
of bed and started getting dressed for
work."

"I'm sure he's planning a
surprise, honey. Don't get aggravated
on your birthday."

"You're right. Jason is really
good about remembering important dates.
Well, Shelly, I have to go get dressed
for work. I'll call you later, okay?"

"You're working on your birthday?
Kirsten, this used to be the most
important day of the year for you. I
can't believe you're going to work."

"It's called being an adult,
Shelly. I will celebrate after I get
off."

"True. Well, enjoy your birthday
at the park with Ryan," Michelle said,
laughing. "Okay, I know that's not
funny. I'm sorry, Kirsten," Michelle
said.

"No, it's not funny. I'm sure
he'll have my surprise waiting for me

when Ryan and I get home."

"Yes, he will, honey. Have a great birthday, and don't forget to call me later and tell me all about it."

"Okay, I'll call you. Bye."

When Kirsten hung up, she couldn't resist the urge to find out if Jason had forgotten her birthday.

"Hey, babe!" she called out to Jason.

Jason walked into the bedroom, "Yeah, baby. What's up?"

"Ryan and I are going to the park today and afterwards we're going out for ice cream."

Jason gave her a weird look. "Ummm, that's what you do every Friday, Kirsten."

"Yeah, but I don't know what time we're getting back home, so—" she said, waiting for something to click with Jason, but he just stared at her like she was crazy. "Well, just in case you have something planned, we won't be—"

"Nah, baby, I have a 6:00 meeting tonight, so I won't—"

"A MEETING! JASON IT'S MY BIRTHDAY," Kirsten exploded.

"Happy Birthday, Ms. Kirsten,"

Ryan said, walking in and interrupting the tension. "Daddy, we need to get Ms. Kirsten a stuffed Poodle for her birthday."

Although Kirsten was angry and her eyes were filled with water, she still managed to give Ryan a nice thank you and a kiss.

Jason gave Ryan a strange look, but he was too busy apologizing to Kirsten to respond to the stuffed Poodle comment. Jason explained to Kirsten how busy things were at work and he promised to make it up to her.

Kirsten started to bring up her past two birthdays that he was also too busy to celebrate, but she figured it wasn't worth arguing over. He told her how sorry he was, gave her a kiss on the cheek, then he and Ryan darted out the door.

After work, Kirsten picked Ryan up and they headed to the park, but after a few minutes of playing, Ryan said his stomach was hurting. They decided to skip the ice cream and go home early. When they got home, Lacey's car was in the driveway.

"What is she doing here?" Kirsten blurted out without thinking. She

189

looked in the rearview mirror at Ryan, hoping he wasn't paying attention. He was asleep.

"Thank goodness," Kirsten said, but she was certainly not happy about Lacey being there. Lacey was nothing but drama and Kirsten wasn't in the mood for any drama on her birthday. She knew Lacey was jealous of her and she was trying to make Jason pay for moving on with his life. Kirsten felt a deep dislike for Lacey, but she knew she had to grin and bear it for Ryan's sake and for the sake of her and Jason's happiness, although, on that day, she wasn't very happy with Jason either.

He didn't even send me any birthday flowers, **she** thought.

She loved Jason very much, so she tried to be understanding of all his obligations. She knew he was very busy trying to establish new businesses and maintaining his current businesses, so she decided not to worry about a silly birthday celebration. Kirsten was just happy that she was going to get to see Jason before he left for his meeting at 6:00.

"I bet he's just pulling my leg

about that meeting. I know he's got
something up his sleeve, BUT LACEY HAS
OBVIOUSLY COME TO RUIN IT," she roared,
as she was hopping out of the car.

Kirsten got Ryan out of his car
seat and put him over her shoulder.
She grabbed her purse and headed
towards the front door. She started to
call Jason to come out and help her
with Ryan, but that meant she would
have to put Ryan back in the car, then
try to find her phone, which she was
sure wasn't in an easy place to find.

"Forget it, I'll just carry him."
She figured Jason and Lacey were in
some sort of argument anyway. "I'll
let him handle that monster and I'll
handle Ryan," Kirsten said. "I'm tired
and not in the mood for Lacey's
shenanigans, especially today," Kirsten
fussed.

The garage was open so Kirsten
decided to just go through there. She
knew Jason hardly ever locked that door
and it would be easier than trying to
unlock the front door with a child
hanging off of her shoulder.

She quietly opened the door,
hoping not to disturb the argument she
was sure would to be taking place.

"Hey, Jason," she said subtly as she walked in the house, but she didn't see anyone. Everything was quiet. *Maybe they're in the back yard. I'm not going out there! I'm trying to get my life back on the right track with God and I really don't want to have to kill nobody today. Besides, she doesn't like me and I don't like her, so why be fake?*

Kirsten went to lay Ryan in his bed on the other side of the house. She checked to make sure he was still asleep, then she took off her shoes and started back down the hallway to go peep in the back yard to see what zoo outfit Lacey was modeling.

Lacey will fit right in on Poodles' doggie playground.

As she crossed through the kitchen she heard a noise coming from Jason's bedroom. At first she thought it was Poodles wanting to go outside, but then she thought, *Poodles doesn't sound like that. What is that noise?*

As Kirsten walked towards Jason's door, she had an empty feeling in the pit of her stomach. Everything started moving in slow motion; it seemed like it was taking forever to get to Jason's room. His door was closed and Jason never closes his door when he's home.

Why is his door closed? What is going on?

Kirsten felt like she was about to have an anxiety attack. She wasn't sure if the door was locked, but she was determined to break it down if it was. With all her might, she burst through the door. It was unlocked so Kirsten almost fell when she rushed in. She let out a huge gasp from the shock of what she saw. "UUUUhhhhhhhhhhh!" She stood there with her mouth opened as Jason and Lacey was enthralled in kisses of passion. They looked like they were trying to bite each other's lips off. Jason's shirt was unbuttoned and so were his pants. Lacey was on top of Jason, completely naked. Her red lipstick was all over his face. Kirsten felt like her heart had stopped completely.

"Kirsten!" Jason yelled with the most fearful sound she'd ever heard. He pushed Lacey off of him and ran over to Kirsten.

"Baby, it is not what it looks like," he said, but all Kirsten could focus on was Jason's lips that were covered in Lacey's red lipstick.

"Oh, it's exactly what it looks like!" mocked Lacey. "It's about time you know the truth."

Kirsten's chest started beating more profusely than it already had been. She was not sure she wanted to hear what Lacey was about to say, but her legs were too heavy to run out of the house.

"We've been sleeping together the entire time you two have been together. Jason knows he can't resist this."

Kirsten looked at Jason for some sign that Lacey was lying, but he just stood there with his head down.

"Every weekend, when he came to visit Ryan, where do you think he was staying? When he went on all those business trips, where do you think he stopped along the way? You shouldn't be surprised; did he ever ask you to come with him? You couldn't see the way he looked at me when he was around me? I bet you thought you guys had something special, didn't you? I'm sorry that you misunderstood; I am Jason's first and last love, suga! There will never be another Mrs. Glaznyte," Lacey said, laughing while Jason stood there like he was having an out of body experience.

Kirsten had only seen Jason and

Lacey together one time and that was
when she dropped all Ryan's clothes in
the yard. How was she supposed to
notice how Jason looked at her? One
thing Kirsten knew Lacey was right
about though was that Jason never
invited her on any of his trips. She
assumed he stayed at hotels, but now
that Lacey mentioned it, why would
Jason spend money for a hotel every
weekend?

Kirsten didn't trust Lacey, but
the fact that she was laying there
naked with Jason made it pretty obvious
that she wasn't lying and since Jason
was just standing there with a dumb
look on his face, Kirsten knew that
everything Lacey was saying was true.

*I knew Lacey still had feelings for Jason just by
the way she acted when she found out that he had a
girlfriend, but never in a million years did I think they
were still sleeping together. Never in a million years did
I think Jason would cheat on me. I never even suspected
that he was still remotely attracted to Lacey. I can't
believe this has happened. I can't believe I didn't see this
coming. God, I feel so weak inside.*

While all of these thoughts raced
through Kirsten's head, Lacey was still
spilling the beans on her and Jason's
love affair. She was standing there,

still naked, yelling, with her boobs flopping all over the place as she bounced around. Jason tried to explain, although never denying anything Lacey was accusing him of.

They were talking so fast that Kirsten couldn't make out anything either of them was saying anymore. It didn't matter anyway; she had seen everything she needed to see.

Kirsten was devastated! She tried to speak, but nothing came out. Her eyes welled with water and she was sure she was no longer breathing. Somehow she found the strength to grab her purse and shoes and head for the door.

Jason grabbed her, "Please, Kirsten, let me explain!"

Lacey was in the background saying, "Oh, I know you're not trying to act like she means more to you than I do, not when you were telling me you love me every time we made love."

Kirsten felt disgusted. She looked at Jason. "You told her you loved her while you were sleeping with me?"

All of a sudden, Kirsten had an **epiphany**. *Jason and I have been together for three years and he has never told me he love me. How could I* *not realize that?*

Jason shouted, "She's lying, Kirsten. Please let me explain."

"You know I ain't lying, Jason. You know I ain't lying."

Jason let go of Kirsten's arms and got in Lacey's face. "Shut up, Lacey! That's enough!"

Jason had never spoken so harshly to Lacey before. She knew he was serious so she quieted down, put her blouse on, slipped back into her tight fitted skirt and threw her bra and panties in her bag.

"Give Ryan a kiss for me," she said, as she headed towards the door.

Kirsten looked over at Lacey with abhorrence. *She didn't even go check on her child!*

"No, Lacey, you stay. This is obviously where Jason wants you to be. I'm leaving."

"No, I don't!" exclaimed Jason. "Kirsten, please don't leave."

Lacey had never seen Jason act so nonchalant towards her, so she slammed the door and left.

"Please, Kirsten, don't go!"

Kirsten couldn't even look at him. "No!" is all she could say as she bolted for the door. That was

Kirsten's first time being able to tell Jason no. When she got outside, she saw that she was blocking Lacey in. Lacey was patiently waiting for her to come out of the house, even though she could have gone around Kirsten's car if she tried hard enough. After all, it was a three-car driveway.

Kirsten went into the back yard to get Poodles and Jason ran to the door after her, begging, "Kirsten, please let me explain!"

"Don't beg now playboy! That's what you get," yelled Lacey. Kirsten grabbed Poodles and jumped in her car. She backed out of the driveway so fast that Jason thought she was going to hit his mailbox. Lacey gave Jason a wink and said, "We'll finish this next time, playa."

"There won't be a next time, Lacey! It's over!" Jason said, angrily.

"Child please, you can't resist me!" Lacey said, laughing. She backed out of the driveway and threw her hands out the window to wave goodbye.

Jason stood in the doorway for about five minutes staring down the street as if he was waiting for some sign that things were not as bad as they seemed. He finally shut the door, went into Ryan's room and got into his bed, forgetting all about the meeting he was supposed to attend at 6:00. He laid there for hours, staring at the walls and holding onto Ryan, who was still sleeping peacefully, totally oblivious to the chaos that just surrounded him.

~ THIRTEEN ~

The next day, Jason made several attempts to call Kirsten, but she would not pick up the phone. He sent flowers to her job, but she just threw them in the trash.

"Oh, now he wants to give me real flowers!" Kirsten said, sarcastically.

There were so many unanswered questions in Kirsten's head, but she wasn't even sure she wanted to know the answers. It was obvious that her world had fallen apart. She had a lot to do that day. She tried her best to forget about Jason, but her heart hurt too badly.

Lena could recognize a broken heart a mile away. She came into Kirsten's office and gave her a hug. Lena didn't say a word and neither did Kirsten. Lena saw the beautiful flowers sitting in the trash. She wanted to take them out and keep them for herself, but she knew Kirsten needed to see them in the trash. Lena could tell that Kirsten was in a lot of pain, so after she hugged her, she just quietly walked back to her desk.

Kirsten knew she had to pull herself together and not be so transparent about how she was feeling. She was a professional and her personal life had to take a back seat, but Kirsten really didn't know how to put her broken heart in the back seat. Good thing Mr. Wayne was away on business and Lance had reverted back to his old ways, doing what he does naturally, avoid work. No one was surprised about Lance, especially not Kirsten.

She tried to get back into the swing of things. She consumed herself with work, trying hard to put what happened behind her. She decided that it was time to get involved in church again. She knew she had to get her spiritual life back on track, but she didn't want to go back to her church just yet. She felt foolish enough without having to bare anything the Pastor's wife was going to whisper to her!

If she knew Jason's heart wasn't right, why didn't she just tell me that instead of all that other stuff? Why not just tell me that the man is a jerk and he's going to rip my heart out and feed it to the dragons? I think I would have appreciated that more.

Kirsten took a deep breath. She knew her Pastor's wife was a good woman and she didn't mean any harm. She didn't know why she was taking her anger out on her. *I'll go ask Lena where she attends Sunday service.*

Just as she walked up to Lena's desk, the phone rang. It was Kirsten's line, but since Kirsten was standing there, Lena went ahead and answered it.

"Hi, Lena, this is Jason Glaznyte. Is Ms. Jabard there?

"Ummmm," is all Lena could come up with. She knew Kirsten did not want to talk to him, but it wasn't her business to get into. Kirsten was staring at Lena wondering why she had this panic look on her face. She didn't realize that it was her phone line that Lena answered. A part of Lena hated Jason too, and she didn't even know what he had done.

"Please, Lena, let me speak to Kirsten," Jason asked, desperately.

Lena took a deep breath. "Hold on, sir, I'll see if she's in."

Jason knew Kirsten was in, but for

some reason, Lena felt the need to protect her from him. Lena never told Kirsten that it was Jason on the phone, but it didn't take a rocket scientist for Kirsten to figure out what was going on.

"I think she must have stepped out; would you like me to have her call you?" Lena asked. Jason knew she was lying, and Lena knew that he knew, but she didn't care. She was sure he deserved it.

"Okay, Lena, can you please tell her that I called? Jason asked, in an aggravated tone.

"Sure will, sir," Lena responded, then she hung up the phone.

"Thank you," whispered Kirsten, as she headed back to her office, forgetting that she came to ask Lena about church.

When Kirsten got back to her desk she noticed that she had several missed calls from Jason.

This ritual went on for about three weeks; him calling her cell phone, her not answering, him calling the office and Lena covering for her, him sending flowers and Kirsten throwing them in the trash. He even

left notes on her car, but Kirsten
didn't bother to read them.

One day Jason just showed up at
Kirsten's job. He passed by Lena and
said, "I know she's here, her car is
outside and I'm going in to see her."

Lena got up from her chair, but
she dared not cross him; after all, he
was still Jason B. Glaznyte, the most
successful business owner in the
region. Kirsten's door was closed.
Jason knocked, while letting himself
in. Kirsten didn't seem to be working.

"Kirsten, I need to talk to you,"
Jason said, while closing the door
behind him.

"How dare you show up at my job,
Jason?" Kirsten asked, angrily.

"Would you have agreed to see me
otherwise?" He responded.

Kirsten didn't answer.

Jason continued, "When I stop by
your house, you won't answer the door,
you won't answer the phone, you won't
respond to my emails or letters or
texts or anything, Kirsten."

Lena tried hard not to listen, but
she really wanted to know what happened
between them. The walls were thick and
Kirsten and Jason were talking pretty

low, so Lena couldn't understand much of anything they were saying.

"Kirsten, please let me take you to lunch, so I can talk to you; please give me a chance to explain."

"You lying on the bed with another woman is explanation enough, Jason. Please leave!"

"No, I'm not leaving."

"Excuse me? Jason, this is a place of business. I don't bring my personal business to my job and neither should you."

"Well, let me take you to lunch then. Kirsten, please let me take you to lunch to explain. I owe you that."

"I'm not hungry and you obviously don't owe me anything."

"Please, Kirsten!" Jason pleaded.

"I'll give you 15 minutes. I have tons of work to do so I will have to ask you to leave in exactly 15 min," Kirsten said. Kirsten hadn't done any work all morning, but she was going to come up with something to make sure Jason didn't get more than 15 minutes of her time.

Jason began his explanation. "Kirsten, I didn't sleep with Lacey every time I went to see Ryan."

Kirsten cut him off, "Ummm, I hope this is not the best you can start off with, Jason."

"Please, just hear me out, Kirsten," he begged. Jason continued, "I once loved this woman very much and I really wanted my family back. When we lived in Vermont, I thought it could possibly work. After we got divorced, she started being nice and making dinner for me, and Lacey was a terrible cook when we were married. It seemed like she was changing, but of course she'd always go back to her ugly ways.

"When I was thinking about relocating to Atlanta, I really wanted them to come with me. Although we were divorced, we discussed getting back together several times so Ryan could have a complete family and I really hated not living in the same house with him. I wanted my son in the house with me; I just wanted everything back. I wanted to believe that there was hope for me and Lacey, but with Lacey there's always drama, all the time. You've seen how she is.

Oh, I've seen more of Lacey than I ever wanted to see, Kirsten thought.

"I eventually decided to just cut

my ties with Lacey and do the best I could to stay active in Ryan's life. When I moved to Atlanta I was done with Lacey, but about a month after I got here she called and said she was relocating to Alabama. She asked if I would come help them get everything set up.

"She's the mother of my son, so of course I was willing to help. I still loved Lacey, but I knew she and I didn't have a future together. A couple of days before I was supposed to go help them, I met you. Kirsten, when I saw you I knew there was something special about you. I knew you were someone I had to get to know. I knew you could help me move on from Lacey."

"SO I WAS YOUR REBOUND?" Kirsten shouted. Lena heard her. She tried to listen for more, but that was the only thing she could make out in the conversation. It was a good thing Mr. Wayne was out of town, Lance was nowhere to be found, and the other employees were on the construction site.

"No, No," said Jason. "You were special; you are special. There was so much I loved about you. The more time

I spent with you, the more I needed you in my life. I was falling for you, but I also still struggled with my feelings for Lacey. I cared for both of you, but for very different reasons. I don't know why I kept sleeping with her, Kirsten. I don't even know why I kept going back to her house when I went to see Ryan. I knew I should have gotten a hotel when I was there and sometimes I did, but even when I got a hotel she would show up in raincoats with nothing underneath. Once, she offered me to sleep in her guest bedroom. I accepted her offer and told her that things were over between us. I told her that there would be no more sex, but I knew she was going to come in the room naked. I knew it, but I stayed there anyway, and of course she came in naked.

"Every time, I told myself that I was not going to let anything happen, that I shouldn't keep doing that to you, but just as sure as she came in, I gave in. I used to justify it by saying, 'Well, I'm a man and she got in my bed naked, so what was I supposed to do?' I knew that was no excuse for what I was doing. I hated what I was

doing to you, but I wouldn't stop. I
don't know why I wouldn't stop, but I
just wouldn't.

"It was like I couldn't say "no"
to Lacey. Right before I brought Ryan
to meet you, I finally made up my mind
that I was ready to stop sleeping with
her. I went to pick Ryan up and I told
Lacey that we were done. She acted
like she was totally fine with my
decision. She said she had moved on
anyway. I wished her the best and said
I just want us to be cordial so we
could raise our son. She agreed and I
thought everything was fine. I brought
Ryan to meet you and we had a great
weekend together, but when I took him
back home, I ended up sleeping with her
again."

"That was the weekend I asked if I
could go with you," Kirsten said.

"Yes, but Kirsten, there was no
way I could take you to Lacey's house.
There's no telling what she would have
done."

"So, did you really have a VIP
party to attend?"

"Yes, I did."

"Did Lacey go with you?"

"No, she didn't. She asked me to

take her, but I couldn't do that to you."

"Did you sleep with her before or after the party, Jason?"

Jason looked down at the floor.

"Yes."

"Which one, Jason? Before or after?"

"Both!"

Kirsten covered her face with her hands. She couldn't believe what she was hearing. "Did you wear a condom, Jason?"

Jason looked down at the floor again.

"Answer the question, Jason!"

"Lacey don't like condoms, so no, but, Kirsten, that was the last time I was with her. I swear! After that, I told her it was over. From then on, when I went to see Ryan, I got a hotel room and I refused to tell Lacey where I was staying. When I dropped Ryan off, I didn't give in to any of her advances and she eventually stopped trying to seduce me. We were done, Kirsten! At that point, it was completely over! That's why I waited so long to introduce you to Ryan. As long as I was sleeping with Lacey, I knew I couldn't let you meet Ryan. I knew I had to be totally done with Lacey before I could bring you around him. Minus that one slip up when I took him back home, I had totally stopped sleeping with her. On our anniversary weekend when I didn't go see Ryan, he told her that I was with you. Needless to say, she flipped out. That's when she showed up unannounced with Ryan's clothes and toys and dumped them all over the yard like a lunatic. I couldn't really respond like I wanted to, because I couldn't bear her telling you that I had been sleeping with her. I knew she would have blurted everything out if I made a big deal about her dropping him off like that.

"I was actually glad she let Ryan come live with me because it kept me from having to deal with her. When I asked her to give me full custody of him, she agreed so I figured I could start concentrating on the two of us without her drama. When I met you, I just had so much baggage that needed to be dealt with, but I was too selfish to let you go, so I tried to maintain both situations and I didn't do a good job with either.

"Since Ryan has been living with us, I have not slept with Lacey. I promise, Kirsten. I know that doesn't take away from all the times I did sleep with her, but please forgive me. Please give me another chance to prove to you that you're the only woman I want. I don't want to lose you, Kirsten; I can't bear losing you."

Kirsten sat there with an empty look on her face. It was like she wasn't even there, except she heard every word Jason said. She wanted to hate him, but she couldn't. In fact she believed him. She honestly believed that Jason tried to stop sleeping with Lacey, and that made Kirsten very angry with herself. *You are such a punk, Kirsten! You better not take this cheater back! He lied to you. He used you for the convenience of having someone there to meet his needs. He never intended to marry you. You did everything for him that a wife would do, but instead of telling you that he loved you, he was telling his ex-wife that he loved her. You slept with him every time he wanted to, but he was still sleeping with her. Every weekend, Kirsten, without a condom, for three whole years he was sleeping with both of y'all. Don't be a fool, Kirsten, don't be nobody's fool!*

She looked over at Jason. "So if you were done with her, why was your tongue stuck down her throat when I walked in the room? Did she make you do that too?"

Jason let out a deep sigh. His eyes swelled with water. Kirsten twisted her lips, because Jason crying was something she never thought was possible. *Okay, he might have gotten me with that sob story, but fake tears is too much, Jason!*

"I want to forget that day, Kirsten. Really, I do. The whole day started out wrong. For one, I totally forgot that it was your birthday and on top of that I almost slept with Lacey again. I just wish that day never happened. I'm so sorry for all of that," he said. Jason sighed again and started to explain.

"Well Lacey called and said she was in town and asked if she could see Ryan. I told her that you guys were at the park and she asked if she could wait at the house for y'all to come home. I hesitated, then she said it was really hot outside and she just wanted to get off her feet.

"Lacey hadn't caused any problems for us since Ryan came to live with us so I felt like it was harmless. She came by and I offered her something to

drink. I told her that y'all shouldn't
be too long and she could watch TV
while she waited. I told her that I
was sorry I couldn't sit and talk to
her, but I had to go get dressed for my
meeting.

"I left her there watching TV and
I went in the bathroom to shave. When
I came out of the bathroom, my bedroom
door was closed and she was lying on
the bed naked. My heart started
pounding, because I knew this was not
going to end well. I told her to put
on her clothes; I told her it was over
between us. She got up and I assumed
she was going to get dressed, but
instead she jumped in front of me and
started unbuttoning my pants. I pushed
her hands off my pants and told her
again that it was over but she started
touching and kissing on me. I pushed
her off several times, then she pushed
me onto the bed and I decided to stop
fighting it. We started kissing and
that's when you walked in. Kirsten,
that's the honest truth. I know it
still hurts, but it's the truth."

Kirsten just sat there silent.
She didn't feel any better now that she
had heard Jason's story. Actually she

felt worst.

"Get out Jason, your fifteen minutes is up," she said, calmly.

"You're not even going to respond?" Jason asked.

"There's really nothing to say to a man who has no self-discipline. It is blatantly obvious that if I hadn't come home early that day, you were going to sleep with her again in the same bed you make love to me in every night. If that wasn't bad enough, you were going to sleep with her on my birthday and when I came home you were going to act like nothing happened, just like you did after sleeping with her all the other times. Without a bit of remorse, you would have turned right around and slept with me too. You call yourself a man of God, yet you have no integrity! Please leave, Jason. We're done here!"

Jason heard someone in the hallway and he didn't want to cause a scene, so he got up and left.

He made several other attempts to make things right with Kirsten, but she ignored him. He knew there was nothing he could do to win Kirsten back.

~ FOURTEEN ~

About six weeks later, Kirsten stopped at the grocery store to get Poodles some dog food. When she turned down the dog food isle, there were Jason and Ryan. She quickly tried to turn around, but Ryan spotted her.

"Ms. Kirsten, Ms. Kirsten," he yelled, then ran and gave her a big hug. Jason ran too, acting as if he was running after Ryan. Kirsten knew she was stuck. She couldn't just walk away from Ryan. He was the cutest thing ever and she loved him like she gave birth to him herself.

"Where have you been, Ms. Kirsten? I miss you," Ryan said.

Kirsten thought she was going to fall apart. "I miss you too, honey bunch."

Ryan was still holding on to Kirsten. She didn't make any eye contact with Jason.

"Well, I have to go, Ryan. I'll see you later, okay?" Kirsten said.

"Can't you come over? I have a new puppy I want to show you."

Kirsten was fighting back tears.

"I can't today, honey, but maybe I'll get to see your puppy another time, okay?"

"Okay," Ryan said, disappointedly. Kirsten put him back down and rushed off without saying a word to Jason.

"Kirsten," Jason called out as she walked off.

She didn't hear you, daddy," Ryan said.

Seeing them made Kirsten's heart hurt. She still loved them very much and hated that she and Ryan had gotten caught in the middle of Jason and Lacey's drama.

"We were both innocent! This is so unfair to Ryan and I," Kirsten said to herself, as she ran to her car, forgetting that she still needed dog food for Poodles.

Kirsten cried all the way home. When she pulled up in her driveway, she realized that she had forgotten Poodles' food.

"Oh, gosh!" Kirsten said. "Well let's just hope Poodles have enough food for tonight and I'll go to a different grocery store tomorrow."

She hated that she still loved Jason. She knew she was nowhere near being over him. She went into the house and tried to pray, but all she could do was cry.

As she lay on the floor, crying uncontrollably, the phone rang. She figured it was Jason so she didn't bother to answer. Whomever it was, they just kept calling, and calling, and calling. She knew there was only one person that would call her repeatedly until she answered. Michelle!

Kirsten leaned over and looked at the caller ID and sure enough, it was Michelle. Kirsten didn't feel like talking to anyone, but she hadn't talked to Michelle in a couple of months so she decided to answer.

"Hey, girl," Kirsten said, trying to sound happy.

"Guess what, Kirsten?

"What?"

"I'M PREGNANT!" Michelle yelled, as loud as she could.

As horrible as Kirsten felt about her own life, she knew she had to put her feelings aside and celebrate with

Michelle.

"That is wonderful, Shelly! I'm so happy for you!"

"I'm four months," Michelle said.

"What? Four months?"

"Yes, Matt didn't want to tell anyone until we got out of our first trimester. He said he didn't want to jinx it."

"You kept a secret from me, Shelly?" Kirsten asked, surprisingly.

"Yes, you know I tell you everything, but I needed to do this for my hubby," Michelle responded.

Kirsten was very proud of this new Michelle. "I'm very happy for you guys. I think that is wonderful, Shelly!"

"IT'S TWINS!" Michelle yelled again.

Kirsten dropped the phone and fell over on the bed.

"TWINS!" she yelled from the bed while the phone was still on the floor.

"YES, TWINS!" she could hear Michelle screaming.

Kirsten picked the phone back up. She heard Matt celebrating in the background as if it was his first time hearing the news.

"Apparently twins run on my dad's side. Who knew?" Michelle said, excitedly.

"Wow, Shelly, that is awesome! So you've talked to your dad again, huh?"

"Yes, we talk all the time, Kirsten. Can you believe that?"

Kirsten heard Matt in the background saying, "Yeah, he'd better be glad he's her father because I don't let no man talk to my woman like that." Kirsten and Michelle both laughed.

"Matt sounds very happy, Shelly."

"Oh, Kirsten, you don't know the half. He's like a kid in a candy store. He can't go anywhere without buying the babies something. Toys, blankets, bibs, bottles, anything that he can get his hands on he's going to buy it! It's crazy, Kirsten. So what's wrong with you?" Michelle asked.

"Huh? Nothing, what are you talking about?"

"Come on, girl, I've known you longer than you've known yourself, so what's up? Tell me what's going on."

Kirsten didn't want to ruin Michelle's good mood, but Michelle said, "If you don't tell me what happened, I'm going to revert back to ghetto-shelly. You know she's still in me."

Matt yelled, "Please tell her, Kirsten. My wife has been ghetto-free for a while now, so don't make her have a relapse."

They all laughed. Michelle left the room so she could listen to Kirsten and so Matt could stop interrupting. Kirsten knew Michelle would get really upset if she told her what happened with Jason, so instead she said, "Girl, it's nothing. Things are just a little stressful at work, but it's nothing I can't handle."

"You liar, what did Jason do?" Michelle responded.

Kirsten knew Michelle wasn't going to let her get off the phone until she told her the truth, so she told Michelle that she caught Jason and his ex-wife kissing in his bedroom.

"I knew it!" Michelle said, "I just knew it! Matt told me how Jason responded when they asked him about marrying you and how Jason went right into talking about his ex. Matt told him he needed to heal from that before it caused problems with you guys, but Jason said everything was fine! Matt knew something wasn't right, Kirsten. He said it wasn't right."

"Matt," Michelle yelled from the other room. "We're about to go to Atlanta to find Jason and kick his butt, so pack up some things," she said.

"What he do? Where he at? Where he at?" Matt started yelling, like he was getting ready for a boxing match. Kirsten didn't want to hear any more so she told Michelle that she had to go and she would call her later.

"Okay, honey! I'm really sorry about Jason. Call me if you need to talk."

"Okay, thanks. Bye," Kirsten said, hanging up the phone.

How did everybody know something wasn't right, but me? Am I that naive? How could I not see this coming?

Three months went by and Kirsten thought about how drama-free her life had been without Jason in it. She welcomed the change. As much as Kirsten loved Jason, she did not need or want the drama anymore, but she still missed him dearly. She wasn't sure how long it was going to take before she would get him out of her system. She almost broke down into tears, but she stopped herself. She decided that she needed to get out of the house for a little while.

"A virgin strawberry-mango daiquiri would be wonderful right now. It is the best substitute for alcohol, because it makes me forget all my troubles," Kirsten said, snickering and wiping the tears from her eyes.

She grabbed her purse and headed towards the door. Just as she was about to leave, her phone rang; she didn't recognize the number, but she answered it anyway.

"Hello."

"Hi, Kirsten, this is Jason."

Kirsten felt like her heart literally stopped. She hadn't talked to Jason in months, but when she heard his voice she got butterflies, just like she did the first day she met him. She forgot about the pep talk she just gave herself about being glad he was out of her life. It seemed as if she also forgot about all the hurt he'd caused her, all the lies he told, and all the cheating he'd done.

She missed him like crazy and his voice sounded so good. She knew then that she was going to say yes to whatever he wanted.

"Can I come see you?" he asked.

Kirsten couldn't get any words out, but her insides were screaming, "**YES!**" She took a deep breath. *Calm down, Kirsten!*

"Ummm, I don't know, Jason."

"Kirsten, I just want to see you. I miss you so much; I just want to talk."

Kirsten figured he'd bring Ryan with him, so it would probably be safe and she really missed Ryan. "Okay, for just a little while."

Within five minutes Jason was at her house and within two seconds of his arrival, they were making out in the foyer. He never even made it into the living room. Lips were smacking and clothes were flying everywhere. Their escapades always seemed to be more animalistic than humanized.

The passion they had was unbelievably breathtaking. Kirsten didn't realize how much she missed him until he was standing in front of her. What a beautiful and irresistible sight he was.

Afterwards, Kirsten just laid in

his arms feeling more helpless than ever. *How could you do this to yourself, Kirsten, after what he did to you? He wasn't good to you, he made you feel like you weren't worthy of being his wife. Why are you letting him back in your life? Why, Kirsten?*

Jason stayed and held Kirsten for the rest of the night. When morning came, he cooked her breakfast and asked if she wanted to hang out for the rest of the day. With a night like that, she couldn't say no. They had a fabulous, passionate, sex-filled day together.

Jason still seemed perfect, although now she had proof that he wasn't. Kirsten couldn't help but wonder if he was still sleeping with Lacey. She felt sad that she let him back in so quickly and without him even explaining what he was going to do differently if she gave him another chance. Matter of fact, he never even asked for another chance. All he did was ring the doorbell. That's all it took to get Kirsten back in his arms. Kirsten was ashamed of herself. *You didn't even play hard to get! That's pitiful, Kirsten,* she thought to herself.

"I want to marry you," Jason said,

interrupting Kirsten's emotional roller coaster of thoughts.

Just then she heard Everett outside mowing the lawn. "Oh, I've got to pay Everett. I changed banks and his money isn't automatically going to his account anymore. I was supposed to pay him last week, but I forgot," Kirsten explained, frantically. She threw on some sweatpants and ran out the door, barefooted with her checkbook. As she was running towards Everett, she fell and stumped her toe. Everett jumped off the lawn mower and ran over to see if she was alright. He helped her up and offered to get his first aid kit from his truck. Kirsten thanked him, but said she was a tough country girl and she'd had plenty of stumped toes in her lifetime. She and Everett laughed while Jason watched them through the kitchen window. Kirsten thanked Everett again, paid him the money and limped back to the house.

"Why do you have a lawn guy?" Jason asked, as soon as she stepped into the house.

Kirsten thought that was a dumb question since she had a house with lawn. "My toe is fine, Jason. Thanks for asking!" Kirsten said, limping to the chair.

"I'm sorry, baby, come sit down. I'll put some ice on your toe for you. I only meant that I could get my lawn guy to take care of your yard for you. You can tell that guy you don't need him anymore," Jason said, trying not to sound jealous.

We dated for three years and he's just thinking about getting someone to cut my yards for me? You're surely not winning any points here, Jason.

"Jason, Everett has been cutting my lawn for four years. He's like family to me and I don't know that I could ever find a better lawn guy than him. I'm not firing him, but thank you for the offer, babe, that is very sweet," she said, then quickly changed the subject.

"Where's Ryan?" she asked, acting as if she never heard what Jason said about getting married.

Jason moved closer to her. She could still smell his breath-taking cologne.

"I'm serious, Kirsten," he said, pulling a ring out of his pocket and placing it on her finger.

"Kirsten, will you marry me?" he

asked.

Kirsten let out a small gasp. It was the most beautiful ring she had ever seen. She wasn't sure what size the diamond was, but it was huge and it looked very good on her finger.

She tried to tell herself that there were too many unresolved issues and she could not accept the ring, but its beauty made her speechless. Immediately, Kirsten felt like she was engulfed under Jason's magic spell again.

She wanted to say no, but the word "no" just didn't seem to exist when it came to Jason. Instead, she just did what she does best. She gave him a silent "yes" as he coaxed her into bed with his sweet and sexual seductions.

A couple of hours later, Jason laid there sleeping and Kirsten laid there staring at her beautiful ring. Her thoughts of walking down the aisle were quickly interrupted when Jason's phone started vibrating. She couldn't help but wonder if it was Lacey calling. She tiptoed to where the phone was and sure enough, it was Lacey.

Kirsten couldn't resist the

228

overwhelming urge to answer it, so she grabbed the phone and stepped out of the room to keep from waking Jason.

"Hello," Kirsten said.

When Lacey heard Kirsten's voice, she immediately started laughing.

"So you took him back, huh? Well, I can't say I blame you. I just might take him back too, because the brotha got skills, don't he girl?" Lacey said, still laughing and mocking Kirsten.

Kirsten's heart sank. She didn't know what to say so she just hung up. She knew she would never win in any match against Lacey; she didn't have the confidence or the ability to handle Lacey.

Kirsten couldn't believe how low her self-esteem had become. She used to be so sure of herself, so confident, to the point that people thought she was snobbish and arrogant.

"What happened to me? I negotiate million-dollar business deals. I go up against some of the most prominent businesses in the region and I win, so why am I letting this dramafied, ghetto-fabulous, psychopath, pole-dancer get to me? Lacey can't hold a candle to what I have to offer in a relationship," Kirsten said, trying to sound tough.

She laughed at the words she just made up. It didn't matter, though, because saying them made Kirsten feel better. It made her feel like her old self again, the Kirsten she longed to be again.

She heard Jason moving around in the other room. "Oh gosh, I've got to get this phone back in there," Kirsten said while running and jumping into the chair where Jason left his phone.

"Hey beautiful lady, you just sat on my phone," Jason said, while yawning.

"Oh, I'm sorry babe."

Kirsten reached down and pretended she was getting the phone from under her. She handed it to him and hoped that Lacey wouldn't call back to tell Jason she answered his phone.

"Hey, you never did tell me where Ryan was," Kirsten said, trying to distract Jason.

"He's with his mom. She came to get him right before I came over here last night." Kirsten's mind drifted. She wondered if he slept with Lacey before he came to see her.

Kirsten already knew Ryan was with his mom, so she didn't know why she got so angry when she heard him say it. She felt herself filling up with rage.

She left her child on your doorstep for Pete's sake, how could you still let her see him? Kirsten was so uncomfortable with Jason being around Lacey, but she knew there was no way around it. They had a child together; they had to see each other. She hated the control Jason, and now Lacey seemed to have over her.

"I hate Lacey!" Kirsten said, not realizing that she was no longer using her inside voice.

"Huh, where did that come from?" Jason said, sounding confused.

"Oh, I'm sorry. I didn't mean to say that."

Jason looked at Kirsten and said, "Kirsten, people don't say things like that and not mean them, so what's on your mind?"

Kirsten knew that no amount of comfort from Jason would make her feel better about Lacey. She wanted to cry, but she couldn't tell Jason what Lacey just said to her, because then he'd know she answered his phone. She wanted to ask him if he was still sleeping with Lacey, but she really didn't want to know the truth. Everything was so dysfunctional. Kirsten didn't even know who she was anymore. She didn't know who Jason was either and she didn't know why she let him back into her life. *How could I be so dumb?*

She looked at the stunning rock still sitting so perfectly on her wedding finger, but she felt so empty. It was as if the ring meant nothing at all. She looked at Jason and said,

"This should be the happiest moment of my life, but I feel so sad and so unfilled. I hate what you've done to us. I hate that I have to deal with Lacey. I hate that I can't trust you anymore. I just hate I got myself caught up in this mess!"

Tears started rolling down Kirsten's face. Jason had never seen Kirsten cry and he wasn't sure how to respond.

"I told you it was over between me and Lacey, you don't have to deal with her anymore. I promise she won't cause any more problems between us."

"That's a lie! I will always have

to deal with Lacey and so will you, so
stop making promises you know you can't
keep or control," Kirsten said,
bitterly. "I can't accept this ring!"

She placed the ring in Jason's
hand.

"Kirsten, please don't do this.
I've changed, baby! I'm trying to get
my life right. I'm praying, I'm
reading my Bible, and I'm spending a
lot of time with God. I know I didn't
do right by you before, but if you give
me a second chance, I will show you
that I'm a changed man and I'm ready to
be the husband you deserve," he
pleaded.

"That's wonderful Jason, it really
is, but—" Kirsten said, stopping in the
middle of her sentence. "I just really
need some time alone, Jason. I don't
know what to think or believe anymore,"
she said walking to the door to let
Jason know that she wanted him to
leave.

Jason grabbed his things and told
her that he'd give her some space to
think things over. He placed the ring
back in her hand and said, "This
belongs to you and if it makes you feel
any better, I took Lacey's name off the

business. Ryan is now 50% part-owner with me." Then he kissed her forehead and left.

Kirsten was very happy that Lacey's name wasn't on Jason's business anymore. She really wanted to believe that he had changed. She wanted to believe that things could work. She loved Jason. They had such a wonderful time whenever they were together and she missed Ryan tremendously. Even if she tried to leave Jason alone, she wasn't sure if she would ever be able to. She felt so addicted to him, but everything just seemed so wrong now.

After Jason left, Kirsten began to think about the three years they had shared. The more she thought about it, the more she saw all the red flags that she had ignored when they were together.

I was too blind to see that he was cheating all along. I thought I was his one and only, but I was competing for him the entire time. I was competing against a woman that wasn't even supposed to still be in the race. I guess this ring is supposed to be my prize for winning? Well, I don't feel like I've won anything. God, I don't know if I can do this anymore. She shook her head.

Kirsten was so disappointed in

herself for sleeping with Jason. She
needed someone to talk to. She called
Beatriz, then Saidah and neither of
them answered, so against her better
judgment, she called Michelle. Kirsten
braced herself.

"Hey Shelly, how are the babies?"

"What's wrong, Kirsten?"

"Gosh, can't I just call to talk
to my best friend without something
being wrong?"

"Kirsten I am pregnant, my sense
of smell, taste, feeling, hearing,
seeing, and knowing have all
increased."

Kirsten laughed. "There is no
such thing as 'sense of Knowing,'
Shelly."

They both laughed.

"Is Matt there?"

"No, but you can call him on his
cell if you need him."

"No, no, I don't need to talk to
him. Something is wrong, though and I
need some rational advice."

"And you called me?" Michelle
asked. "Saidah, Beatriz and your mom
and the rest of the universe must not
be available," Michelle said, laughing.
"I'm just playing, what's wrong, girl?"

"Well, Jason came over last night and—" was all Kirsten managed to get out of her mouth before Michelle started screaming through the phone.

"O.M.G., I can't believe you're still sleeping with that birdbrain. Tell me you're not sleeping with him, Kirsten? He cheated on you! Please tell me you did not take him back. He doesn't want to be in a committed relationship with you, because he's still in one with his ex-wife. He's a whore, Kirsten, and he's just going to keep stringing you along for as long as he can. I can't believe you've sunken to this level. What has happened to you? You obviously have lost all self-worth and self-esteem. I really feel sorry for you."

Kirsten wanted to defend herself and she wanted to defend Jason, as well, but it wouldn't have done any good to mention that Jason proposed to her or the fact that he said he had change. The old Michelle had obviously returned and she was enraged more than Kirsten had ever seen. At this point, Kirsten felt it was best to just tell Michelle bye and hang up the phone.

She loved Michelle dearly and knew

that reaction was only because Michelle didn't want to see her get hurt, but Michelle was a walking time bomb and although she had changed a lot, Kirsten still knew that she could benefit from a few anger management classes.

Kirsten didn't know why she even called Michelle, knowing she was pregnant, but Michelle had become so calm lately. Kirsten figured she was able to communicate rationally now.

What was I thinking?

She knew that Matt was not going to appreciate her calling and upsetting his wife. Kirsten felt really bad for getting Michelle all worked up; Lord knows it doesn't take much.

Shelly will always be my best friend no matter what, but from now on, I will wait until Beatriz, Saidah, or my mom is available before I share any more of my problems.

On Monday morning, when Kirsten went to work she saw roses on Lena's desk. She didn't think much of it.

Maybe it's Admin Appreciation Day or something, but then she noticed how unusually happy Lena was. She quickly turned around and went back to Lena's desk. She looked Lena in the eyes and said, "Who is he?"

Lena laughed like a little school girl with a crush.

"Lena, are you dating somebody?" Kirsten had been so lost in her own world that she didn't even notice that Lena had found herself a man.

"Hold on, let me go outside to see if it's snowing," Kirsten said to Lena.

"It's August in Atlanta, Georgia; there ain't no snow on the ground, girl." They both laughed.

"Well, I want to hear all about him." Lena got up from her desk and assured Kirsten that she'd tell her everything, but she had to go to a parent-teacher conference, so they would have to put that conversation off until later.

"Well, can you tell me anything about him before you go?"

"He's wonderful!" Lena yelled, as she was leaving. Then she said, "Oh," and ran back to Kirsten. Lena leaned over and whispered, "When I got to work this morning, Lance was in Mr. Wayne's office balling like a little baby. Apparently Mr. Wayne told him that he would be working in the mail room from now on."

Kirsten's eyes grew so big, they

looked like they were about to disconnect from their sockets. Lena continued. "Mr. Wayne told him that he needed to work his way up like everybody else. He said, "If you're too lazy to go to college and get a degree, then I'm too lazy to keep paying you like you have one. Then he told Lance that he had two months to find an apartment, and he suggested that he start saving his money."

Kirsten's mouth fell open. "He's kicking him out of the house too?" Kirsten asked.

"Yep, but I gotta go now," Lena said, and ran back towards the door. Kirsten begged Lena to come back, but she said, "Sorry, I have to go."

"Being a receptionist definitely does have its perks," Kirsten said, as she walked towards her office. As she was opening her door, Mr. Wayne ran into the hallway.

"Kirsten!" he said, like he was happy to see her. "I'm glad I caught you before I left. I'm gonna stop by your office later so we can talk about that little project I had you working on. I found a better solution that won't cause you any headaches. I have

to run to a meeting now, but let's get
together this afternoon to discuss,
okay?"

"Yes, sir," Kirsten said, trying
to pretend she didn't know what he was
talking about.

Since Mr. Wayne and Lena were both
gone, Kirsten decided to walk down the
hallway where Lance's office was.

The office was totally empty. It
didn't even have a desk or a chair;
nothing but carpet and walls. Kirsten
sort of felt bad for Lance, but then
she snapped out of it and said, "A
little bit of hard work and a slice of
humble pie never hurt anybody; he'll be
just fine. At least he still has a
job."

As she was walking back down the
hallway towards her office, she saw
Lance with the mail bin. He was
happily delivering everyone their mail.
Kirsten didn't want Lance to see her so
she took the side hallway and quickly
ran back into her office.

She sat at her desk and thought
about all the changes that had taken
place around her. *Lance was demoted, Jason
and I broke up, and Lena got a man. Who would have
thunkit?*

Kirsten laughed, turned on some music, and worked diligently for the rest of the day.

~ FIFTEEN ~

"Ding Dong, Ding Dong." The
doorbell chimed, as Kirsten lazed
around the house one evening. She
looked through the peephole and saw
that it was Jason.

"Hey," she said, surprisingly, as
she opened the door.

"Hey, baby," he replied, letting
himself in and giving her a hug and
kiss, as if they hadn't broken up.
Kirsten just stood there looking
dumbfounded.

"I have a gift for you," he said,
smiling. "I saw it and knew you had to
have it. Here," he uttered, while
shoving a box in her arms.

Kirsten carefully tore open the
beautifully wrapped box.

"A Coach purse, Jason?"

"Not just a Coach purse, it's the
one with the pink on it, just like you
wanted. I saw it at the mall. It was
the last one there, so I had to get it

for you."

Kirsten really wanted to stand her ground and remind Jason about the space he was supposed to be giving her to think things over, but he got her a Coach purse for goodness sakes; the same, exact Coach purse she'd been wanting for years. As far as Kirsten was concerned, there really wasn't anything else to think about, other than this beautiful purse and all the outfits she could wear with it.

He looked at her and smiled; he could see the joy in her eyes. Then out of the blue, he kissed her. She wanted so badly to resist him, but she didn't, she couldn't. Within a few minutes, there she was again, helplessly ensnared in Jason's trap of pleasure and passion and heartache and pain.

Week after week, Kirsten tried to distance herself from him, and week after week, he found ways to get back into her life. Kirsten didn't know how to get rid of him, but to be totally honest, she didn't even know if she wanted to. She truly loved Jason. When he was around, all his faults seemed trivial, regardless of how significant they were in reality.

Kirsten could no longer talk to her friends about Jason. They all knew he had cheated on her and she was way too embarrassed to let them know that not only had she taken him back, but that they were now engaged.

Michelle was the only one with some awareness that Jason had crept his way back into her life, but there was no way Kirsten was going to ever talk to Michelle about Jason again. Kirsten knew that Michelle and Matt were both crazy and they would actually attempt to come to Atlanta to try and beat Jason up. It didn't matter that Michelle was pregnant; she would still fight if need be and Matt would be right beside her, daring anyone to touch her.

Kirsten was unhappy about her situation; she seldom wore her ring. She normally kept it in her purse, though, just in case Jason made one of his surprise visits, which he'd been making a lot of lately. Kirsten wasn't sure what was going to happen between her and Jason. She decided it was best to keep their engagement a secret, at least for the time being.

One day, Kirsten was sitting on her couch and she glanced over at her beautiful ring, which was lying on the coffee table. She looked down at her bare ring finger and let out a huge exhale. *A year ago, I would have done anything to be Jason's wife, but so much has happened now. I don't know if a ring means anything to me anymore.*

Kirsten stared up at the ceiling. *What if Jason really has changed? What if he really has left Lacey alone? What if he really is ready to treat me the way I deserve to be treated? God, I love this man more than anything, but I'm so confused right now.*

"I don't know if I can do this!" she said, out loud.

Tears ran down Kirsten's cheeks. She put one hand over her face. "God, I want so badly to believe that Jason and I can somehow get past this and we can still make things work, but I'm just not sure any more."

Kirsten continued to cry. She couldn't help but feel stupid for even accepting the ring. The thought of marrying Jason and finding out that he was still cheating would be awful. Kirsten felt trapped; she didn't know how she was going to get herself untangled from Jason's web, but she knew she had to.

Three days past, with no calls or visits from Jason. It seemed as if he was finally giving her the space she needed to clear her head. She sat down and began making a list of pros and cons of all the things she liked and didn't like about her relationship with Jason. She told herself that if the cons outweigh the pros, that would give her the strength she needed to walk away from Jason for once and for all. Just as she grabbed her pen and paper, Jason called.

"Hey, babe, I know I'm supposed to be giving you some time and space to think things over, but I was wondering if Ryan and I could stop by to see you when he gets back from seeing his mom?"

"Jason, you know I would love to see Ryan, but I just can't drag him back into this situation until things become a little bit clearer between us."

"Kirsten, things couldn't be any clearer. You are the woman for me, that's not going to change, but I do understand your concerns," he said. "Is it possible for me to stop by your place for a little while so we can talk?"

246

Kirsten took a deep breath, "Ummm, Jason, I don't—"

"Kirsten, there's nothing to be afraid of. I want to marry you. Have you at least thought about a timeframe for when you want to get married?" Jason asked, interrupting.

"I try not to think about it; it makes me an emotional wreck, Jason. I can't keep doing this."

"Kirsten, let's just talk."

"Jason, every time we talk, we end up naked."

"No sex, Kirsten. I only want to talk, okay?"

Against Kirsten's better judgment she told Jason that he could stop by.

"Kirsten, no matter how good he looks or smells, you will not give in to him," she said to herself.

When Jason rang the doorbell, Kirsten let him in and said "No sex, Jason!" He threw his hands up to try and persuade her that sex was the farthest thing from his mind.

Yeah Right, she thought, as she closed the door behind him.

"I want to marry you, Kirsten; you're the only one I want!" Jason said. He grabbed her hand and led her to the couch. "Please sit down, let's talk," he said.

For the first time, Kirsten didn't feel her body parts jump when Jason touched her. "I need to tell you about my relationship with Lacey," Jason said softly, still holding her hand.

Kirsten's heart started pounding with anger. Inwardly she screamed, *REALLY, JASON? You just said you wanted to marry me, now you want to talk about Lacey? I'm not sure how those two things go together!*

Kirsten didn't want to hear anything else about him and Lacey, but she knew Jason was going to somehow talk her into listening, so she decided not to prolong it.

"Go ahead," she said to him.

I might as well have dated Lacey; that's the only person I'm thinking about and talking about these days. Kirsten was getting angry with herself for letting Jason back in her life. *A relationship shouldn't be this stressful,* she thought as Jason began talking.

"Kirsten, my relationship with Lacey was always bizarre, even from the beginning. Lacey was only 17 when I met her but she told me she was 21; I was only 20 myself. She was a waitress at a fancy night club in Vermont. I

248

was on a business trip up there, and that evening I decided to hang out and relax a little.

"I went to the club where Lacey worked. She noticed that I came in alone and brought over a free drink. She struck up a friendly conversation and told me she got off at midnight. She asked if I wanted her to show me around the city. I told her I had to get up early the next morning and I was very tired from work that day. She said, 'Jason this is Vermont, there's not that much to see at midnight. I assure you, it's not going to take that long.' I thought she was beautiful and feisty. She had on fiery red lipstick and very small shorts that barely covered the bottom half of her butt."

Kirsten interrupted the story, "Ummmm, am I supposed to be getting something valuable out of this story, because I'm not seeing the value added right now, Jason."

Jason could tell that he probably shouldn't have mentioned Lacey's booty shorts.

In Kirsten's opinion, Lacey sounded like a stripper and her opinion of Jason had drastically dwindled as well. Kirsten let out a huff to let Jason know she was getting perturbed.

"Kirsten, please just listen to me," Jason begged, as if he desperately needed to get this story off his chest. He took a deep breath and continued.

"When Lacey got off from work, she changed into a nice dress and we rode all over town. I was amazed at how elegant she looked when she dressed up. She was very intelligent and articulate. Not at all what I imagined when I first met her. The town was awesome and I just felt like I was in another world. By the end of the night, I thought Lacey was indeed a lovely lady."

Lacey, a lovely lady? He must be kidding me! Lacey is nowhere near "lovely lady" status. A monstrous beast, perhaps, but not a lovely lady.

Jason went on with his story. "The next morning when I got up to leave for my flight, Lacey gave me her number and asked if we could we keep in touch."

"When you got up from where, Jason? Please tell me you didn't sleep with her on the first night you met her? Is that what you do, Jason? Sleep with people you don't know?"

Kirsten was shocked! She didn't know why she was so shocked, but she was. She thought Jason only had animalistic chemistry with her, but now she knew Jason was just an animal...PERIOD!

"Good-bye, Jason, you're not the man I thought you were!" Kirsten said, with her hand pointing to the door.

"Wait, Kirsten! Hear me out. I was just an old, country boy from Mississippi. One night stands were something I'd never experienced. It made me feel grown up, like a man. I knew it meant nothing to her. I had no intentions of ever calling or seeing her again, but a few months later, I had another trip to Vermont so I called her. She sounded very happy to hear from me. She told me she no longer worked at the night club. She said she wanted to do something better with her life and she used her cashier skills to land a job as a bank teller.

"When I got to Vermont she seemed like a totally different person from the woman I met at the night club. Her relationship with her mom was very problematic and she never knew her dad, so she needed someone to talk to. She treated me so special and made me feel like I was the best thing that ever happened to her. She told me I was her savior. She made me feel wanted and it was nice to feel wanted.

"I made several more trips to Vermont and I just fell in love. One day out of the blue I popped the question. She said 'yes' and I got a job transfer to Vermont. I didn't want to tell anyone because I knew they would think I was crazy. I only knew her for five months before I married her and out of those five months, I only saw her six times."

Kirsten wasn't really impressed with anything Jason was saying and she really didn't see the point of Jason sharing this story with her. Hearing about his and Lacey's five month relationship that quickly blossomed into marriage was not helping her feel any better about their three-year, no commitment, live-in partnership. She wasn't even sure if the story had a point or even an end to it, for that matter. It seemed like Jason just wanted someone to listen to him talk...about Lacey.

If you need to talk about Lacey, a better choice

would've been to call your friends, not the woman you just proposed to, Jason.

Jason didn't seem to notice the hateful looks Kirsten was giving him; he was way too focused on what he needed to say.

"The first three months of our marriage were wonderful. Lacey wasn't much of a cook, but I was a great cook, so it didn't matter."

Ummm, when did you become a great cook, Jason, because you sure didn't do any cooking when I was there! Kirsten thought, while giving Jason another evil eye.

He kept talking.

"After a few months passed, I noticed how distant Lacey had started to become, but I loved her, Kirsten. I really loved her. I didn't even ask what was wrong; I just hoped things would get better.

"I desperately wanted to start a family, but Lacey insisted that we wait. A year went by and I mentioned having kids again; Lacey was still adamant about waiting. Two more years went by, and one day I just got upset. I asked her why she kept making excuses every time I talked about having kids. She said, 'Baby, you know I love you and I want to have lots of babies with you, but I think we should focus on our careers right now.'

"I tried not to argue with her, because I knew I put in a lot of hours at work. I knew Lacey would be the one spending most of the time with the baby, but after four years of marriage, Lacey decided that she no longer wanted to work. That was fine with me because I didn't need her to work anyway. I was doing very well in my career and I had no problem supporting both of us. I figured if Lacey wasn't working, we could finally start on all those babies she promised me.

"She quit her job. I paid off all her bills and told her she could start a business, go to school, or do whatever she wanted with her free time.

"About three months later I brought up the subject of kids again, but she still resisted the baby talk. My family and friends told me that Lacey was a gold-digger and she was only using me for my money. They told me that she would never have any kids, so I might as well stop asking, but I didn't believe them. I felt that Lacey and I had a great relationship. She

254

had a rough childhood and she was
probably just afraid. I told them that
they just didn't understand her, but
things got to the point where Lacey
didn't even want to have sex anymore.
I would come home for lunch, her car
would be there, but she would be gone.
When I asked where she'd been, she'd
get agitated and start screaming. At
night I'd try to romance her, but she
wasn't interested. She claimed she was
too tired. I'd say 'From what? You
haven't done anything all day,' but of
course that started another argument.
I just got tired of begging my wife for
sex.

    "One morning before I went to work
I said, 'Lacey, I want to have sex with
you and I would like to do it right
now, please.' Needless to say, she got
really mad. She started throwing
things and she accused me of treating
her like a slut. She said she knew
working at the night club would come
back to haunt her. She told me I never
valued her as a woman and she was tired
of being unappreciated. I said, 'All I
want to do is have sex with my wife.
When did that become a crime, Lacey?'

    "Kirsten, it had been ten months

since I slept with her. Ten months, Kirsten! Women were all over me at work, I could've had any of them, but cheating on Lacey was never an option."

This made Kirsten furious, because cheating on her was definitely an option! She jumped up and asked Jason to leave. He said, "Kirsten, I know this is difficult for you, but please sit back down, sweetheart, and hear me out. I'm just trying to paint the picture of where I was with Lacey, so maybe you can understand why I did some of the things I did with you. I was a very broken man. I was very confused concerning Lacey. I somehow still felt like it was my obligation to make her happy. I'm just trying to show you where I was with her, Kirsten, and why it was so difficult for me to let her go.

"She sex-deprived me, but I stayed. She spent all of my money, but I stayed. She wouldn't give me any kids, but I stayed. She would disappear for hours, without any explanation, but I still stayed. No matter what she did, I could never bring myself to leave her. I knew I was a fool for her, Kirsten, but she was my wife and I loved her. I've just always felt like it was my job to take care of her, and it didn't matter if we were divorced or not. To me, she was still my wife. Kirsten, I know I've messed things up with us. I never allowed myself to get over Lacey and I'm very sorry for doing that to you, baby. Really I am." Jason said, with tears in his eyes.

Kirsten reluctantly sat back down and Jason continued.

"Eventually, I had had enough and Lacey sensed that I was distancing myself from her. One day, out of the blue she said she was ready to start a family. I had given up on having any kids, so I was totally shocked, but it had been ten months, so of course I wasn't going to ask any questions. On our first try, she got pregnant."

Kirsten raised her eyebrow because that sounded very suspect to her.

"I was so happy, Kirsten! I couldn't believe I was finally going to have kids, but during the pregnancy Lacey grew very resentful of me. She barely talked to me and I felt extremely disconnected from her. I did my best not to upset her. When we found out we were having a son, I was ecstatic and Lacey agreed to name him after me."

Kirsten gave Jason a funny look because his son's name is Ryan, not Jason, but she decided not to interrupt since the story was finally getting interesting.

Jason continued, "I thought things were getting better between me and Lacey. Then out of the blue again, she started accusing me of not loving her, telling me I was using her just to have a child, saying how my family and friends have never liked her, and the list went on and on. Of course, she stopped having sex with me, again. Matter of fact, she only allowed me to touch her that one time and that's when she got pregnant. It seemed like there was nothing I could do to make her happy. I figured it was just emotions, but every attempt I made to make her feel better, she would turn it around to make me feel worse. I said, 'Just tell me what you want, Lacey. Tell me how to make you happy.' She looked at me and said, 'I want a divorce, Jason.'

"I couldn't believe what I was hearing. I said, 'A divorce? You're seven months pregnant! What about our family? What about our son?' Lacey screamed as loud as she could, 'I don't like children, Jason. I never have and I never will.'

I was in total shock. I responded, 'You don't like children? You're seven months pregnant. What do you mean you don't like children?' She said, nonchalantly 'I'm not the motherly type, Jason, sorry.' Then she got up and left the house without saying another word.

"For the first time in my adult life I broke down in tears. She stayed gone for five hours. For the sake of the baby, I didn't want to argue, so I didn't even bother to ask where she'd been. It didn't matter anyway; I knew she wouldn't tell me the truth. I wasn't even sure who I had married. The only thing that kept me afloat was the fact that my son needed his parents to stay together. That's what mattered most to me. I asked Lacey to tell me what I needed to do to make it work, but she said to me, 'there's nothing to make work Jason.'

"We didn't even speak for a long time after that. Sometimes she didn't even come home. I filed a missing person's police report on her once. She showed up the next day, angry because her friends told her the police were looking for her. Eventually I just stopped trying to find her; the only thing I could do was pray that the baby was fine.

"When we finally had the baby, she seemed happier than ever. The baby was healthy and I was very glad about that. He looked just like me, so needless to say, I was relieved. I hoped she had changed her mind about the divorce, because I couldn't wait to get Jason Junior home. I loved him so much, Kirsten. I couldn't imagine us living in two separate houses.

"After two days, we were finally able to take him home and everything seemed wonderful. Lacey and the baby were both doing great. Lacey's natural maternal instincts kicked in and she seemed to be enjoying motherhood.

"A few weeks later, the baby's birth certificate came in the mail and I bounced and sang all the way from the mailbox, 'Jason Bernard Glaznyte, Junior is in the house' but when I looked at the name on the birth certificate, it said Ryan Jeffrey Glaznyte.

"I was HOT, Kirsten! I thought the hospital made a mistake. I got on the phone and called them. I was yelling and screaming, telling them they needed to get it fixed immediately. I yelled and screamed until my throat was sore, but Lacey didn't seem bothered at all by it. The hospital apologized about the mistake. They said they would pull the records and resubmit the paperwork to get it corrected. The nurse who delivered Jason Junior was on duty; she overheard the other nurse talking to me and asked if she could speak with me.

"She said, 'Mr. Glaznyte, I'm Glenda. I was your wife's nurse when your son was delivered. You are correct, your son was to be named after you, but you should probably speak with your wife because before she checked out, she changed his name to Ryan Jeffrey Glaznyte. I may get fired for telling you this, but I feel that I should save you the trouble researching what happened.'

"I said 'RYAN JEFFREY? Who is Ryan Jeffrey?' Kirsten, I was so angry. I hung up the phone and turned and looked at Lacey. She handed me the baby and said, 'You can have his name changed back if you want. I just thought it would be nice to name him after my father who passed when I was younger.'

"I said, 'After your father? He was supposed to be named after his father! That's what we agreed on, Lacey.' Then she said with an attitude, 'Well at least he's yours.'

"I put the baby in the crib. I looked at Lacey and I knew I wanted to strangle her, so I jumped in my car and got a hotel room so I could cool off for the night. When I came back the next morning, Lacey had packed up her and the baby's things and they were gone.

"I called her. I didn't think she would answer, but to my surprise she did. I asked her what was going on. She told me she was back at her mom's house and she had filed for divorce a few days ago. I said, 'Divorce, Lacey?' She said, 'Yes, Jason. Please don't make it ugly. Just sign the papers when you get them so we can both move on.'

"I didn't know how to move on, Kirsten. I loved my son so much. A few days later I got the divorce papers in the mail. I tried to talk to her again, but she was adamant about me signing the papers, so I did. I asked her if I could have custody of the baby. She responded, 'Not as long as I'm alive.' I felt like a truck had run over me.

"After a year of trying to get Lacey to come back home and her refusing, I just consumed myself with work. I eventually stopped trying to make things work with her and I just focused on raising Ryan as best as I could. Then all of a sudden, Lacey wanted to make things work again, so I moved her and Ryan back in with me, but within a few months it was the same old drama. I would come home some days and she'd be gone. I told her I couldn't live like that anymore, but every time she wanted to come back, I let her back in. No matter what she did, Kirsten, I'd let her come back. We went back and forth like that until I moved to Atlanta."

Kirsten just shook her head.

I knew he wasn't right in the head when he gave

me that stupid fake flower. I should have followed my gut feeling. I should have listened to my friends. All I cared about was that he had the looks of what I wanted, but I ignored all the other things he wasn't. The signs were there, I just chose to ignore them.

Jason continued. "When I met you Kirsten, I knew you were special, but I had so much baggage. I was in so much pain and turmoil over my marriage and divorce and my son. I didn't know how to fix any of it. That's the part that hurt so bad. I just didn't have a clue how to fix it. I just hoped it would go away, but it didn't. Kirsten, I'm so sorry I dragged you into my dysfunctional life with Lacey. When I moved here I thought I could get a fresh start, but then she moved too, and as soon as she came back in the picture, I caved in. I'm so sorry that I wasn't honest with you, but I knew you wouldn't give me a chance if I told you about all my drama with Lacey.

"I was so happy with you, Kirsten, more than I have been with anyone, but whenever I was around Lacey, I just gave into whatever she wanted. Kirsten, I promise if you give me another chance, I will treat you the way you deserve. I will get counseling. I'll do whatever I need to do to prove to you that you're the only woman for me. I have not slept with Lacey since you left me. I'm done with her, Kirsten! You won't ever have to worry about Lacey again. Please give me another chance; give us another chance."

Kirsten wasn't sure if she believed that Jason was truly done with Lacey, especially if Lacey had that kind of hold on him. She loved Jason so much and desperately wanted things to work, but it was obvious that he was a fool for Lacey and Kirsten no longer wanted to be a fool for him.

In a way she felt sorry for him.

At some point, everyone has to seek and discover their own way out of the mess they create, **she** thought.

Kirsten looked up at Jason.

"I can't save you from Lacey, Jason."

"I don't want you to save me from Lacey. I told you I am done with her," he responded.

"Jason, you still love her. I can feel it when you talk about her."

"Kirsten, just let me prove to you that you are the only woman I need;

you're the only woman I want. I'm tired of dysfunctional relationships. I'm ready to give you what I should have given you a long time ago. I promise you, I'm a changed man, Kirsten."

She sighed and asked Jason to give her some more time to think things over. He agreed and told her to just give him a call when she was ready to talk. He kissed her on the cheek and said goodnight.

~ SIXTEEN ~

Kirsten was so confused; she decided to go to the one place where she always found comfort, her parents' house.

She called her mom and asked if she could come home for the weekend.

"Do you need to ask?" her mom said, excitedly.

"Thanks ma, I'm leaving right now," Kirsten responded.

"Okay, baby, I'll see you in a couple of hours. Your dad is gone to a fishing tournament this weekend so he won't be here."

"Great, I really need some alone time with you anyway. See you in a few, momma."

Mrs. Jan was a little puzzled as to why Kirsten seemed happy that her dad wouldn't be home that weekend, but she quickly brushed it off. She was happy to spend any time she could with her baby girl.

Kirsten threw some clothes in a bag and headed to Fountainwater. When she drove up to her parents' house, Mrs. Jan was standing in the doorway as if she had a radar that told her when Kirsten was near.

Going home always made Kirsten smile. It was a small, three bedroom log cabin with lots of shaded trees and farmland for the animals. Mrs. Jan had beautiful flowerbeds that ran along the sides of the house and Mr. Jabard always kept the lawn nice and green. The house was nothing to brag about, but there was no other place Kirsten would rather call home.

As Kirsten parked the car, her mom waved excitedly and Kirsten waved back. She grabbed her bags, then heard her mom yell, "Come on in, baby. I just fried up some chicken for ya."

"No thanks, ma. I'm not hungry."

"You're not hungry? What's wrong with you, child? You're always hungry," Mrs. Jan said, giggling at her own joke. She looked in Kirsten's eyes and said, "Come sit down, baby."

Mrs. Jan sat down on the sofa and patted the seat next to her for Kirsten. Kirsten sat down beside her mom, laid her head on mom's lap and began to cry uncontrollably.

"Momma, I don't know what to do."

"About what, honey?" Her mom responded in a worried tone.

"Jason," Kirsten said.

"What's wrong with Jason?" Mrs. Jan asked, thinking Jason had gotten into some sort of accident or trouble.

Kirsten knew her mom liked Jason. Her dad liked him too, but Mr. Jabard was never sure that Jason could cherish his little girl the way she deserved to be cherished. Of course, Mrs. Jan knew that if it was left up to Mr. Jabard, no man could cherish Kirsten the way she deserved. He didn't think anyone would ever be worthy of his baby girl.

Kirsten was no angel, but she knew she didn't deserve to be cheated on. Cheating was where she drew the line, except it seemed like she wasn't drawing any lines at all. She'd never loved a man as much as she loved Jason, but she'd also never been hurt by a man as much as she'd been hurt by Jason. She still couldn't get over the soul connection she felt with him, though. It was the type of bond that Kirsten

269

wasn't sure would ever be broken or
that she would ever experience with
anyone else.   Jason B. Glaznyte made
her heart sing, if there was such a
thing.

As Kirsten lay there sobbing on
her mother's lap, she began to tell her
mom everything that happened with
Jason.   She told her how she walked in
on Jason and his ex-wife kissing and
how Lacey told her that they were
sleeping together every time he went to
see Ryan.

"Well, did he say it wasn't true?"
Her mom asked, angrily.

"Momma, he just stood there with a
dumb look on his face. He didn't even
try to deny it. Later, he had the
nerve to tell me that the reason he
kept sleeping with her was because she
kept coming into his room naked, trying
to seduce him. He actually had the
nerve to use that as an excuse, momma.
That only showed me that he has no
self-discipline. It definitely didn't
make me feel better about him as a man,
that's for sure," Kirsten said, with
anger.   Then she shamefully dropped her
head and said, "But even after all of
that. After I knew he had lied, and

cheated, and deceived me, I still went
back to him."

Mrs. Jan let out a small gasp of
surprise.

"I know, momma. I'm so ashamed of
myself," Kirsten said. Then she told
her mom how Jason came over and
promised that he was done with Lacey,
he promised that he was going to
change, he promised to go to counseling
and do whatever it took to make things
work between them. Kirsten told her
mom how Jason asked her to marry him.
She said, "But when he mentioned that
Lacey came to pick up Ryan right before
he came to my house, I just cringed,
momma. I wondered if he'd slept with
her again. The thought of him sleeping
with her then coming over to my house
and sleeping with me was unbearable. I
felt so stupid, but the worst part of
all this is, I still want things to
work. I still want to be with
him. How can I be so dumb? I'm a
smart girl, momma, but when it comes to
Jason, it seems like I have no common
sense at all."

Mrs. Jan took a deep breath,
rubbed Kirsten's hair out of her face,
which was soaked with tears and said,

"It's okay, you loved him...and you looked like a fool."

Kirsten looked up at her mom, puzzled as to what she meant by that. Mrs. Jan went on to say, "Baby, sometimes love makes you do some crazy things; things you never thought you'd do. Love can make a complete fool out of you and sometimes you know you're being a fool, but you stay there anyway. It's like the person has a hold on you and you can't break free.

"Some people say they're gonna change and they do, and sometimes they say they're gonna change and they don't. It's a risk you take. Relationships are about faith, Kirsten. You make a commitment to someone based solely on a promise they've made to you. If they mess up, and they probably will, then you have to decide if they deserve another chance. There is still no guarantee that you won't end up looking like a fool, again, so it's still a risk. This is where you have to pray, search your heart, and decide if the person is worth the risk. Only you can make that decision, because you're the one who will have to live with whatever decision you make."

Kirsten felt so discouraged. She
didn't know what she should do. When
she looked at her parents' marriage,
she saw two people who were still very
much in love after 30 years; two people
she'd never even heard argue. She
didn't understand why she couldn't just
have a relationship like theirs.

"You and daddy are so perfect.
Why couldn't I find someone like him?"
Kirsten said, sobbing.

Mrs. Jan shook her head, "Honey,
there is no such thing as a perfect
relationship. You'd best believe me
and your father have had our share of
ups and downs. I considered divorcing
him once, and for a long time I wasn't
sure if I made the right decision by
staying, but we made it work and I'm
very happy we did. He didn't cheat on
me, but he still violated my trust and
when trust is violated, it's very hard
to get it back."

Kirsten said, "Tell me what
happened with you and daddy."

Mrs. Jan smiled, "Well, about a
year after your dad and I got married,
he decided to take all of our money and
invest it in some cow farm in Tifton.
The guy told him that the cows were the

best in South Georgia and if he
invested half of the cost, he could
triple his money within two months.

"Your dad wanted to have a farm so
bad, Kirsten, but I knew in my heart
that he was making a mistake. You were
only one month old. I tried to tell
him it wasn't a smart decision, but he
was bullheaded and stubborn. He told
me that when our money tripled he would
give me the world. I told him I'd
rather have peace of mind. He just
shrugged his shoulders like I was being
dramatic. He invested the money
anyway.

"All of it?" Kirsten asked.

"Every penny," Mrs. Jan responded,
"And the investment turned out to be a
hoax, just like I thought, leaving us
with nothing. We had no way to buy
food, no way to pay our bills,
nothing. Good thing you were breastfed
because we wouldn't have had a thing to
feed you. I hadn't gone grocery
shopping yet, so there wasn't much food
in the house. I didn't know what to
do. Part of the money he invested were
wedding gifts from family and friends
and the other part was what we had
saved up for a rainy day. It wasn't

just his money, Kirsten. We both saved
that money and he blew it all.

"He tried and tried to find the
man who swindled him, but he couldn't.
He filed a police report, but the cops
just shook their heads at him and said
he should have known better. He knew
he had failed me, Kirsten. I trusted
him to take care of me and he didn't.
It was a month before he would get paid
again from his job and neither of us
knew how we were going to survive until
then. He knew he had really messed up
and he felt terrible about it, but it
didn't make me feel any better about
him or our marriage.

"I was angry because I begged him
not to invest in that stupid farm, but
he felt like women should just remain
silent and let a man be a man. I
didn't feel like he honored me as his
wife and his partner, so it took
everything in me to stay married to
him. I said to myself, 'There's no way
I want to be married to a man that has
no regard for his family.'

"The whole town heard about what
happened. Of course, my dad offered to
help us, but your daddy would not
accept anyone's handouts. He said to

my dad, 'You gave her to me to take care of and I'll do just that.'

"My dad was furious with your father and the people mocked me for staying by his side. They told me I was stupid for staying with him. People tried to give me money, but I wouldn't take it. I told them that we were just fine, but we weren't.

"I did the best I could to make the little food we had last. Some days we had eggs and water for dinner and some days we just had crackers. We would both lay in bed and cry, trying not to let the other one hear. It was the longest month of my life and even after that, we had gotten so far behind in our bills, we still struggled. I would only buy rice and grits because I needed a meal that would last a while. If I bought meat, I'd just buy one pack, cut it up in small pieces, and cook a little of it each night for dinner. This went on for months and I didn't know how much more I could take. I felt trapped and helpless.

"Your daddy made a mistake, Kirsten, and I knew he was truly sorry. It still didn't change the fact that his selfishness is what put us in that

situation, but to me, he was honestly
worth a second chance. On the weekends
he would cut folks' yards and wash
their cars to try to make a little
extra cash, but all of that money had
to go towards our mortgage payment.
The bank was calling every other day
wanting some money. They agreed to
take partial payments until we could
get caught up. By the time we paid one
bill, the next month's bill was due.
The light bill was due, the water bill
was due, and the insurance bill was
due. Everybody seemed to want money,
and we just didn't have it to give. I
told him we could let my mother keep
you during the day so I could get a job
and help him, but he said it was his
job to take care of me. He told me he
let me down and he would work all day
and all night if he had to to make sure
you and I were taken care of, but
Kirsten, it was a very long time before
I felt taken care of. The only thing
that kept me going was that I truly
believed he had learned his lesson. We
eventually got back on track. Your dad
started his own farm business and it
was doing very well. He knew I liked
looking at land, so he asked me to go

around and pick out property for him to invest in. I knew he only did it to make me feel better about what happened, but before long, he was making a lot of money off of the land. At one point, people even considered us rich. I wouldn't say we were ever rich, but I never needed or wanted for anything again."

"Wow," Kirsten said. "I can't imagine daddy making such a bad decision like that. He seems so business savvy."

Her mother responded, "He is now, but it wasn't always that way. It took us a very long time to get out of the mess he made, but we survived. He's my husband and I know he loves me with all his heart. I love him too, Kirsten. I've never loved anyone more than the man I married. He thought I was going to leave him, though," Mrs. Jan said, giggling. Every time I went into my closet to get something, he'd asked, 'What are you doing, Jan?' I'd always respond, "Nothing, Jacob." Maybe he thought I was going to kill him; I don't know," Mrs. Jan said, laughing. "I decided to take the risk, though. I stayed with him because I believed he had changed."

Kirsten's eyes filled with water. She had no idea that her parents went through this.

Her mom said, "Kirsten, when it comes to matters of the heart, there's really no advice anyone can give you. Ask God to open your eyes and let you see this man's heart. If you honestly believe he's changed and you still want to be with him, then forgive him, let the past go and don't ever bring it back up again. If you don't believe he's changed, then cut your losses and move on with your life without any regrets. Kirsten, the question is, do you believe he's changed?"

"I don't know," Kirsten said, still sobbing.

Mrs. Jan said, "The question is not if he has changed, Kirsten, but do you BELIEVE he has changed."

"I really don't know, momma," Kirsten said.

"Well, the fact that you don't know means you do know," Mrs. Jan responded. "Come on, let's get you something to drink before you dehydrate yourself. You're getting to be like

Michelle with all that crying and carrying on." They both laughed.

Kirsten knew she needed to call Michelle and apologize for hanging up on her, but if anyone understood Kirsten, it was Michelle. They were truly kindred spirits, and Kirsten knew, Michelle wasn't holding any grudges.

After Kirsten got something to eat and drink, Mrs. Jan said, "Get in the car. I want to take you somewhere so you can clear your head."

She took Kirsten downtown. In the center of Fountainwater was a huge fountain. Kirsten and her mom visited it quite often when she was a little girl. The fountain was in honor of the great theologian writer, François Fénelon, placed there in 1815 (100 years after his death). The fountain was to encourage kids to use their imagination through writing. At the bottom of the fountain was one of Fénelon's great sayings, "If all the crowns of Europe were placed at my disposal on condition that I should abandon my books and studies, I should spurn the crowns away and stand by the books."

When Kirsten was younger, she
didn't really understand what the quote
meant, but she knew she loved sitting
at the fountain. There was a great
sense of peace surrounding it. Her mom
told her that the sound of water helps
people to think clearer. Mrs. Jan sat
there quietly, while Kirsten lay on the
bench, staring up at the pretty blue
sky. The fountain was so peaceful to
Kirsten. It made her feel like she
didn't have any problems at all.

As Mrs. Jan sat there, she was
silently praying for God to give
Kirsten wisdom. They stayed for two
hours without saying a word to each
other. When Kirsten finished thinking,
she gave her mom a hug and said, "Thank
you, mom. You always know just what I
need."

Mrs. Jan smiled and they went back
to the house. The rest of the weekend
they spent washing and folding clothes,
picking up pecans, and tending to the
farm animals. Although Kirsten was a
city girl now, there was something so
wonderful about being in the country.

Kirsten's dad came home right
after she left to go back to
Atlanta. Mrs. Jan was sad that he

missed Kirsten by only 20 minutes. He brought in a cooler full of fish for Mrs. Jan to clean.

He said, "Darn it, I sure wish I'd caught Kirsten before she left. I would have given her some of this fish to take home with her."

Mrs. Jan opened the cooler and saw all those fish with their heads still attached; some of them looked like they were moving. She laughed and said, "I think those fish have a better chance of getting eaten if they stay here with us, honey."

Mr. Jabard laughed and said, "Yeah, she never was much of a blood and guts kinda girl. She'd probably faint on the way home if one of those fish moved."

They both laughed. Mrs. Jan told him about Kirsten and Jason breaking up and how Jason came back and asked Kirsten to marry him.

"I hope she doesn't marry him," he said.

"Why do you say that, honey?"

"Because any man that dates a woman for three years and she has to break up with him to get him to propose to her, isn't worth marrying. A real man appreciates a woman when he has her, not after he's lost her."

Mrs. Jan never thought about that before. She just looked at him and said, "That sure is the truth, baby. That sure is the truth." Then he sat down at the table and she brought him his food and jar of sweet tea like she's done for 30 years; Mrs. Jan wouldn't have it any other way.

~ S E V E N T E E N ~

When Kirsten left Fountainwater she felt like a heavy load of emotional turmoil had been lifted off of her shoulders; she felt free.

Kirsten knew what she had to do and for the first time in three years, she was ready to do it. She wasn't quite sure how she would give Jason his ring back, but she knew she no longer wanted to keep it.

"The fact that I do not want to keep this beautiful rock is my confirmation that it's time for me to move on with my life," Kirsten told herself.

She felt her entire relationship with Jason had been a lie. She had no confidence that he would ever stop sleeping with Lacey. "Talk is cheap!" Kirsten said. "For three years, I sat at home almost every weekend by myself while he went off and laid up with his ex-wife. I became a mother to his son, loving Ryan like I birthed him myself, and the first chance Jason got to go back to his ex, he did. If I hadn't come home when I did, they would have had sex right there in the same bed he and I sleep in every night. He wouldn't have said one word, NOT ONE COTTON-PICKING WORD!" Kirsten screamed.

She felt herself becoming hysterical, but she didn't care. She decided that it was best to just get it all out.

"I loved him and he refused to love me back. Whenever my friends questioned Jason's strange behavior, I got upset with them. I moved in with him and played his wife, without a ring or any real commitment. He used me for his convenience so he could have someone local to cater to all of his needs. He kept me there so he wouldn't have to be alone. I was his shield to keep him from dealing with his own insecurities.

Her eyes filled with tears. "I BECAME A TOTAL FOOL FOR HIM!" Kirsten yelled, hitting the steering wheel, and mistakenly blowing at the truck in front of her. The driver moved over to the other lane, but he threw up his middle finger as Kirsten passed by. She looked over at the man, but she was so upset about her relationship with Jason that she wasn't bothered by his gesture or the ugly face he was making at her.

"I never want to see Lacey again," she said. "And at this point, I'm not sure that I ever want to see Jason again either. Life with Jason will be full of drama. It will be nothing but unwanted surprises, and as much as I love surprises, I think I'll opt out of Jason's kind of surprises."

Kirsten had several heart-to-heart talks with herself as she drove back to Atlanta. She was ready for change! This made her think of a poem Beatriz wrote for English class in high school.

It said, "Change is inevitable. Sometimes the process feels wonderful and sometimes it feels horrible, but change always leads to an endless possibility of something better. It leads to the possibility of a better situation, the possibility of a better future, and the possibility of a better you. Embrace this creature called change! Fall in love with it and let it fall in love with you, for in its

arms lie the transition to where you
stop wishing and start achieving."

When Beatriz finished reciting the
poem, she got a standing ovation. Even
the boys in class stood up and clapped.
Everyone knew the struggles Beatriz and
her family faced when they moved to
America. Her parents could not speak
English and Beatriz spoke very little.
Saidah tried to help, but Saidah's mom
was so adamant about Saidah learning an
African language that she barely had
time to figure out the English language
herself.

Beatriz eventually picked up on it
and became a straight "A" student. She
said the poem represented how sad she
was when she first left Puerto Rico and
how afraid she was when they moved to
America. She said the change that she
resisted and hated actually opened the
door for her to make wonderful new
friends, friends who were closer to her
than her own sisters.

If it worked for Beatriz, it will work for me,
Kirsten thought.

"Beatriz told us that coming to
America was the best decision her
parents could have ever made and
deciding to leave Jason is the best

decision I could ever make," Kirsten
said.

Kirsten was almost in Atlanta when
she got a call from Michelle.

"Hey Shelly," she said, trying to
hide how depressed she was.

"Hey, honey, I had the babies!"
Michelle said, sounding excited and
exhausted, as if she forgot all about
the ugly conversation she and Kirsten
had.

"Oh my gosh, Shelly, I'm so happy
for you. I know they're beautiful,"
Kirsten said, deciding to forget too.

"Yes, they are. They look just
like you, Kirsten." They both laughed.

Matt was in the background
yelling, "Kirsten, you know these
babies look just like they're daddy!
They look just like me, Kirsten, just
like me!"

Kirsten was very happy for Matt
and Michelle. She knew how much they
went through to get those babies. She
was very happy that Michelle did right
by Matt.

"Kirsten," Michelle said, sounding
serious.

"Yeah, Shelly, what's wrong?"

"I love you and I just want you to be happy. Whatever that is and with whomever that is, okay?"

Kirsten knew this was Michelle's way of apologizing for going ballistic on her the last time they spoke.

"I love you too, honey, and I have come to grips with what I need to do so I can be happy," Kirsten responded.

Michelle knew what Kirsten meant. She said, "Okay, honey, do what you gotta do. I will always be in your corner, no matter what."

"I know you will, Shelly, even if you're glued to a hospital bed and can't move right now, I still know that you've got my back," Kirsten said, teasing.

Michelle laughed, then she said, "Well, I gotta go feed these starving babies. I'll call you later."

"Okay, Shelly. Congratulations! I can't wait to see my sweetie pies. I'll come visit you very soon, okay?"

"You better come, and bring Beatriz and Saidah with you so we can have another girls' night out."

Kirsten laughed. She knew it would be a long time before Michelle went anywhere.

"Okay, later gator," Kirsten said, as she hung up the phone.

Kirsten pulled up in her driveway and Everett had just finished cutting the lawn.

"Hey, Ms. Jabard," he yelled.

"Hey, Everett, how are you? It's Sunday evening, why are you cutting grass?" Kirsten asked.

"Well, I came by yesterday, but my lawn mower broke, so I fixed it and came back today. Oh, Ms. Jabard, I bought you a walker. I even put some green tennis balls on the back legs to help keep you balanced."

Kirsten looked at him as if he had grown three extra eyes. "Huh?" she said. "Why in the world do I need a walker?"

"So you won't trip over your feet and stomp your toe again," he said, laughing, as he held his grandma's walker in the air. "It's my grandma's, but she said you can have it." Everett laughed some more.

"Don't quit your day job, Everett, you suck at comedy," Kirsten said, laughing as she walked in the house. She thought Everett had forgotten about that little fall she had or at least she was hoping he'd forgotten.

When she went inside she knew she needed to go ahead and officially call things off with Jason, but she wanted to relax her nerves first, so she decided to soak in the tub. Kirsten ran the bath water, turned on the tub jets, poured in bubble bath and then lit some candles; she didn't care that it was still daylight outside. Kirsten knew that it would not be easy to get rid of Jason. He was dogmatic and didn't take "no" for an answer. After all, he was a prominent business owner, so of course he knew how to get what he wanted. She also knew that Jason wasn't going to accept the ring back and he was going to keep trying to find reasons to stay in her life. If she wanted to move on, she would have to be stern and to the point so Jason would know that she was serious.

I can't believe I wasted three years of my life on a meaningless relationship, Kirsten thought, as she lay there soaking in the tub. Then something clicked. "I AM JASON!" she screamed, dropping her mouth open. She knew that sounded stupid, but she said it as if it was something really profound.

Kirsten continued with her metaphor. "Jason is trapped in an unhealthy relationship with Lacey, just like I am trapped in an unhealthy relationship with him. Lacey manipulates and controls Jason the same way he manipulates and controls me. Jason is just as stupid as I am because as evil and as hateful as Lacey is to him, he keeps going back to her. Actually, Jason is way more stupid than I am." Kirsten sat there quietly. "Well, I'll be darned; Jason is fool for love too," Kirsten said, laughing at her newfound discovery. "He's so good looking, though. He's well-rounded, and established and so, so smart; I just don't know how he ended up in that toxic situation."

All of a sudden she didn't hate Jason anymore. She actually kind of felt sorry him. She began to realize that anybody can play the fool.

"Hmmm, it doesn't matter who you are, what your title is, where you live, what you drive, or how good you look, because anybody, at any time can find themselves playing the part of The Fool," Kirsten said, with amazement.

"I have never let myself fall in
love like that," she said. "I'm
Kirsten Denise Jabard. What do I look
like being somebody's fool? I am
always in control, I stay in control,"
Kirsten said, as if she was trying to
convince herself that she was never in
love with Jason.

Kirsten let out a deep breath.
"Who am I kidding? I was a fool; a
plain old fool who lost all her common
sense. That man sure was fine, though!
He was everything on my list that I
wanted. Dark chocolate, checked.
Tall, checked. Muscular, checked.
Bald, checked. Smart, checked. Rich,
checked. Good Sex, yes, Lawdy checked.
Involved in church, checked. WAIT A
MINUTE!!!!!" Kirsten shouted, abruptly.
"Number one on my list said I wanted a
committed Christian not just someone
who attends church. Anybody can go to
church and now that I think about it,
not once have I even seen Jason read
his Bible. What committed Christian
never reads their bible? Shoot, I've
never even seen Jason pray! And
although Jason said he respected my
decision to wait until marriage, every
chance he got he was rubbing up against

me, trying to get me in his bed. He never really respected my decision at all. It was all manipulation! He even went as far as fencing in his back yard for Poodles, just so he could get laid, and the sad thing is, he was already getting laid..by Lacey. Jason must be a sex-addict. Nah, he's just a self-addict; he only cares about what he wants. He has no self-discipline. Just because it's offered, doesn't mean you have to take it, Jason!" Kirsten said, sarcastically.

She continued, "Number two was someone who makes me feel like I mean the world to them." She twisted her mouth. "Well, that definitely wasn't Jason, so let's just move on to number three, which was LOYAL AND FAITHFUL, JASON!" Kirsten said, loudly, as if Jason was standing in front of her.

She felt herself getting riled up. She stopped. "Nope, no more anger, Kirsten. He's not even worth it. He's a fake, a phony, and one big façade, but if the truth be told, I really deceived myself. I got so blindsided with all the superficial, outward things that he possessed that I totally ignored the red flags. Jason didn't

have any of my top three desired
traits. NOT ONE OF THEM! I was so
naïve. Just because he was in church
didn't mean he was a Christian or that
he wanted to live a life that would be
pleasing to God. He wasn't loyal or
faithful and he didn't have a lick of
integrity. Jason wouldn't know
integrity if it bit him in the butt. I
have to be honest with myself though,
it was all my fault! I ignored all the
signs that told me he was not the one
and I insisted on making him the one.
I totally deceived myself!" The
thought of that made Kirsten sad, but
she knew it was true.

   After Kirsten took her bath, she
knew it was time to say goodbye to
Jason, the man she once thought she
couldn't live without. Kirsten
couldn't believe her hands were shaking
as she dialed his number.

   "Hey, baby!" Jason answered,
sounding all cheery.

   "Hey, Jason, this is Kirsten."

   "Babe, I know who you are. I'm
glad you're back, although I didn't
know you were leaving, but we can
discuss that later. I stopped by this
weekend. I saw your lawn guy, E-Thug.

He told me he thought you were out of town. He must be very loyal to grass-cutting, because he seems to always be cutting your grass."

Kirsten shook her head at Jason having the nerve to be jealous. "Jason, stop it. His name is Everett, not E-Thug and yes, he is very loyal. I've never once had to call him and tell him that my grass was getting high. He does an awesome job and I wouldn't trade him for anything."

"Hmmmmm, wouldn't trade him for anything, huh? Well, I'll just keep my eye on him. So, Kirsten, I was thinking. Maybe you can make a key for me this weekend, so I can check on your house when you're out of town and check on Poodles so you won't have to take her with you."

Kirsten laughed again and said, "Everett is harmless, Jason. There's no need for you to scout out my house while I'm away. I assure you, Everett isn't the least bit interested in me. If he was, I would know it. There's absolutely no need to be jealous and I enjoy taking Poodles on my trips with me. Besides, she wouldn't have it any other way."

"I told you, I'll get my lawn guy to take care of your yard for you."

"And I told you, I already have a great yard guy, Jason. Everett is not attracted to me. As far as I know, he could be married, so please stop acting all weird."

Jason had gotten her so wrapped up in defending Everett that she almost forgot that she called to break up with him.

"Anyway, we need to talk for a minute. Is now a good time?" Kirsten said to Jason, sounding like she was still aggravated from the Everett conversation.

"Yeah, what's up?" Jason asked, although he wasn't quite ready to change the subject.

"I can't marry you," Kirsten said, confidently. "You know I love you more than anything, but I have no more faith in us."

"Whoa!" Jason responded. "No more faith in us? Where did all this come from? We were fine on Saturday before you left. What happened while you were gone?"

"Jason, you know we were not fine before I left. I gave your ring back to you and everything."

"Yeah, but I thought that was just about Lacey. You've had time to cool down since then so I don't understand what the big deal is now."

Kirsten rolled her eyes. "Jason, you're so clueless when it comes to women."

"Well, I can't argue with you there, baby. I really don't have a clue, but maybe you can help me. How about I come over so we can talk? You sound stressed. Maybe I can rub your feet for you so you can relax."

"No, Jason! My decision is final. Every time you come over, we never get around to any talking."

Jason giggled as if he had just received a compliment. "That's not true, Kirsten. We did a lot of talking the last time I came over."

"No, you did a lot of talking. We're done, Jason! It's over! I'll mail your ring to you, certified mail of course."

"Come on, Kirsten! Don't do this, baby!" Jason said, right before Kirsten hung up on him.

"If I give him a chance to talk, he's going to woo me right back in his

arms and into his bed. I'm done! I **AM
DONE!**" Kirsten shouted, as she threw
the phone on the bed and walked out of
the room. She could hear the phone
ringing as she was walking; she knew it
was Jason, and she had finally made up
her mind to close that door for good.
She knew there was something better for
her.

*I don't trust him any farther than I can throw
him and I definitely can't throw him.*

Kirsten laughed at her joke. "It
sure feels good to laugh again. I
didn't realize how depressed this
relationship had made me. I wonder if
people who are grouchy and moody all
the time are that way because they're
in unfulfilling relationships. I just
refuse to keep subjecting myself to the
roller coaster ride Jason, and now
Lacey, would constantly have me on."

Kirsten vowed that drama-filled
relationships would not be a part of
her life. She wanted security; someone
who made her feel safe and protected,
emotionally and physically. Now that
she could see things more clearly, she
realized that Jason had never made her
feel protected. She was finally ready
to admit that there was always an

uneasy feeling she had about him. She was never sure of his motives, even from their first date with that ridiculous silk rose.

"As soon as he gave me that fake flower, I should have run in the other direction." Kirsten laughed, then she said "but no need to dwell on that now, I will just learn from the mistakes I've made so I can become a better person.

~ EIGHTEEN ~

Since the break-up was official, Kirsten decided that she was going to take a mental vacation to redirect her energy in a more positive manner.

She had dedicated so much of herself to Jason that she didn't even know what she liked to do anymore. She had somehow lost herself in the relationship and desperately needed to get to know herself again. She knew she needed to heal from the relationship, but she didn't know where to start. People always said, "The only way to heal from a relationship is to start a new one," but Kirsten was a witness that that wasn't true.

"When you're still in love with someone, you only bring baggage into that new relationship and cause an innocent person to get hurt," Kirsten said. "But, I do need to get out of this house, though. I'll plan a trip to go see Shelly and the babies!"

Kirsten said, excitedly. "Maybe I'll ask Shelly how her cousin Caleb is doing." Kirsten laughed.

She really did wonder how Caleb was doing, but she wouldn't dare call him. She figured he didn't want anything else to do with her after she stood him up. "Well, I tried to apologize, but he never called me back. It probably wasn't meant to be anyway," she said.

The next couple of weeks went by fast and before she knew it, it was the weekend she planned to visit Michelle.

"I can't wait to see Shelly and my little babies!"

Kirsten already had her bags packed in the car, so after work she changed into something more comfortable and headed to Michelle's house.

When she pulled up, cars and people were everywhere. They were eating and laughing and seemingly having the best time of their lives.

"Oh my goodness, I think I picked a bad weekend to come," Kirsten said.

Just then Michelle came outside, waving frantically at Kirsten. Kirsten slowly got out of the car and spoke to everyone.

"This is my best friend, Kirsten, everybody," Michelle told her family. Michelle's mom came out and gave Kirsten a big hug. "I haven't seen you in years, Kizzie."

Kirsten hated that nickname, but she loved Michelle's mom, so she did her best to ignore it. Michelle laughed because she knew Kirsten hated when her mom called her that.

Michelle whispered in Kirsten's ear, "Kizzie, I know you're nervous around all these white folks, so let me get you inside."

"Yes, I am, let's go," Kirsten said, jokingly and they both giggled. Michelle's mom gave Kirsten another hug and grabbed her bags. "Kizzie, you've got to see these babies, they look just like me," Michelle's mom said.

"I thought they looked just like Matt," Kirsten said, laughing.

"Honey, Matt is a liar, my grandbabies look just like me." They all laughed.

When Kirsten got inside, a group of guys were sitting around the table playing cards. They were so noisy that she didn't know how the babies were coping. As Kirsten passed the table, this very good-looking, strawberry blonde-headed guy with pretty green eyes spoke to her.

"Hey, Kirsten!"

Kirsten looked at him strangely. She had no idea who he was, but she tried not to act weird.

"Hey," she said, as she followed Michelle into the sunroom.

Michelle didn't seem to notice and neither did anyone else, so Kirsten just acted like it was no big deal. Michelle gave one of the babies to Kirsten and they sat down to catch up. Kirsten looked at the babies and said, "Girl, these babies look just like me, I don't know what Matt or your mom is talking about." Michelle let out a huge laugh.

Eventually, Michelle's family started leaving and Matt finally popped his head into the sunroom. "Hey, Kirsten!" he said, coming to give her a hug.

"Ewwww, get away!" both girls screamed. Matt was soaked with sweat from playing basketball with Michelle's cousins.

"You guys have been playing basketball all this time?" Michelle asked.

"Yeah, your cousins tried to gang up on me, but I had to let them know, I'm the papa of twins. You can't produce twins unless you got stamina, baby," Matt said, not waiting for their response. He left the room, still shooting air hoops.

"Shelly, I thought twins ran on your dad's side," Kirsten asked.

"Yeah, they do, and two sets were playing basketball with Matt, but I guess he couldn't put two and two together to come up with four."

Kirsten giggled and said, "He's just a proud dad."

"Can you guess who else was here today?" Michelle asked.

"Who, Caleb?" Kirsten guessed.

Michelle laughed, "My dad, silly. You didn't want Caleb, remember, so why are you thinking about him?"

"Oh, wow! Your dad was here? That is awesome, Shelly," Kirsten said, ignoring Michelle's sarcasm about Caleb.

Just then the strawberry blonde-headed guy came into the room and started making small talk.

"How have you been, Kirsten?" he asked.

"I'm good, how are you?" Kirsten asked, trying to not make it obvious that she didn't know who he was. Kirsten stared at Michelle, trying to get her attention, but Michelle kept watching television like there was nothing unnatural taking place.

Maybe he's someone from high school, Kirsten thought. She started pinching Michelle's leg in hopes that Michelle would give her some hint of who this guy was and how he knew who she was, but Michelle acted like she didn't feel a thing.

I know Shelly feels me pinching her! I'm going to kill her if she doesn't help me!

The guy sat and talked to Kirsten for about twenty minutes. Kirsten did her best to not be awkward. People were coming in and out saying goodbye to him and Michelle, but Kirsten still didn't have a clue who he was. Then all of a sudden Michelle gave the guy the baby that she was holding and started walking out of the room. She looked back at Kirsten; Kirsten was staring back at her with a helpless look on her face.

Michelle quickly looked away, but when she got to the doorway, she stopped, turned around and asked abruptly, "Do y'all want something to drink?"

What I want is for you to tell me who this guy is! Kirsten thought.

"No, thank you," Kirsten responded, with an attitude.

"Hey, cuz, bring me some sweet tea, please."

"No problem, Caleb, do you want ice in it?"

Michelle looked over at Kirsten and rolled her eyes. Michelle didn't understand why Kirsten couldn't figure out who Caleb was.

"Who else could it be, numbnut, pinching my leg like she's crazy. I better not have a bruise," Michelle mumbled, as she walked into the kitchen, not even waiting for Caleb's response.

Kirsten couldn't believe that was Caleb. *Now, I just asked her if Caleb was here. I swear I'm going to kill Shelly! First, I'm going to kill her for not telling me he was going to be here, then I'm*

*going to bring her back to life and kill her again for
ignoring me when she knew I was trying to find out who
he was.*

Kirsten knew that Michelle had
intentionally let her suffer for the
past twenty minutes. Kirsten couldn't
help but laugh at Michelle's poker
face, though. She laughed out loud.

"What are you laughing at?" Caleb
asked.

"Caleb, I'm so sorry. All this
time, I had no idea who you were. I
didn't ask because you acted like you
knew me so I was trying to remember
where I knew you from."

"Michelle didn't tell you I was
going to be here?" Caleb asked,
surprisingly.

"No, she did not. Matter of fact,
I didn't know any of her family would
be here."

"Oh really, well she called us up
and told us to come over for a cookout.
Then she told me that you were coming
and told me not to screw things up this
time, like I did last time."

Kirsten and Caleb both laughed
because they knew it was Kirsten who
screwed things up, but Michelle would

never blame Kirsten for anything, at
least not to anyone else.

"Besides, she showed me a picture
of you a long time ago."

"She did what?" Kirsten yelled.

"She showed me a picture of you."

"But it was supposed to be a blind
date!"

"Who said that? I always knew
what you looked like."

"I'm going to kill Shelly,"
Kirsten responded, heatedly.

"So you never knew what I looked
like?" Caleb asked.

"No, Shelly would never show me a
picture. She only said I wouldn't be
disappointed."

"Well, are you?" Caleb asked,
with a sexy grin.

Kirsten tried not to flirt back,
but she couldn't help it. "Not at
all," she responded, with a huge smile
on her face.

"Good," Caleb said, then they
started talking about something else.

Kirsten was so happy that she
finally knew who she was talking to,
especially since Michelle decided not
to come back, and didn't bother telling
Caleb that he would not be getting that

iced tea he asked for. She wasn't sure where Michelle ran off to, but the babies had gone to sleep so Kirsten and Caleb sat on the couch, talking and watching movies; they got along great.

After their second movie was over, Caleb said he had to hit the road before it got too late. He told Kirsten that he would still like to take her out some time, then he kissed her. Caleb's kiss totally caught Kirsten off guard. She eventually stopped him, but only after she got a good feel of his lips. She had never kissed a white guy before, but it was a very nice experience.

"Sorry for being so forward, Kirsten. I've wanted to do that ever since you walked through the door."

"It's alright, but I'm just coming out of a crazy relationship and I really don't think I should get involved with anyone right now."

"I understand. Maybe we can still keep in touch, though, since we're both in the Atlanta area. I'll give you the time and space you need to get over your relationship. Just consider me your support group," Caleb said, laughing.

Kirsten smiled at how thoughtful Caleb was. She definitely needed a local support group. She knew she was going to need help getting over Jason, but she definitely didn't want to jump into another relationship. She didn't want to do to anyone what Jason had done her.

Kirsten wished she had gone out with Caleb instead of Jason, but he was still white and she wasn't sure if that would work anyway.

Growing up in South Georgia, blacks and whites weren't supposed to be mixing like that. Maybe it was okay up North, but definitely not in the South. Caleb was quite the catch, though, and he didn't seem to mind at all about dating Kirsten. He was from California, and to Kirsten, that was the difference. No one cared in Cali; everyone cared in Georgia, especially Fountainwater, Georgia.

When Caleb left, he gave Kirsten a hug and vowed to keep in touch. As he was leaving, Michelle finally showed her face again to say goodbye to him.

Once Caleb was gone, Michelle laughed so hard at Kirsten. She told Matt all about how she refused to tell

Kirsten who Caleb was. Michelle was literally on the floor crying while laughing.

Kirsten didn't think it was funny, but Michelle and Matt were acting like it was the highlight of the night.

Matt said, "Michelle, show me again how Kirsten kept pinching your leg." Then he and Michelle both laughed some more.

"I better not have a bruise," Michelle responded.

"I hope you do," Kirsten said.

Michelle and Matt laughed some more.

"I'm going to bed," Kirsten replied.

"Oh, don't go to bed, Kirsten. We still need to talk about the old, ugly, bald guy."

Kirsten knew she was talking about Jason. "Oh, there is nothing to tell. It's over between us. For good!"

Matt interrupted, "You dumped Jason?"

"He needed it," Michelle and Kirsten said at the same time.

"You two are scary when you're together! Y'all think way too much alike," Matt said, shaking his head and walking out of the room.

"Well, he did need it and I'm very proud of you, Kizzie." Michelle said smiling.

"Uggghhhh, I hate that name. I can't believe your mom still calls me that."

Michelle laughed. "Are you okay, Kirsten?"

"Yes! I'm so peaceful without Jason. I know I did the right thing."

"What about Caleb? You guys hit it off pretty good, even if you didn't know who you were hitting it off with."

Matt laughed from the other room. "Michelle, come show me how Kirsten was staring at you while you were trying to watch TV."

"Matt, she looked so pitiful. Her eyes were saying, 'Help! A stranger keeps talking to me and I don't know what to do.' It was hilarious. I wish you were there, baby." Michelle and Matt kept laughing.

"Matt, do you always listen to conversations between me and Shelly?" Kirsten yelled down the hall.

"Yep, there's never a dull moment with you two," Matt responded.

Kirsten shook her head and started talking to Michelle again. "Caleb seems like a great guy. Why didn't you tell me how good-looking he was? You could have at least showed me a picture, Shelly, my goodness."

"It was a blind date, Kirsten. You aren't supposed to see pictures."

"You liar, Caleb knew exactly who I was because you showed him a picture."

"She sure did," Matt yelled! "I told her that wasn't right, Kirsten, but you know how your friend gets."

"Hush, Matt," Michelle responded. "Kirsten, I know you. If I had shown you a picture, you would have found something wrong and some reason not to go. You know I'm telling the truth."

"Yeah, you're probably right," Kirsten said, laughing.

"But you told me he was white!"

"Yeah, because I know how we grew up. I don't know why, but interracial dating is such a big issue down here so I felt I owed you that. I didn't want you passing out when you saw him, or anything."

Kirsten laughed. "Yeah, that's true, but he's so good-looking, though, Shelly!"

"Kirsten, I don't know why you're acting all surprised. I'm good-looking; I don't have ugly people in my family."

Kirsten laughed, "Well, I am definitely surprised, but it is a pleasant surprise, that's for sure. I would like to get to know him better, but I'm just scared that I'll do him just like Jason did me. I know I need to get over Jason before I date anyone else. It wouldn't be fair to Caleb, but he seems so nice, Shelly. I'd hate to let this opportunity pass, but then there's the race factor to deal with as well."

"Who cares about race? You're a grown woman, he's a grown man. All that matters is if y'all make each other happy. Caleb is a great guy, Kirsten, but if you're not completely ready or able to move on with your life, then you shouldn't get Caleb involved."

"Yeah, you're right, Shelly."

"Besides, if you hurt my cousin, you'll never hear the end of it from me. I'll bring it up every time I talk to you."

"You know she'll do it," Matt yelled from the other room.

"Be quiet, Matt," Kirsten and Michelle yelled back to him.

"Let's go to bed, Kirsten. I'm tired, and you know we have to get up at 2am with the babies," Michelle said.

"What do you mean, we?" I didn't help you get those babies, so I'll see y'all in the morning," Kirsten responded.

As they walked down the hall they heard Matthew pretending to snore.

"Oh, you're getting up at 2am, proud papa. You can stop pretending that you're asleep," Michelle said.

Kirsten and Matt laughed.

"Good night, y'all, and if you need me to wake up with you, you know I will, Shelly," Kirsten said.

Michelle responded "I know, honey, but I'll let you get some rest. You had to drive here and my baby daddy would be so upset if I let someone else take his place feeding the kids during our 2am feeding session."

"No, he wouldn't" Matt responded. They all laughed.

"Good night, y'all," Kirsten said.

"Good night, Kirsten," Michelle and Matt responded.

The next day, Kirsten and Michelle lounged around the house doing nothing. Kirsten loved babies. When she lived with Jason she really didn't see herself having kids because she didn't think Jason wanted any, but now that she and Jason were over, she knew she wanted kids of her own. Kirsten also wanted a wonderful marriage like Michelle and Matt's. She knew they had gone through a lot but the love between them was so real; what they had was genuine. Kirsten wanted something that was real and genuine, too. She knew Jason would never give that to her. She just hated she wasted so much time trying to make things work when it was obvious that she and Jason wanted two different things.

"Well, you win some and you lose some, but at least I've learn from the experience and I'm ready to embrace change."

~ NINETEEN ~

As Kirsten headed back to Atlanta she thought about Caleb's kiss; she couldn't believe she let him kiss her. She figured there would be a big difference between the way black guys and white guys kissed, but using Caleb as her only example, she said to herself, "He's as great a great kisser as any other great kisser I've kissed."

Kirsten laughed. She didn't know why she was thinking about him so much, but she couldn't get him out of her head. His breath smelled like Bubble Yum bubble gum. It felt so good to be wrapped up in somebody's arms, but Kirsten knew she was vulnerable. She knew she desperately wanted to feel loved and wanted again, and that's how Caleb made her feel. She also knew she would be asking for trouble if she allowed herself to get caught up with emotions.

"I am way too vulnerable right now and I'm not going to jump into another relationship. I know I need time to heal," she said to herself.

Dating outside of her race was another huge factor for Kirsten. She wasn't ready for all the drama that goes with interracial dating in the South. The way white and black people stare at you like you have three arms and four legs. She had been through enough drama with Jason and she didn't have enough strength to slay the interracial dating dragon just yet, but, if nothing else, she finally felt that she was no longer restricted by the absurd notion that her "ideal" guy had to be a dark Chocolate Hershey Bar.

Although I'm not ready to completely cross over to a different race yet, I am definitely ready to go outside this dating box I've placed myself in. Being with Jason made me realize that having this "list" of what my ideal man should look like was dumb. That stupid list only caused me to look at Jason for his outside appearance and not see him for who he really was. People put way too much value on what a person looks like! Looks don't matter a whole lot if that person is not treating you right.

Kirsten was no longer looking for a certain type of guy, but she wanted a guy who would not try to manipulate her, a man with character and integrity, a man who loves God and who loves her. She didn't want someone who didn't have any self-discipline, nor did she want someone who couldn't say no to their ex. Then on the flip side, she also didn't want to date someone that she had to constantly explain to people how "Love has no color" and "If two people love each other, everyone should just be happy for them." A drama-free life is what Kirsten was looking for. Kirsten took a deep breath.

"God, I want the man you've chosen for me, not the man I've chosen for myself," Kirsten said, as she pulled into her driveway.

"Good grief, Charlie Brown! Why is Everett always at my house whenever I come from out of town?" she said, grumbling.

Everett came running up to Kirsten's car as she was getting out.

"Hey Ms. Jabard, I'm really glad I caught you. Up the street from you a lady said she saw some snakes in her back yard. I came over to put some Snake-Be-Gone around the edges of your yard. Please be careful, we don't need to take any chances."

Kirsten looked at Everett, who was always dingy, but this time she didn't care; she gave him a big hug.

"Everett, thank you so much! I am deathly afraid of snakes. I don't know what I would do if I saw one," she said in a frightened tone.

"You would call me and I would take care of it for you," Everett responded.

"Everett, I don't think I've ever met someone as nice as you, other than my dad. I really appreciate you thinking about me. What do I owe you for the Snake-be-gone?" she asked.

"Oh, no ma'am, it is my job to protect you. I wouldn't dream of asking you to pay me," he said, waving his hand back and forth like he was offended that she even asked.

"Everett, thank you so very much, you're such an awesome lawn guy."

"Lawn Care Technician."

"Huh, what are you talking about?"

"My title is Lawn Care Technician, Ms. Jabard," said Everett, with a smirk.

"Oh, I'm sorry, Mr. Lawn Care Technician," she responded and they both laughed.

"Okay, Ms. Jabard, let me finish putting this stuff down. I've got to go take care of the lawn at church. I didn't get to it yesterday."

"That's nice Everett, where do you go to church?"

"Grace Temple, you should visit sometime. You'll love it."

"I just might do that, thanks for the invite."

"No problem. I gotta run, sorry I can't stay and chat."

"Bye, Everett," she responded.

As Kirsten went into the house she couldn't help but laugh at how dedicated Everett was to his grass cutting business.

"Thank you Lord for letting Everett be my "Lawn Care Technician." I will never complain about him being at my house again. He can sleep out there for all I care, as long as he keeps those snakes away," Kirsten said, still laughing.

A few weeks went by, and Kirsten really wanted to go back to her church, but she didn't want the Pastor's wife to see her.

I just don't feel like being bothered. She knows God didn't send Jason to me, she knows I was sinning;

she knows I wasn't being led by God. I feel guilty enough. I don't need anybody making me feel worse about myself.

Kirsten decided to go to church anyway. When she walked through the door, standing in the church foyer was the one person she didn't want to see, the Pastor's wife. There was nowhere for Kirsten to run; she had nowhere to hide.

"Hey, Kirsten!" the Pastor's wife said, running and giving Kirsten a big hug. "How have you been? It's so good to see you!"

Kirsten braced herself for the "Be led by God" spiel, but there wasn't one, so Kirsten decided to go ahead and get it over with herself.

"Jason isn't with me this time; it turns out that he wasn't the man that God had for me," Kirsten said, looking off like she was embarrassed.

The Pastor's wife turned Kirsten's head back towards her and smiled. "Don't be ashamed because you made a bad decision. We all make bad decisions. The key is to learn from those decisions. God already knew how the story would end; He just needed you to learn the lesson. If you learn the lesson, then your mistakes and failures make you a better person."

Kirsten's eyes filled with tears. "I thought you would be disappointed in me because you tried to warn me about him."

"What do you mean? I never tried to warn you about Jason."

"Yes, because you would always tell me to be led by God."

"Oh, girl, I tell everybody that. That's just my greeting. Instead of saying hello, I say 'Be led by God or Let the Lord lead you.' Kirsten, I never meant any harm by that." The Pastor's wife laughed so hard that she was holding her stomach. "Is that why you would go the other way when you saw me?"

"Yes, ma'am." Kirsten gave her a puppy dog face. She laughed even harder. This time Kirsten laughed too. She hugged Kirsten again.

"I'm sorry I made you feel that way, honey. We obviously need to spend more time together so you can get to know me. Once I tell you about all my mistakes and failures, you will never avoid me again." They both laughed some more, then went inside.

Months went by and Kirsten hadn't heard a peep out of Jason, so she figured he had obviously come to grips with her decision. Kirsten knew he had gotten the ring back because she sent it Certified Mail. It was funny to Kirsten that she barely even thought of him anymore. *This was a man who once consumed my every thought, now I barely think about him at all; funny how things can change with time.* **Kirsten had** finally realized that Jason was not at all what she wanted in a man; he was only what she thought she wanted.

She and Caleb got together from time to time for dinner or a movie. Caleb stayed true to his word about allowing Kirsten time and space to get over her relationship, and over time they had become more like friends than potential lovers. He never tried to kiss her again and she never wanted him to. Eventually they started calling each other cousins. They developed a wonderful friendship! She told him everything that happened with her and Jason, and he came to her for advice about the girls he were dating. Kirsten liked it better with Caleb being her friend. She could just relax and focus on herself instead of trying to make someone else happy or keeping them satisfied.

Caleb enjoyed Kirsten's friendship as well. Some people looked at them weird when they were together, but they didn't care. She no longer looked at Caleb as being a "white boy." He had become a friend who just so happened to be white. Race no longer carried any weight with Kirsten and it would no longer be a factor with anyone she dated. "It doesn't matter what a person's color is, what matters is how they make you feel when you're with them."

Kirsten's whole mindset had changed and it was very liberating. She liked not putting herself in a box anymore, she liked being free to think differently than how she was taught to think. Kirsten didn't realize how many limits she had placed on her life. She didn't realize how unrealistic some of her beliefs and thoughts were. Caleb was a free spirit who chased the wind. If he felt it, he did it. Kirsten admired his love of freedom. Caleb was always taking Kirsten on some adventure with him. Kirsten was a Southern "homebody" and Caleb was a fast pace

Cali man. They knew a relationship
between them would never work, but what
they provided to each other as friends
could not be topped.

Soon it was time for Caleb to
leave for his next duty station.
Kirsten really hated to see him leave,
and she hated that she wasted three
years on Jason when she could have been
hanging out with Caleb and having the
time of her life.

When Caleb got his orders, he
called Kirsten to let her know that
they were sending him to Germany.

"Oh, I'm so jealous, I would love
to go to Germany," Kirsten said.

"Well, come with me," Caleb
responded.

They both laughed. She wasn't
sure if Caleb was serious or not but
she sure hated that he was leaving.
Caleb taught her a lot about men, about
relationships and about life. He
taught her to stop judging people by
their outward appearance and get to
know their heart. Caleb helped her lay
to rest all her crazy beliefs about
what good relationships should "look"
like. He even helped her have a
funeral ceremony for all the warped

thinking she allowed to hold her back.
She wrote everything she could think of
on a piece of paper and buried it in
her back yard. Caleb made a wooden
tombstone for the list that said, "So
long suckas, you're not welcome here
anymore."

Kirsten laughed harder than she
ever had when she saw that tombstone.
Caleb was as nutty she was, but Kirsten
knew she needed him to help her get
through all the pain.

He did what a lover couldn't do;
he allowed her to heal without
requiring her to give him anything in
return. Caleb allowed her to talk and
cry and scream as much as she needed
to; he let her get out all the anger
and the hurt. Kirsten knew that God
sent Caleb into her life to be her
friend.

She wasn't sure how they became so
close, but she knew she wouldn't have
been able to get over Jason without
him.

Kirsten hadn't seen Jason since
they broke up and she didn't even miss
him. She wasn't sure what her reaction
would be if she ever saw him again, but

she knew she wasn't the same girl she was when they were together.

Before Caleb left for Germany he stopped by to see Kirsten.

"I came to get you," he said. Kirsten laughed.

"You're crazy Caleb. I'm sure gonna miss you, though."

Caleb gave her a big hug. He said, "Kirsten, these last few months in Atlanta have been wonderful. I'm so glad we got a chance to get to know each other. I guess it wasn't meant for us to be in a relationship, but you're an impeccable friend and one great woman. I will always be grateful for your friendship. I want you to come see me in Germany whenever you want. I mean that; I'll pay for your ticket."

Kirsten was surprised by Caleb's offer because he had recently started dating someone and Kirsten knew that offer wouldn't go over well with his new love.

"Caleb, I don't think your girlfriend would like me coming to see you in Germany."

"Kirsten, she didn't like you coming to see me in Atlanta, but I told her that we were great friends and you were like family to me. Of course she didn't believe me, but you are, Kirsten. You're like family to me. I can't describe it, but I feel like I'm leaving home for the first time and I don't know when I'm going to see my family again. It's not a cool feeling, ya know?" Kirsten knew exactly what Caleb meant. She felt the same way.

"I am like family, aren't I?"

"Yes, Kizzie, you are."

"Oh gosh, never call me that!"

They both laughed. Then Caleb said, "Well, I gotta run. We'll keep in touch, okay? Oh, and don't forget to send me an invitation to your wedding."

Kirsten laughed and said, "ditto." Caleb grabbed her and held her like he didn't want to let go. He looked at her like he wanted to kiss her. Kirsten got nervous; she wasn't sure what Caleb was about to do next, but he just smiled and said, "Bye, Kizzie," then he left for the airport.

Kirsten was very sad that Caleb had to leave, but she knew their time together was God-sent. He came into her life when what she needed most was a true friend.

"He came when he was supposed to come and he left when he was supposed to leave. I guess that means this chapter in my life is over, but I'm definitely a better person now. Having Caleb in my life has surely prepared me for the next chapter of my life. Speaking of which, I wonder what is coming next," Kirsten said.

A few weeks went by and Caleb called to tell her how much he loved Germany. He and his girlfriend had since broken up and he had found a new love. Kirsten laughed at how fast Caleb moved on. He never cheated on women, but if it didn't work out, he didn't shed any tears or waste any time on a relationship that wasn't working. She wished she was more like Caleb in that regard.

If you know it's not working, just move on, but that's easier said than done.

Kirsten had shed a lot of tears over Jason and hadn't come close to dating anyone since they broke up, unless she wanted to count the time she and Caleb kissed at Michelle's house, but she didn't. She was glad that she was finally over Jason. She felt like she was back in control of her life again and she was eagerly awaiting the next chapter.

~ TWENTY ~

Kirsten was staring out of her
kitchen window daydreaming when her
phone started ringing. It was across
the room and she was being lazy that
day, but she begrudgingly got up and
answered it.

"Hey, Kirsten!" Beatriz, Saidah,
and Michelle all yelled when she
answered the phone.

"Hey, guys! To what do I owe the
pleasure of a phone call from my three
best friends?"

Saidah said, "Well, Michelle told
us that Caleb got orders to Germany and
we didn't want you to fall back into
the loving and capable arms of Jason B.
Glaznyte, so we decided to call and
give you some phone support."

Kirsten laughed, "It would be so
much better if you guys were here in
person, but I guess phone support is a
wonderful alternative. Thank y'all and
no worries, I'm completely over Jason.
I don't know how in the world I allowed

myself to be such a fool for him. That
wasn't me, I am not that girl. She was
dumb and you guys know I'm smart,
beautiful, classy, intelligent, and
God-fearing! It had to be another
person who temporarily took over my
mind and body."

"Like temporary insanity, huh,
Kirsten?" Michelle asked.

"Yes, exactly! I was temporarily
insane." Kirsten chuckled, "I don't
think I'll ever understand how I became
so blind to the point where I made such
bad—"

Michelle cut her off, "There's no
need to dwell on that now, sugafoot!
You've learned from that whole
experience and you're a better person
for it. Everybody is blind when
they're in love, Kirsten, you're no
exception."

Just then Saidah broke out into a
song by Aaron Neville.

♫ ♪ ♫ Everybody plays the fool,
sometimes. There's no exceptions to
the rule; listen baby. It may be
factual, it may be cruel, I ain't
lying. Everybody plays the fool ♫ ♪ ♫

All the girls joined in and sang
along. Kirsten couldn't help but

laugh. Then she said, "So, I'm not the only one who's been a fool for love, huh?"

Beatriz chimed in, "Nope, not at all. Everybody has played that role, male and female. There's no exceptions to the rule." All the girls laughed again.

Kirsten wiped tears from her eyes while she was laughing, and said, "I'm very grateful that I went through all of that, because now my whole outlook on relationships has changed."

"Yeah, she's even willing to date white guys now," Michelle chimed in.

"Don't push it, Michelle! Saidah said. "Kirsten has never dated outside of her race. I know your cousin is fine and all, but I don't think anyone can get Kirsten to cross the race line."

"Why not?" asked Beatriz, "People should never limit themselves. If they find happiness with someone, then that's who they should be with, regardless of race."

"Kirsten, why are you so quiet? Did you sleep with Caleb?" Saidah asked.

"No, I never slept with Caleb. The only thing we've ever done was kiss and that was at Michelle's house the first day I met him."

"What?" Michelle yelled, "You kissed Caleb at my house and you didn't tell me? What else did you do while y'all were left unattended, Ms. Hottie pants? Y'all were supposed to be watching the babies for me, but obviously the babies should have been watching y'all."

They all laughed. "Nothing else happened, I swear!" Kirsten said, "Caleb was truly a wonderful friend. If it wasn't for him, I don't think I would have gotten over Jason. But Saidah, to answer your question, yes, I'll date outside of my race now. I'm ready for whatever life has for me."

"Yep, she slept with him," Saidah responded.

"No, I did not!"

"Well, was he at least a good kisser? You know I've always heard that black guys' kisses are different than white guys?"

"That's the dumbest thing I've ever heard," Michelle said, "There's no difference! People are people. Either you're a good kisser or a bad kisser!"

"Actually, Shelly, I've heard the same thing," Kirsten responded. "But, yes, Saidah, he was a great kisser."

"And you didn't sleep with him?"

"No, Saidah, I didn't sleep with him. We never even came close to sleeping together. I didn't need to become emotionally attached to anyone, and Caleb promised to give me the space I needed to heal and he did, but now I'm ready to try new things. I don't want to limit my happiness any more. I still prefer my own race and y'all know I still like my men tar-black, but if God sends me someone who is snow white, then so be it."

"That is so awesome, Kirsten," Beatriz responded. "I told you a long time ago to just let God send the man that's right for you. All that superficial stuff will only get you everything you don't want."

"That's for sure," Kirsten agreed, "Now, I'm just going to go with the flow, no matter what color he is," Kirsten said.

"Upendo hauna rangi," Saidah said to Kirsten

"WHAT?" Kirsten and Michelle shouted.

"I said, love has no color!" Saidah responded.

"Well, what language did you say it in?" Michelle asked.

"Swahili," Beatriz replied.

"Oh, my God! You can speak Swahili, Saidah?" Michelle asked surprisingly.

"Saidah, why didn't we know you could speak Swahili?" asked Kirsten. "And Beatriz, how did you know she could speak Swahili?"

"Duh, I know everything about Saidah!" Beatriz responded.

Michelle and Kirsten ignored Beatriz.

"Saidah, how long have you spoken Swahili and why haven't we ever heard you speak it?" Kirsten said.

Saidah responded, "Why are you guys acting like you didn't know that my mom made me learn Swahili?"

Michelle chimed in, "Yeah, we knew she was trying to teach you, but everybody knows you're unteachable, so we didn't think you actually learned anything."

"Well, I didn't really have a choice, I was given a test each week, but the reason I never spoke it at school is because the only language we were allowed to speak at home was Swahili. By the time my brothers and I got to school, we were Swahili'd out."

They all laughed. "I just can't believe we never knew that about you," Kirsten said.

"Except Beatriz, she knows everything about Saidah," Michelle said, sarcastically

"Well, there's one thing she doesn't know," Saidah said.

"What do I not know?" Beatriz asked, as if Saidah was lying.

"I'm going to Africa!"

"You're going where?" Beatriz asked.

"I'm going to Africa. It hit home when you mentioned how some African-Americans want to claim their African heritage, but they've never stepped foot in Africa. Well, I'm stepping foot in Africa," Saidah said.

Michelle said, "O.M.G., I can't believe you're going to Africa, Saidah, can I please come with you? Please, please, I would love to go to Africa."

"Michelle, I love you like a sister, but I will stop believing in Santa Claus before I take a white girl to Africa with me. It's just not going to happen."

Michelle said, "Oh, a white girl can't visit the Mother Land? How do you know I don't have heritage there too, huh, huh?"

"Hush, Michelle! You're not going." Saidah responded.

Michelle and Kirsten were laughing so hard that their stomachs were hurting.

"What are y'all laughing at?" Beatriz asked.

Kirsten said, "I'm just picturing Michelle in Africa with her two white babies, asking people if they can help her find her heritage."

Beatriz let out an aggravated sigh. "Africa doesn't just have blacks living there. A lot of white people live there too, ya know?"

"Get outta here," Saidah responded. "There are no white people in living in Africa."

"Actually there are," Kirsten said, "But it's still funny just picturing Michelle and Matt there.

They will stand out like a sore thumb, even if they are surrounded by other white Africans. Y'all know they don't know how to act, but Saidah, please tell me you knew Michelle was just joking. She is not going to Africa."

"Kirsten, I swear you know me too well," Michelle said. "Y'all know Matt is so white and redneck, he would have all of his hunting gear with him, asking folks when deer season was. They would have kicked all of us out of Africa anyway. By the way, Saidah, what's the Swahili word for Hunter?"

"Mwindaji," Saidah said.

Michelle and Kirsten burst out laughing again. "Girl, Matt wouldn't even be able to pronounce that. Please keep him in the United States where he belongs," Kirsten said to Michelle.

Michelle and Kirsten laughed some more. Beatriz and Saidah didn't find the humor in anything they were laughing about, but it was hard to stop Kirsten and Michelle once they were on a roll.

"Well, laugh all y'all want! I am going and neither Michelle, Matt, nor those pretty blue-eyed babies will be going with me."

341

"When are you going?" Beatriz asked, sounding concerned.

"This summer and you can't go either, and neither can Kirsten because she doesn't care anything about her heritage," Saidah said.

Kirsten responded, "Saidah, it's not that I don't care about my heritage but my grandmother, great grandmother, and great, great grandmother were all born and raised in America. They are my heritage, but if you want to go to Africa, then I support you whole-heartedly. I just don't need to go visit Africa. I have a copy of my family tree and I know enough about my ancestors to be able to pass my heritage on to my children and that's what matters most to me."

Saidah rolled her eyes. Beatriz laughed as if she saw Saidah.

"Well, definitely keep us posted on your trip, Saidah," Beatriz chimed in.

"Yes, please keep us posted, but I have to go now, ladies. Matt and the babies are finally up from their naps. I swear I have three babies, not two."

"I heard that!" Matt yelled from the other room.

Kirsten laughed and said, "Matt
has the best listening ears known to
man. Well, ladies, I'm getting off the
phone too. It was great talking to you
guys, as always. Let's do it again
real soon, okay?"

They all agreed and hung up the
phone.

A couple of days later, Kirsten
and Poodles were sitting on the couch
watching a movie and the doorbell rang.
"Who could that be?" Kirsten wondered.
"Lord, please don't let it be Jason,
please don't let it be Jason," Kirsten
begged. She looked out the peep hole
and it was Everett.

"What is he doing here? My grass
is already cut," she said. She threw
on some sweatpants and opened the door.

"Hi, Ms. Jabard."

"Hey, Everett, is something wrong?
Any more snakes loose?" she said,
laughing. Everett smiled a little, but
he wasn't his normal self.

"Hi, Ms. Jabard," he said again as
if he was nervous.

"What's wrong, Everett?"

"Nothing, ummmm, I know I'm your
lawn guy and all, but there's this
banquet going on at one of the hotels

downtown tonight, and I was wondering
if you'd like to accompany me?"

First, Kirsten was shocked that
Everett even thought of asking her to
go with him and second she didn't know
that Everett was the type to even hang
out at hotel banquets. She'd always
seen him in dirty jeans and a dirty
white t-shirt. She looked at Everett
standing there shaking waiting for her
answer. He looked like he hadn't
shaved in a few days, but Kirsten
didn't really care.

*I am no longer going to live my life according to
some stupid, unrealistic list. Jason was everything I
thought I wanted and in the end none of that mattered
because he was nothing that I wanted.*

Kirsten had buried that list and
now she was ready to live a life
outside the box. She was ready to not
judge a book by its cover. She was
ready for a new life and a fresh start.

Everett interrupted her thoughts.
"I'm sorry I'm looking so rough, but I
just got done mowing yards and I wanted
to get over here to ask you so you'll
have enough time to think about it."

"Lawn Care Technician, Everett."

"Huh, what do you mean?"

"Well, you said you were my lawn guy, but you're actually my Lawn Care Technician, and sure, I'll go with you."

Everett grinned a little. "You will?" he said, as if he was surprised, and obviously still nervous. As much as Everett liked to joke around with her, he seemed like a total stranger standing at her door. *That was a perfect joke and he totally missed the opportunity to laugh,* **Kirsten** thought.

She had never seen a man act like this around her. She'd known Everett for years, but he was standing there shaking like she was the Queen of England when he asked her to go to the banquet with him. Everett thanked her for accepting his invitation and told her he'd come pick her up at 6:00.

"I know I don't have to tell you this, but the banquet is pretty fancy. I'll be wearing a tux. I know you'll look beautiful in anything you put on, but I just wanted you to know what to expect," Everett said, and then turned to walk back to his dirty truck with lawn equipment on it.

Kirsten smiled at Everett's compliment. "Why thank you Everett," she said. She couldn't imagine Everett in a tux. That was going to be a sight to see. She had nine hours to get dressed.

"I've been to plenty of banquets before, so I'm sure there's something in my closet to wear." Kirsten said, letting out a big sigh. She was excited to be getting out of the house. Everett had been cutting her lawn for five years, but she had never paid attention to him until today. He'd always crack some joke to make her laugh, but she never really noticed him. He was about 5'11" which was a good height for Kirsten who was 5'5."

Kirsten started to wonder if Jason's suspicions of Everett were valid. Indeed Everett had always been attracted to Kirsten, but she never knew it. She was too caught up in Jason to notice that anyone else existed. Everett had several employees working for him but he always made sure he took care of Kirsten's lawn himself.

Kirsten sat and played back all her memories of Everett to see if there were any signs that he liked her, but nothing stood out for her, other than him being at her house so much and doing extra work for free.

"I just thought he loved his job," Kirsten said laughing, "But, there's really no time to rehash all of this now, I need to figure out what I'm wearing and what I'm going to do with my hair," she said.

Before Kirsten knew it, it was 3:00. "Oh gosh, I need to start getting dressed!" she exclaimed. Kirsten decided to go with a dress that was her favorite color, royal blue.

"I look very good in blue," Kirsten said with her nose up in the air. This made her feel like her old self again. She was starting to see the woman she lost. Her dress was a halter top with sparkles around the neck. She chose her long diamond earrings, diamond bracelet, and silver shoes with diamonds across the straps. *My feet look simply exquisite in these shoes.*

When Kirsten put her outfit on, she couldn't believe how pretty she looked. All the formal affairs she went to were work related. This was the first formal affair that she was invited to as a date. Just as she finished doing her hair and makeup, the doorbell rang.

"Is it 6:00 already?" Kirsten looked at her clock and it was 5:59. "Okay, I guess it is," she said.

She answered the door and what she saw almost made her gasp for breath. Everett had tossed aside his dirty jeans and t-shirt and shaved off all his stubble. This is the first time she'd seen him with a clean face. She didn't realize how light his skin was, but there stood Everett more handsome than ever in his black tux; Kirsten was speechless.

"You look so beautiful, Ms. Jabard."

"Everett, please call me, Kirsten."

"You look so beautiful, Kirsten," Everett said, like he was still in a daze.

"You look very handsome yourself; you clean up pretty good!" Kirsten said.

Everett shook his head, "You know I'd rather be in jeans and a t-shirt, but I have to do this formal stuff to celebrate my people and the community."

Kirsten didn't know what he was talking about, but she figured she'd find out soon enough. Everett walked her to the car and opened her door for her. Kirsten didn't know what kind of banquet they were going to and she didn't care. She was just ready for something different. When they got there she discovered it was a Lawn Care banquet where they honored customers with the best yards and employees who got the most referrals. Kirsten laughed because if she was looking for something different, this would be it.

They had a wonderful evening. Everyone was so dressed up. Kirsten couldn't believe that these people spent most of their time cutting grass and planting flowers, but that night, they looked like they wanted nothing to do with grass, flowers or dirt.

Everett alone looked like a total transformation. Kirsten found out that Everett was the Chairman of the banquet. They presented him with a plaque and he had to say a few words. She noticed that Everett was a man of very little words, but when he spoke, he was very authoritative.

I can't believe my Everett has full control and command of this entire room.

Kirsten looked around and not one person seemed distracted, other than herself. She looked back at Everett, with his head held high and his shoulders up straight, telling people the importance of taking care of their lawn. *He's almost got me convinced,* Kirsten thought as she did an inward chuckle.

After the banquet was over, a lot of people came up to thank Everett for putting on another wonderful event. Everett kept Kirsten close to him and proudly introduced her to several people that worked for him.

"How often does this event occur?" Kirsten asked Everett.

"We've been doing it for about six years and it gets better each year," he responded, with a smile.

Everyone seemed very pleased with the banquet turnout. They were all so nice and Everett had thoroughly impressed her as well. When it was time for the night to end, Kirsten sighed. Everett asked if she was ready to leave. She said yes, but she really wasn't. She knew that as soon as she hit the front door of her house, she would be like Cinderella. Her beautiful outfit and glass slippers would all disappear and she'd go back to scrubbing floors and picking up dog poop. Kirsten laughed at her silly thoughts.

Everett asked what she was laughing at, but she said, "Nothing. This night has been wonderful, Everett. Thank you for the invitation." He thanked her for accompanying him as well and asked if he could take her out again sometime. Then he said, "But next time I won't make you dress so fancy."

Kirsten laughed. "I would love to, Everett, even if I had to dress fancy! I had a really great time." They walked to his car and Everett took Kirsten home. He walked her to the door, thanked her again for the lovely evening and hugged her goodnight.

~ T W E N T Y ~
O N E ~

When Kirsten got to work on Monday, Lena came to her office. "Hi, Kirsten, I have something for you," she said with a big smile.

"Leeeeena!" Kirsten said excitedly. It's been forever since I've talked to you. Now that you've gotten your little, fancy promotion and all, I never get to see you. How's the Support Agreement folks treating you over there?"

"Awesome, I love it Kirsten. I'm so glad Mr. Wayne made me take that job. He told me that if I didn't accept it, he would fire me."

"Yes, I remember that. You were pouting like a little baby and Mr. Wayne was screaming, 'I can't even give this woman a promotion, who's ever heard of nonsense like that?'" Kirsten said, trying to sound like Mr. Wayne. "The whole thing was hysterical. You have a lot of potential, Lena, and it shouldn't be spent behind a desk, answering phones all day. He should have made you go a long time ago."

"Yeah, you're right. Now that my kids are older, I'm okay with working late if I have to. Mr. Wayne knows that I don't like change, but he told me that I'll never know if I never try and I held onto those words. Moving over there was the best decision I could have made. Well, it was the best decision Mr. Wayne could have made for me," Lena said, chuckling. "So, Kirsten, how's the new receptionist working out?"

Kirsten frowned. "Oh, she's great if you like staring at boobs and thighs all day. She does good work, though, so I suppose I should give her credit for that," Kirsten said, as she rolled her eyes. "Lena, I miss you terribly. Oh! You will not believe what I did this weekend."

Lena smiled, "What did you do?"

"I went to a lawn care banquet and I had an awesome time!"

Lena laughed, "You went to the Annual Community Lawn Care Banquet? How on earth did you end up there?

I've gone for the past two years, but this year I decided not to compete for Yard of the Month. The banquets are always very nice, though."

Kirsten fell over laughing. "You participate in Yard of the Month, Lena? That is hilarious!"

"Girl, yes. Everett and his team give outstanding gifts."

Kirsten paused. "You know Everett?" she asked, trying not to sound too suspicious.

"Yeah, he goes to my church," Lena said, nonchalantly.

"Really? Well, he seems like a great guy."

"Oh, he is, Kirsten. I don't know why he's not married. He's so good-looking. I heard that several women have tried to date him, but he told them that God already showed him who his wife is and he's just waiting until God prepares her heart for him. He said he didn't think it was fair to lead them on knowing their relationship would never go anywhere. Of course, that just made the women want him more. They couldn't help but have respect for him because he wasn't out there trying to sleep with everything that moved just because he could. I never talk to him whole lot but I love the little bit I do know about him. He seems very honest and genuine and everyone has a lot of respect for him."

That whole conversation sent chills up Kirsten's spine. She didn't know what to think so she didn't bother telling Lena that she went as Everett's date.

"So, what did you want to give me?" Kirsten asked, trying to change the subject.

"Oh," Lena replied, handing her an envelope. "Go ahead, open it," she said, waving her hands excitedly.

Kirsten opened the envelope and pulled out a card. "You are cordially invited to the wedding ceremony of Lena Renee Jessup and Jethro Joseph Wade..."

Kirsten's mouth fell open. "Lena, you're getting married? I thought you hated men. When did you have time to get rid of all that bitterness, give this Jethro guy a chance, fall in love, get proposed to, say yes, and plan a wedding? Where have I been?" Kirsten asked.

Lena said, "Kirsten, true love can flush out all bitterness and it doesn't take forever to get married if you know a person is right for you. He's so right for me, Kirsten. I never thought I'd even talk to a man again, and now here I am planning a wedding. I know God put us together. It had to be God to heal me so I could love again."

"Indeed it was. I'm very happy for you, Lena. I'll definitely be there." Kirsten gave Lena a big hug and Lena giggled like she was a kindergartener.

"Thanks," Lena said. "Oh, let me give you an update on Lance, too, while I'm here. He is doing very well in the mailroom, better than anyone expected."

"No way!"

"Yes way! He got his own apartment too, just as Mr. Wayne told him to do. He had to sell his Corvette. He has a Honda now, but it's nice and he seems to be okay with all of his changes."

"Oh, that's his little blue Honda out there? I was wondering who got a new car. It is nice," Kirsten said, shaking her head in agreement. She and Lena both wanted to laugh but they didn't.

"Mr. Wayne did the right thing; he was causing Lance more harm than good by letting him mooch off of him and his wife," Lena responded.

"Yeah, you're right about that. Wait! Lena, you're not even our receptionist anymore; how do you still know what's going on around here?"

"A receptionist always maintains her connections, Kirsten," Lena said in some type of Scottish accent.

Kirsten laughed, then Lena said, "Well, I have to run, I can't hang out and chat like we used to. They actually expect me to work over there."

"Good, they should. Bye! I'll see you in about two months at the chapel, Mrs. Jethro." Lena laughed.

"Isn't that the ugliest name you've ever heard, Kirsten? He's sweet as pie, though."

"Yes, it is, but if he makes you happy, then Jethro is the sweetest name anyone could ever have."

"Yeah right," Lena said, laughing as she was leaving Kirsten's office.

Just then, Kirsten got a text from Everett. All it said was, "Morning." Kirsten smiled. She liked how simple Everett was.

As she and Everett began to hang out more, they quickly discovered that they were like two peas in a pod. For their lives to be so different, she couldn't believe how well they got along. Everett always kept her laughing about something. It felt like they had known each other all of their lives.

Kirsten would often think, *I feel like I can tell Everett anything. Kind of like the way I felt with Caleb, except when I think of Everett, the word "cousin" doesn't cross my mind,* then she would snicker to herself.

The whole thing was very weird to Kirsten. She felt such a friendship connection with Everett, but she was also very attracted to him. Outwardly, he wasn't anything close to what she would have chosen for herself, but inwardly, he was everything she needed and wanted. Everett didn't have any kids and no ex-wives.

Thank God, no baby momma drama, Kirsten thought.

About a month and a half after Everett and Kirsten started dating he asked if she wanted to go to a wedding with him that following Saturday.

"Yeah sure, I'll go. No, wait, I can't," she said. "My co-worker is getting married Saturday, but what time is yours? Maybe we can go to both," Kirsten responded.

Everett looked at her with one eyebrow raised, "Kirsten I'm not a spring chicken anymore, I don't think I can do two weddings in one day. How about we just get together after church on Sunday?"

"Okay, that's fine," she said.

When Saturday came, Kirsten lazed around the house most of the morning, then she began to get dressed for Lena's wedding. She was so happy for Lena. *I never thought that Lena would open up her heart to love again. She's living proof that anyone can heal from a broken heart and a bad relationship and goes on to find someone who truly loves and cares for them.*

When Kirsten got to the church, it was packed. She could barely find anywhere to park. She made her way to a seat near the back. *Thank goodness I have somewhere to sit. I didn't know Lena and Jethro were so popular,* Kirsten thought, as she laughed quietly.

The ceremony began promptly at 4:30. The wedding party started making their way down the aisle; everyone

looked so lovely.   The colors were peach and purple.   *Peach and purple? Hmmm, those colors really don't look that bad together. Look at Lena trying to be creative!*

When the wedding party had all taken their places up front, the flower girl came in and spread two gigantic baskets of petals all over the aisle. *My goodness!   That's a lot of petals, but maybe Lena wanted it that way so I'll just keep my thoughts to myself.*

Jethro was standing there with great anticipation of his bride. Kirsten was so glad his looks did not match his name.

Right before it was time for Lena to walk in, the Pastor said, "All rise please, as Minister Everett Larson sings for the bridal entrance."

Everett Larson? That's my Everett! Minister? When did Everett become a Minister?

Sure enough, Everett got up and did a solo on his guitar.

Well, ya don't say! This man can sing and play the guitar? Wow! I do love a man who plays the guitar, but I just don't know about this Minister stuff. Lord, you know I love you, but dating a Minister is a lot of right-living and no more sinning. **Kirsten laughed at her silly thoughts.** *Lord, I'm just teasing. You know I want to live right.*

Kirsten could not believe what she was seeing. Everett's voice was amazing. She had no idea that he had all those gifts and talents.

This is not the lawn guy I've known for five years. This is simply not the same man.

As Lena walked down the aisle, through her field of flower petals, she seemed very happy, and her groom even happier. Lena was such a beautiful bride. Everything was wonderful! She and Jethro exchanged vows, then the Pastor told Jethro he could kiss his bride. Jethro picked Lena up and gave her the longest kiss Kirsten had ever witnessed. *Good grief, is all that necessary?*

When the wedding was over, Kirsten went over and quickly hugged Lena and Jethro. Lena was so busy hugging everybody that she barely even noticed who Kirsten was. Kirsten didn't mind, though, because she was anxious to get over to Everett. His back was turned because he was putting his guitar back in its case. He had no idea that Kirsten was there.

Kirsten walked up behind him. "I didn't know you could sing, dance, and play the guitar, Minister Larson."

Everett turned around quickly. "Hey, what are you doing here?" he asked, while giving Kirsten a hug. "Correction," he said. "I only sing and play the guitar, dancing is not my forte."

"Ummmm, Minister?" Kirsten said with a surprised look on her face.

"Yes, I'm guilty of all the above, now what are you doing here? I didn't know you knew Jethro and Lena."

"Lena is my co-worker."

"Oh, okay. Lena and Jethro are my church members."

"Yes, that's right, how could I possibly forget that?" Kirsten said hitting herself on the forehead, "Lena did tell me she knew you."

"You talked to Lena about me?" Everett asked with a smirk on his face.

"NOOOO! Well yes, well kinda. I told her that I went to the Lawn Care banquet and you were very nice. That's when she told me that y'all went to church together. I just didn't put two and two together when you invited me to a wedding."

"You look beautiful, let's go dance," Everett said.

"I thought you couldn't dance?"

"I can't, but you can teach me."

Kirsten laughed. They left the church and walked to the reception hall across the street. They could hear the music as soon as they stepped outside.

"The bride and groom aren't here yet, so we can't dance," Kirsten said.

"Oh, we don't wait for bride and groom at this church. If there's a wedding, we go ahead and break the dance floor in before they even get there."

"But you're a Minister," Kirsten said.

Everett gave her a weird look. "And? Are Ministers not allowed to dance and have fun? There's freedom in God, Kirsten. Don't let anyone make you think that you have to be uptight and boring when you give your life to God. There's a lot of fun to be had, now let's go have it."

"That's so true! I think I like this church," Kirsten responded.

"You'll love it! We are one big happy family here. Come tomorrow. You can sit with me."

"I like that idea," she said.

Kirsten and Everett went to the dance floor and began to dance the

night away. The bride and groom
eventually joined in with the
festivities and Lena made her way over
to Kirsten and Everett.

"Well, well, I see you've met
Everett Larson," Lena whispered in
Kirsten's ear.

Kirsten turned around, "Hey lady,
you look so beautiful and yes, I've met
the Minister. He's an awesome guy."

"Yes he is! Perhaps you're the
woman he's been waiting for. Hmmmm."

"Get outta here and go dance with
your husband, Lena."

"I'm just saying, Kirsten, I'm
just saying," Lena said as she walked
away, laughing.

"What was all that whispering
about?" Everett asked.

"Oh nothing, just girl chat. You
know how we do."

"Yes, I do, I have five sisters."

"Five sisters, oh my gosh! Any
brothers?"

"Two."

"Wow! Your parents definitely
enjoyed each other's company, huh?"

"Yes, they did and still do. I've
never seen a couple who loves each
other so much."

"You too, huh? My parents are sickening."

"Love is never sickening, Kirsten," Everett responded.

Kirsten smiled. Everett was such a great guy, but she didn't want to fall for him, nor did she want him to fall for her.

No love for me! No! No! Love makes you do crazy stuff. You lose all your common sense, and become an emotional lunatic. No, Thank You! **Then Kirsten thought about the list she and Caleb buried in her back yard and how she agreed to forgive Jason, forgive herself, and let the past go and embrace her future.**

Hmmm, on second thought, I do want to fall for Everett and I want Everett to fall for me. I will give my all, as if I was never hurt.

As far as Everett was concerned, he had fallen for Kirsten on the first day he met her. He knew then that she was the one for him, even if she didn't pay him any attention. He knew that one day he would get the nerve to ask her out.

Five years ago, if Everett would have asked Kirsten out, she would have said no. She never would have given him a chance. He wasn't dark skinned, he wasn't rich, and he didn't drive a fancy car. He was always dirty, and since he was a lawn guy, she would have assumed that he wasn't intelligent enough to be in the business world. Back then, Kirsten equated intelligence with having accolades and degrees and being a "big wig" in corporate America, which Everett knew nothing about.

Everett's world was totally different from Kirsten's world, but now she welcomed the change. She didn't realize how wrong she was about Everett. All that "superficial magnificence" she thought she needed in a man no longer mattered. She didn't care what color his skin was, she didn't care how much money he made, what kind of car he drove, or how many degrees he had hanging on his wall. Kirsten just wanted someone who would take care of her heart, someone who would be true to her and give her the love she deserved. She loved how special Everett made her feel and how consistent and stable he was. What you saw was what you got with Everett; there were no hidden agendas and no pretenses.

Everett loved taking Kirsten down
to the lake, where they would just sit
and talk for hours. Actually, it was
mostly Kirsten doing all the talking
and Everett mostly listening. Some
days he would bring his fishing pole
and Kirsten would sit and read a book
or just lie on the blanket and stare at
the sky. Kirsten loved being near
water. Poodles loved the lake, too.
She and Everett didn't have the same
doggie bond that she and Jason had, but
they still managed to get along fine.
Everett didn't care for dogs because he
was bitten by one when he was younger,
but he tolerated Poodles enough to let
her lick his feet whenever she wanted
to. Kirsten always got a kick out of
watching Everett squirm when Poodles
licked his toes.

Kirsten's relationship with
Everett was much different than the
sexually-driven relationship she had
with Jason. Everett was taking things
very slow and Kirsten couldn't be
happier. She really didn't want to
rush into anything.

Everett was such a handyman,
always carrying around tools of some
sort. Anything Kirsten needed fixing,

he'd fix it. He kept her car clean, and of course he kept her yard maintained. He even tried to talk Kirsten into entering the Yard of the Month contest, but she would look at him like he was crazy; he'd just laugh.

Everett reminded her so much of her dad and she loved that about him. Kirsten was in no hurry for love but she was thoroughly enjoying Everett's company.

Kirsten found out later that Everett was the owner of the lawn business. He didn't have to ever cut grass, but it was something he genuinely loved, and it didn't take long for Kirsten to start loving to see Everett in his dirty t-shirt and jeans.

Everett was full of surprises, but they were all very good surprises. Kirsten knew that Caleb played a big part in helping her stop judging people without getting to know them first. Without Caleb, she would have never accepted Everett's offer to go to the banquet and she would have missed out on a wonderful time and a wonderful man. She was seeing a side of Everett that she never had a clue existed.

Everett was more than she ever imagined him to be.

She said one day she would definitely call Caleb and thank him for making her a better person, but until then she was going to enjoy this journey with Everett, wherever it ended up taking them.

~ TWENTY-TWO ~

As Everett and Kirsten's relationship and attraction for each other grew stronger, Everett told Kirsten that he needed to talk to her about something. Everett typically didn't talk much, so his wanting to talk made Kirsten kind of nervous. He took her to their favorite place, the lake.

He put a blanket on the ground and asked her to sit down. Then he said, "Kirsten, we've been dating for almost three months and I think you are so beautiful, inside and out. God knows I'm so attracted to you, but it is really important to me that we don't have sex unless we're married."

Everett stopped abruptly and held his hand up. "Now, don't get me wrong, I'm not saying we need to run off and get married, but I need you to understand that I must refrain from sex unless we are married. I know people may think I'm crazy, because it's definitely hard to stay focused when I'm around you. Trust me, it's hard, but it's something I need to do for my spiritual wellbeing. I just thought I should let you know before we get too far into this."

When Everett stopped talking, Kirsten was fighting back tears. All she could say was, "Wow, me too, Everett. I really want that too," and she gave him a big hug.

Five months passed and things grew pretty rapidly between them. Jason was long gone from Kirsten's thoughts and she knew she wanted Everett in her life for a very long time.

She could even see herself settling down with him and having lots of kids; as many as he wanted to have. Kirsten even entertained the thought of giving up her career and being an at-home mom like her mother.

I can't believe I'm having these kinds of thoughts. I have never thought about quitting my job and having a house full of crumb snatchers before.

Kirsten laughed. Never in a million years did she see herself as a homemaker when she was with Jason. She

was never secure enough to make such a
bold move like that, nor was she sure
enough of his love or commitment to
her. She had no doubt of Everett's
love, though. Although it had only
been five months and they hadn't
exchanged the "L" word yet, she knew
what she and Everett had was real. He
was a real man and she would follow him
to end of the earth if he asked her
too; she knew he would never let
anything happen to her. Everett was
stable and predictable, and as
independent as Kirsten thought she was,
she didn't realize how much she loved
stability until she met Everett.

*Hmmmm, stability was never on the list of things
I wanted in a man. I never even looked at it as being
important until now. I never looked at a lot of things as
being important until now. I guess you can't miss what
you've never had, but now that I have it, I don't want to
ever live without it.*

Everett made her feel safe and
secure. On top of all that, he loved
the Lord. He didn't just go to church,
he truly lived his life according to
God's word. She'd never met a man like
him before. She knew Everett wanted to
throw her on the bed and make love to

her, but because of his dedication to
God, he didn't.

*If he has self-discipline with me, then I know he'll
have self-discipline with other women when they try to
sleep with him, and as good as he looks, I know those
little hoochies will surely try.*

She loved that Everett had self-
control and she loved that when he made
a vow, he kept it. When things became
sexually tense between them, he'd stop,
kiss her forehead and tell her it was
time for him to leave. Sometimes
Everett would be sweating profusely
from all the excitement, but he never
let it get past the kissing stage,
although he sure did want it to.
Kirsten hated when he left so abruptly
like that, well she just hated when he
left, period.

One Friday night they were sitting
on the couch and he told her he had to
go because he had to get up early the
next morning to mow the church lawn and
to clean the inside of the church.
Kirsten didn't want him to leave, so
she began to whine and complain.

"Everett, why are you the only one
who cleans the church every Saturday?
You spend your entire Saturday morning
at the church. You don't get paid or

anything. Looks like someone else would step up to the plate sometimes and at least help you."

Everett put his finger across his mouth like he was thinking about what Kirsten just said.

"Do I not show you enough attention?" he asked her.

Kirsten frowned, "Yeah, of course you do. Why would you ask me that?"

"Well, I do your yards and clean your car every Saturday as well and you don't pay or help me either.

Kirsten, cleaning the church is my pleasure. It is my gift to God because I love him. Cleaning your car and taking care of your yard is my pleasure. It is my gift to you because I love you. When a man loves a woman, he takes pleasure in doing things for her. He doesn't have to be asked, or helped or compensated. Just like the tree branch that fell in your yard, I saw that it needed to be moved so I moved it; you didn't have to ask. If I see something that needs to be done, I do it, with nothing required in return. I take care of the House of the Lord and I take care of the house of my woman. It's the least I can do for the people I love."

Kirsten felt really bad for complaining and she was very embarrassed that she didn't think of it like that, but there was something Everett said that caught her attention and she needed clarification.

"Did you say you love me?" she asked.

He looked at her, "Kirsten, I have always loved you, but the timing wasn't right. One day I was praying and I asked God to show me what I needed to do to have you. Then I turned to a scripture in the Bible that said, "Love always protects, it always trust, it always hopes, and it always perseveres." I knew that was God's answer to my prayer, so that's what I did. I protected you, I trusted that God would give you to me, I hoped that you would see me as the man who could make you happy and I never gave up until I got you."

"You definitely got me," Kirsten said, smiling.

"Yes, and I'll bet you my life I won't let anything take you from me."

"There is nothing that could ever take me from you, Everett. Now go home, you've got to get up early in the morning and take care of the Lord's house. Do you want me to come help you?"

Everett laughed at Kirsten's drastic change in attitude. "No baby, I'll stop by later tomorrow, okay?"

"Okay," Kirsten said as she walked Everett to the door.

A couple of weeks later, Everett remembered that Kirsten's thirty-fourth birthday was coming up. He wanted to throw her a surprise party and invite all of her family and friends, whom he hadn't met yet. He had talked to Michelle on the phone once and had even spoken to Kirsten's dad about some fertilizer he should use for his cow pasture; needless to say, Mr. Jabard loved Everett because Everett could talk farm language.

The bad thing was that Everett didn't know how to get back in touch with any of them. *Lena may be able to help me contact them. Let me get her number from Jethro.*

He called Jethro, but he couldn't reach him, so he called the church secretary and got Lena's work number.

It was Lena's old number, so when he called it, the new receptionist answered the phone.

"Hi, I'm looking for Lena Wade."

"Sir, she no longer works in this area, but I can pass on a message for you," she responded.

"Yes, if you will, it is very important that I speak with her. My name is Everett Larson and—"

"Everett Larson, aren't you Ms. Jabard's boyfriend?"

"Shhhhhh! Yes, now I'm trying to plan a surprise birthday party for Kirsten, so please don't tell her I called. I need to get in touch with her family and friends and I was hoping Lena would have their numbers."

"Her friend Michelle called this morning. I still have her number on caller ID. Would you like me to get it for you?"

"Oh, yes! That would be great. Thank you!"

"No problem. Ms. Jabard has quite a few pictures of you on her desk, you're very photogenic. Love the dimples," she said.

Everett could tell that she was trying to flirt with him, so he responded with a cold, "Thank you."

"Do you have any brothers?" she asked, while laughing.

"Hey, I'm sorry to cut you off, but I really need that number if you'll be so kind to get it for me."

The receptionist rolled her eyes, "Hold on for a minute." She put Everett on hold and got the number off of caller ID.

Everett made it clear that he didn't want to have any more small talk so she just gave him the number.

"I would really appreciate it if you didn't let Kirsten know about the party," he said.

"Oh, I'm good at keeping secrets, Mr. Larson. You can tell me anything you want and I won't tell a soul," she responded with a smile.

"Thank you. Goodbye," he said, before she had a chance to say anything else.

Everett shook his head at how transparent she was. He was used to women flirting with him, but he thought it was sad how some of them demean themselves. His mother taught him to respect women, so any woman who disrespected herself never got much attention from Everett, and this was even before he met Kirsten. Now, Everett only had a heart for Kirsten. He waited five years to get her and he had no intention of messing that up for any cheap thrills.

He called Michelle and told her about the surprise birthday party for Kirsten and asked if she could give him everybody's number. Michelle was so excited. "Everett, do you know that Kirsten has never had a surprise birthday party?"

"Oh, really? No, I didn't know that. Well, in that case, I'll make it the most memorable birthday she's ever had."

"I know you will and that's why we love you."

Everett laughed, "I love you guys, too."

Michelle gave him all the numbers and asked if he needed help, but he told her no, he had it all taken care of. He called all the girls, Kirsten's parents, and his family and friends, and invited them to Atlanta for the weekend. He rented a farm house where

everyone could stay. It had a
beautiful pond, with a white gazebo and
a reception hall for special events.
Everett hired a professional decorator;
the place looked fabulous.

Kirsten thought they were just
going to go to dinner, but when Everett
started heading towards the country,
she had a flashback of Jason's lunch
surprise where she ended up naked.

*I'm sure Everett isn't taking me somewhere to try
to have sex with me, but this is definitely not a restaurant
either. What does this man have up his sleeves?*

Everett parked the car and she
gave him a funny look.

"Come on," he said.

She didn't say a word; she just
smiled and followed him into the house.
When she walked through the door, all
of her friends and family were there.
They all yelled, "SURPRISE!" and
Kirsten burst into tears.

She said, "Everett, no one has
ever thrown me a surprise birthday
party before. Thank you so much!"

"Yeah, I know. Michelle told me,"
he said.

"How did you pull this off?"

"Shhhhh! No questions, we have a
party to attend."

Everyone hugged Kirsten and sang
Happy Birthday to her. She was in
tears most of the night, but they were
tears of joy. She was so excited to
see everyone. They had never all been
to Atlanta at the same time before.
Words couldn't describe how special
Kirsten felt being surrounded by all
the people who loved her. Even Lena
and Jethro was there.

Kirsten had stopped celebrating
her birthday because she and Jason
never did anything special. He was
either out of town or sick or there was
always something that caused him to not
be in a celebratory mood, so her
birthday had become just another day to
her. Within three years, Jason had
caused her to not even think of her own
birthday as special anymore, yet, he
was always ready to celebrate his
special day.

How could I let him do that to me?

She looked over at Everett and he
gave her a smile, showing his deep
dimples. He had the prettiest white
teeth and a smile to die for. Kirsten
didn't know how in the world she'd
missed this man who was right in front

of her face the entire time. She gave him a big hug and kiss.

"I appreciate you so much. You are more than I could have ever imagined. I will love you always," she said.

That was the first time Kirsten told Everett that she loved him.

"And I have loved you always," he responded, while kissing her forehead.

The rest of the night was fabulous. Kirsten's and Everett's family and friends all got along great. It was like they had all known each other forever.

The next day, all the ladies went to get massages and all the guys went golfing. Although Kirsten's family and friends liked Jason, there was something they loved about Everett. Everett and Kirsten were total opposites, yet they seemed perfect for each other.

Kirsten was very happy that she got a chance to meet Everett's parents. They reminded Kirsten so much of her own parents. Two of Everett's sisters, one of his brothers and Everett's best friend all came to the party as well. Kirsten was delighted that they would come to her party, seeing how she'd never even spoken with them before, but it didn't matter because she was planning to be around them for a very long time.

When it was time to go, they all joked that the next time they would see each other, it would be for Everett and Kirsten's wedding. Kirsten and Everett looked at each other and smiled; neither seemed to have any objections to that idea.

~ TWENTY-
THREE ~

After Kirsten's birthday celebration, it took everything in her not to have sex with Everett. At this point, they had been dating six months and they were running out of things to occupy themselves with. He wanted her very badly and she really wanted to experience being with him as well.

Everett was every woman's dream, but Kirsten was haunted by thoughts of Everett not being good in bed, when/if they ever slept together. She honestly wanted to wait until marriage because spiritually, it was the right thing to do, but she didn't want to be dissatisfied either. "There is nothing worse than bad sex," she said, out loud.

God, I know I shouldn't even be thinking about sex, but you created it and I'm really trying to do this the right way. I am so scared that I will not be satisfied if we wait to have sex. Lord, that would be a nightmare!

Please help us to honor you and do the right thing. If you have destined us to be together, then please help me to stop worrying over it and when/if we get married, please bless us with a fulfilled sex life.

Kirsten let out a deep breath. All of a sudden Beatriz came across her mind.

"Let me call Beatriz and see if they made it home safely, since they had to travel a little farther than anyone else.

"Hello," Beatriz answered.

"Hey, ladybug, how's it going?"

"Hey, Kirsten, I'm so glad to hear from you. We adore Everett and your party was wonderful and did I tell you that we adore Everett?" she said, laughing.

"Yes, it was and yes you did. I adore him too. I couldn't stop crying. I felt more in love with him that night than I ever have."

"Well, yeah, he was looking HOT!" Beatriz said, laughing, "I can't believe he was your lawn guy and you never noticed him. I really can't believe that, Kirsten."

"I know, me either. Beatriz, he was always dirty and I just never saw him like that."

"Girl, you couldn't look past all that dirt and see that hunk of burning love?"

Kirsten laughed, "No, I guess I couldn't, but I'm so glad he washed up and put on a tux, so I would notice how good-looking he is."

"He is good-looking, Kirsten, and he's nothing on your list."

"That's the thing, Beatriz, he's everything on my list; everything that's important and everything that I need. He is it."

"Yep, you're right, Kirsten. He is everything that's not superficial."

"Exactly," Kirsten agreed, "But I actually just called to make sure you guys made it home safely. I know that was quite a drive for you, especially with the kids."

Beatriz laughed. "It sure was, but we'd do it again if we had to."

"Beatriz, I really am glad y'all were able to come. I can't believe Everett called you; he's so shy."

"Hmmmm, the way he was all over you, he didn't seem shy to me and I noticed how in shape you look these days. Would Mr. Shy have anything to do with that by chance? Before work,

386

after work, before lunch after lunch, before—"

"No, Beatriz, he's nothing like Jason. Everett has vowed not to have sex until he gets married."

"HE'S A VIRGIN?" Beatriz screamed.

"No! No! Well, actually I don't know, but I believe when he became a Christian he made the same vow for purity that I made, except, he actually stuck to his vows. I stuck to my vows, too, until the devil escorted a fine man across my path," Kirsten said, shaking her head. "That's really sad, isn't it," she said, about herself.

"Awwww, don't beat yourself up, Kirsten. You loved Jason and you were just trying to please him as his woman should."

"No, as his wife should, which I was not. Besides, he had his ex-wife who was also just trying to please him, too."

"What? Are you serious?"

"Oh, I thought I told you about that. I don't want to rehash it, but yes, that's the reason we broke up; he was still sleeping with his ex-wife."

"OH MY GOSH! Kirsten, I'm so sorry. I didn't know that. I knew it was something involving another woman, but I didn't know it was his ex-wife."

"Girl, it is fine. And he actually does own the Jazz restaurant in Atlanta."

"He does? And he never told you?"

"No, he didn't, but after I talked to you and Saidah, I asked him and he said it was complicated; his ex-wife owned part of it, although they were divorced when the place was built.

"Wow, Kirsten. That is crazy."

"Girl, I don't even know who Jason really is, but who cares? Leaving him was the best thing that could have ever happened to me. I just hate I wasted so much time with him when I could have been with a man who's absolutely wonderful to me and wonderful for me. Everett was right there the entire time and I never knew it. He makes me feel so beautiful and so secure. I didn't realize how low my self-esteem had gotten with Jason. I no longer thought I was attractive and I was starting to think I wasn't good enough to be anybody's wife. I just thought that all I'd ever be was a convenient girlfriend, and I accepted that role. There was even a point where I still

slept with him knowing that he was
probably still sleeping with his ex. I
can't believe I stooped so low.
Beatriz, it is so sad how people can
kill your self-esteem and you never
even realize it's gone. With Everett,
I feel so confident. I have never once
wondered what he's doing when we're not
together. I just trust him. I don't
question who he talks to while he out.
I don't feel the need to go through his
phone and I love that. Everett loves
God; he is so committed to living a
holy life. He's not perfect, but he
makes me feel safe, but—" Kirsten said,
pausing, as if she didn't want to
finish her sentence.

"But what?" Beatriz asked.

"Okay, I need to talk to you about
something. Beatriz, you know I really
care about Everett. He's fantastic!
He's like my best friend and my soul
mate all wrapped up in one."

"Yes, now get to the point,
Kirsten. What's the problem?"

"Ok, so, you know how we agreed to
wait until marriage before we have sex,
right?"

"Yeah, are you guys talking about
marriage?"

"No! No way! We've only been dating six months. I'm just saying, what if we get married and the sex isn't good? What if it's terrible? Beatriz, I don't know what I would do. I care so much for him. Sex isn't everything, but girl, you know good sex is important! You know it is!"

"Yeah, it's important," Beatriz said, laughing. "Kirsten, do you really want to wait until you get married to have sex? Because it sounds like you don't. Have you changed your mind?"

"No, I haven't and Beatriz I do want to wait. I really do, but I want to make sure it's good before I commit. Am I wrong for thinking that way?"

"Yes and no, Kirsten. From the spiritual side yes, because you have to trust that God will take care of you in every aspect. He made sex, so surely he knows what will satisfy you. On the flip side, you're human and it's natural to want to test everything out before you commit."

"Exactly!" Kirsten said. "Beatriz, you know a guy will enjoy sex, regardless. It doesn't matter if the woman is blind, crippled, or crazy.

If she's lying in the bed next to him, he's going to have sex with her, but for women it's different. What if he is a virgin? What if he doesn't know what he's doing? What if he doesn't know how to please me? Beatriz, I love God, I really do and I want to live holy, but I kinda think I should know what I'm getting before I get stuck with it, ya know?"

Beatriz laughed. "You sound like a man, Kirsten."

"I know! Oh my gosh, I know, but this is something I think about all the time. It's torturing me, Beatriz. I'm so nervous about it. I asked God to send me a man who wanted to wait until marriage and he sent me the best man in the universe and all I think about is having sex with him. What does that say about me, Beatriz? Sometimes I wonder if I'm really even a Christian. Some of the things I have done and the things I think about are so ungodly."

Beatriz could hear the torment in Kirsten's voice and she was trying very hard not to laugh. "Of course you're a Christian, silly, but you're also human. You have desires just like anyone else. When you become a

Christian, you don't turn into a robot. You still have feelings and desires but you've made the decision to not give in to those desires until you get married. That is very noble, Kirsten. A lot of people say they're a Christian and they are out here humping anything that moves. Stop being so hard on yourself; nobody said living a holy life was easy."

"You are so right, Beatriz. I want to please God, but sometimes I feel like I can't or that I just don't know how."

"Kirsten, it's a step-by-step process towards holiness. No one has arrived. Your heart is pure and that's a great place to start."

"Yeah, I guess you're right. Besides, I only want to have sex with him one time, then we can go back to waiting."

Beatriz let out a huge holler, "Girl, now you're talking crazy! If you let that beast out, you'll never get it back in the cage. If you want to wait until marriage, then leave that thing locked up!" Beatriz said, still laughing.

Kirsten laughed out loud, too. "Girl, I feel it rising up whenever he kisses me! I'm like, 'Good grief, what is that, a python?' He kisses me so passionately, though, like he's savoring every second. When he gets too excited he tells me that he has to go home before he throws me over his shoulder and conquers me. When he says that, girl I want to scream, 'CONQUER ME TARZAN, CONQUER ME!' I know he wants to have sex with me so badly and sometimes I feel like I'm tempting him. He really wants to wait though and so do—"

"Listen, Kirsten," Beatriz interrupted, "This man has got it going on. You don't have to worry about whether he's going to be good in bed or not. He will!"

"Beatriz, no one can be sure of that unless they—"

"Yes, Kirsten, you can be sure, so stop trying to find reasons to sleep with him. Guys who are passionate kissers are also very good in bed, even if their package is small, they will know how to work with what they've got, but you just explained that he seems to be working with a lot. Great kissers make great lovers, period! If he's savoring every moment with your clothes on, he will savor every moment with your clothes off. You don't have any worries with this one, honey, so just enjoy the love y'all have. You'll have plenty of time to get naked, I promise. If he loves God and he loves you enough to wait, then don't mess it up, Kirsten. When a guy knows he's not going to get any sex, he will show you who he really is. When we start having sex with them is when they start lying because they don't want us to take away the sex. They just tell us what we want to hear or just enough to keep us holding on to their lies and false promises."

Kirsten laughed, "You're so silly, Beatriz. Are you some kind of psychiatrist or something?" Kirsten asked, jokingly.

"Girl, you know I was majoring in Psychology, but I dropped out when we got to Abnormal Psychology. The instructor started talking about multiple personalities and stuff. I was like, 'Oh no! This chic can only deal with one personality at a time, from one person at a time.' I knew then that that was not a career field I needed to be in." They both laughed.

Beatriz got serious. "Kirsten, this man cherishes you for who you are, not for what you can give him. This is the man you deserve; this is the man you've been waiting for."

"He really is Beatriz. He is everything I want and need."

"Well, let him love you with your clothes on."

Kirsten smiled, "Let him love me with my clothes on, huh. I love that, Beatriz. Okay, I will. I promise! Thank you for always being there for me. Your advice is the best."

"You're welcome," Beatriz said. "Well, I have to go, honey, but let's talk later, okay? Keep me posted."

"Yes, I sure will."

"Okay, bye, Kirsten."

"Bye, Beatriz. Love you!"

"Love you, too."

Kirsten was so glad she and Beatriz had that talk. Beatriz was always the perfect person to talk to when Kirsten was confused about an issue. She was never judgmental, never condescending, and never argumentative. Kirsten loved that about her.

Michelle was the total opposite of
Beatriz. She was all of those things,
judgmental, condescending, and
argumentative, but she had a heart of
gold and she was very loyal to her
friends. Michelle was what some would
call, "a ride or die chic." She was
always there for Kirsten, it didn't
matter what time, day or night. If
Kirsten needed Michelle, she knew
Michelle would drop whatever she was
doing to be available. Kirsten loved
her as much as she loved herself. She
could not imagine life without Michelle
in it.

Saidah was a combination of
Michelle and Beatriz. She always spoke
her mind, but she also knew when to
hush and listen. Kirsten knew she had
the best friends in the world and she
wouldn't trade them for anything. She
also had the best parents in the world
and the best co-worker, Lena, and her
boss, Mr. Wayne wasn't half bad either.
Now, she had Everett, and he made
everything complete.

~TWENTY-FOUR~

It was two months later and Kirsten and Everett had been dating for almost eight months. They were very much in love and living Holy seemed to be getting harder and harder as each day past.

One evening they were both lying on a blanket at the beach, and the sun had just finished setting. Everett thought about how beautiful Kirsten looked under the sun, then all of a sudden, he started thinking about how beautiful Kirsten would look under him. He tried to erase those thoughts, but his mind was racing with all kinds of perverted thoughts. Before he knew it, he was on top of Kirsten kissing her. They could both feel the sexual tension rising between them. Things were getting pretty intense and this time Everett wasn't stopping himself.

"Everett, I really don't think we should—" was all Kirsten could get out of her mouth before Everett covered it with his lips. To Kirsten, it seemed like Everett had been taken over by some aliens. He seemed to have forgotten all about his vows, as well as the fact that they were at a public beach. That was until a little boy passed by with his mother and pointed at them.

"Yuck!!!! Momma look, they're making out on the beach!"

The little boy's mom seemed disgusted! "Cover your eyes!" she huffed. "Some people have no morals, respect, or standards! Let's go," she said, grabbing her son's arm and running towards the beach exit.

Kirsten and Everett were so embarrassed. They didn't know what came over them. Everett laid his head on Kirsten, still huffing and puffing. He wanted so badly to continue where he left off, but the interruption from the kid slapped him back into reality.

Lord, you've got to help me! He thought as he shook his head in disbelief at his actions.

Everett couldn't take it anymore. He knew Kirsten was the one for him and he honestly didn't know how much longer he could resist wanting to rip her clothes off. He was ready to marry her and he was definitely ready to have sex with her.

She was so beautiful to him. He would give her the world if he could. He wasn't sure if Kirsten was ready to get married, but he knew it was time to take things to the next level.

It's been almost eight months and that's a long time to have a beautiful woman in front of you and you can't touch her. I don't know how much more of this I can take. Lord, I'm trying to do the right thing, but a brotha has really gotten weak in the knees lately.

He and Kirsten packed their things to go home. When he got to Kirsten's house he told her that it was best that he didn't come in. She smiled and nodded her head in agreement. He apologized for how he acted at the beach. He told her that he loved her more than anything and he never meant to disrespect her or make her feel like she didn't have morals or standards like the lady said.

Kirsten smiled, "Everett, we have more morals and standards than anyone.

We just wanna have sex. Is that so bad?" she asked, looking at Everett with her puppy dog expression.

Kirsten's puppy dog look turned Everett on even more. He put the car in park and jumped over into the passenger seat with Kirsten. Everett was kissing all over Kirsten and his hands seemed to have had a mind of their own.

"Everett, I wasn't trying to tempt you," Kirsten finally managed to say, while Everett was still sucking her lips down like he was eating Southern pig feet soaked in vinegar.

"I love your flavored lip gloss, Kirsten. It makes your lips taste like peach cobbler," he said.

Kirsten pushed him off of her. "Everett, get a hold of yourself, we are in a parked car in my driveway for goodness sake and as much as I would like you to take me right here, I don't want our first time to be in a car like we're some horny teenagers."

Everett laughed. He climbed back to his side and rubbed his hands over his face. "I'm so sorry, baby; really I am. Please go in the house, because I can't be responsible for my actions as long as you're in front of me," he said, as he laughed some more.

Kirsten looked worried. "Should I let you go home alone? Are you going to go call an old girlfriend or something to get you some relief?" she asked.

Everett looked at her like he was appalled. "What? I would never cheat on you, how could you ask me something like that?"

"I'm sorry baby, I wasn't really serious, but Everett, you're obviously needing to have sex right now, so don't get mad at me for wondering how you're going to relieve all that tension."

"Do you think this is the first time I've wanted to have sex with you and couldn't? I assure you, I've had built up tension before and I've never thought about sleeping with another woman. Do you really think I'm like that?"

"No, no baby I don't, I—"

"And correction," Everett said, cutting her off, "I don't need to have sex, I want to have sex, and I want to have it with you, but since I can't do that, I'm going to go home, take a shower and watch sports."

"I'm sorry, baby. I should have never made that accusation."

"Kirsten, don't you think I know you want to sleep with me just as bad as I want to sleep with you? Would it really make sense for me to break my vows to God and jeopardize what we have by sleeping with someone else when I have you right here? If I'm sinning, it's going to be with you, right here in this car, right now, in your driveway, in front of all your neighbors," Everett said, smiling.

Kirsten laughed. She felt bad for what she said to Everett. She didn't know why she even brought it up, but she was glad it hadn't totally ruined Everett's mood.

She touched his hand. "I know you would never cheat on me, baby. Please forgive me," she said leaning over to give him a kiss.

"Kirsten," he said, placing his arm in front of her. "I love you more than anything, but if you kiss me, then Lord help us both."

"Okay, baby," she replied, as she un-puckered her lips and got out of the car. "I love you so much," she said, leaning in the window.

Everett tried very hard to look at her face, but his eyes kept going down to her boobs.

"Everett, what is wrong with you? Stop it!" she said, shaking her head, as she walked away.

Everett got out of the car and grabbed her arm, while laughing, "I'm so sorry, baby. I don't mean to stare, but I've always stared at your boobs because they're always talking to me, but today I want to talk back to them." He chuckled.

Kirsten didn't like how he was gawking at her. It reminded her of how Jason always wanted sex like she was some sex slave, but she remind herself that Everett was not Jason and it was natural for him to want to have sex.

"You're beautiful, baby. Do you expect me not to look?" Everett asked, interrupting Kirsten's thoughts.

She smiled, "Yes, I expect you not to look!" They both laughed, then Everett gave her a quick and dry kiss good night.

"Well, I can't promise you I won't look, but I'm trying very, very hard not to touch, Kirsten. Really hard."

He gave her a wink and walked back to his car.

"Yes, I know baby, you're doing a good job," Kirsten yelled, sarcastically. "Good night, Everett."

"Good night, baby," he said, as he put the car in reverse and started backing out the driveway. He made an abrupt stop and got out of the car. "Oh baby, I'm sorry, I didn't even walk you to the door. Dang! I'm losing it."

Kirsten laughed, "It's okay, baby. Go on home."

"No, it's almost dark out here. I can suppress my testosterone enough to make sure you get in the house safely. I haven't gone completely crazy."

"Yes, you have," Kirsten responded, as Everett walked her to the door. He made sure she got in the house okay, gave her another light kiss and said good night again.

The next day, Everett decided to stop by the church to talk to the Pastor.

"Hey, Pastor, how are you doing?" Everett asked.

"Hey, Minister Larson, come on in," the Pastor responded.

"Am I disturbing you?"

"No, never! Have a seat. You want some water? I also have some Pepsi in the—"

"No, I'm good, Pastor, thank you. I need to run something by you."

"Sure, go ahead."

"Ummm, how soon is too soon to get married?"

The Pastor laughed. "Ahhhh, I see. Well, if you know someone is the one for you, there is no such thing as too soon to get married. All relationships will have their ups and downs, it doesn't matter how long you date before you get married. If you love the woman and she's good to you, marry her. It's just that simple. You've been waiting for the woman God has for you, right?"

"Yes, I've waited a long time," Everett said.

"Is Kirsten that woman?"

"Absolutely, Pastor. I have no doubt about that."

"Well, go get your license and I'll marry y'all today."

They both laughed. "I don't think we can get married today, but I would like to start making preparations for marriage counseling, once I propose, of course."

"Okay, y'all can do counseling if you want. I think it's good, but it's not required."

"What do you mean, it's not required? I thought Pastors wouldn't marry you without marriage counseling."

The Pastor looked over his glasses at Everett. "Can I be honest with you, Minister Larson?" he asked.

"Yes, please, Pastor."

"Years ago, there was no such thing as marriage counseling and those marriages lasted forty, fifty, and sixty years. Now we got all kinds of marriage counseling and marriages aren't even lasting sixty days. Either you're going to be committed to staying married or you're not. Counseling gives you an idea of what to expect and how to cope with certain things, but there are still going to be surprises. There will still be disappointments, and sometimes you're still going to wonder if you did the right thing.

"We are talking about two people trying to merge their lives together and that's hard to do unless you're committed. The key is commitment, not

counseling. However, in saying that,
please let me know if you guys want
counseling and I'll be happy to provide
it for you," the Pastor said, with a
big smile.

Everett sat there pondering what
the Pastor just said.

"Minister Larson, some men already
know how to love and treat a woman and
some women already know how to love and
treat a man. They learned it from
positive male and female influences in
their lives. However, some do not,
because they were never taught. They
didn't have great role models, so they
learned to manipulate their partner to
get what they want. They start off
being sweet and kind, but they can't
endure. The reason they can't endure
is because it was never from their
heart. Their kindness and their
compliments were never real.

"So many people jump in the sack
with someone who has no commitment or
loyalty to them, then they have the
nerve to get angry when the person
doesn't take them seriously or when
they get dumped for the next good
looking thing that comes along. They
think they're gonna wake up to the same

person they laid down with, only to
find out that the person they laid down
with was a façade. That's why it's
important to build a foundation with a
person, have a friendship connection
with them first, then pursue a
relationship.

"If you really care for someone,
you don't play silly games with them.
You don't do things just to press their
buttons or just to get a reaction out
of them! That's childish; that's what
lil kids do! When you love someone, it
will make you happy to see your partner
happy. Grownups don't jeopardize what
they have at home for what's in the
streets. You would be amazed by how
many people intentionally jeopardize a
good relationship simply because they
are not used to someone treating them
good. They become comfortable with
abuse, and if someone isn't abusing
them, mentally, physically, or
emotionally, then they don't want to be
in the relationship," said the Pastor.

"Wow! Pastor, that's pretty
deep." Everett responded.

"I'm sorry, Minister Larson. I got
a little off track," the Pastor said,
chuckling. "Everything you need to

know about love and marriage is in the Bible. A commitment to living out First Corinthians, Chapter thirteen is what it's going to take for y'all to stay married. Couples need to read this chapter together, and often. Marriage gets fuzzy and it takes a commitment to God's word and a commitment to each other to get through the hard times, but it is possible. I assure you, it's possible."

The Pastor sat back in his chair and rubbed his hand across his eyebrows. "My wife and I have been married for 49 years and I've never cheated on her. There were plenty of opportunities, though. Women will strip down in the middle of church service if you let them. They don't care that you're a Minister of the Gospel. Sometimes they come from every direction and they ain't all ugly either. It will be women from your past, women from your present, and women from your future. Whether you're a Pastor, trying to live holy or whether you sin every second of your life, you will always be surrounded by temptations, but it's up to you to remember the big picture.

"I'm going to be real with you for
a minute," the Pastor said in a very
serious tone. "You must always think
with your big head. Trust me, the
little one will always be speaking, but
you need to have enough wisdom to
realize that if you listen to him, it's
going to lead you down a road of
regret.

"You are the head of your house,
so it's not up to your wife to keep
your marriage alive; it's up to you, as
a man of God. Don't ever stop wooing
her! Don't ever stop making her feel
beautiful. Don't ever stop making her
feel safe and secure! Women need that.
In return, you're going to get a woman
who lives to satisfy you in every way
possible. Make her feel good about
herself during the day and she'll have
no problem with you tapping her on her
shoulder during the night. It's really
that simple."

"Wow!" Everett said, again.

The Pastor chimed in again, "I
sure hope I haven't discouraged you
from getting married. It's a beautiful
thing to have someone to share your
life with, but it's not always easy.
That's the only point I'm trying to

make here, but go, marry her! Marry
her! She's a great gal. You've found
a jewel!"

"Yes, I have, Pastor!"

"Well, make her yours then," the
Pastor said, tapping his pencil on his
desk.

"Okay, thank you for the talk. It
was great; I needed to hear it."

"Well, there's more of that in
counseling if you and the future Mrs.
Larson decide y'all want it."

Everett smiled. He liked the
sound of Mrs. Larson.

"I think we may, but maybe for a
quick recap and overview," Everett,
said laughing.

"Well, come on back and we'll fix
you right up. The Mrs. helps me with
all the counseling sessions, so we can
give you the male and female
perspective on things. Besides, we
wouldn't want Kirsten to be
outnumbered," the Pastor said, smiling.

"Yes, she will like having a woman
in there, but Pastor, I haven't
proposed to her yet so—"

The Pastor cut him off, "I know
how to keep a secret, that's what
Pastors do. We keep lots of secrets,

thank God! No worries, now go propose!"

Everett laughed. "Thanks again, Pastor; have a good one!"

"You too, Minister Larson, you too," the Pastor said, chuckling.

~ TWENTY - FIVE ~

The next week Kirsten went out of town for work. Although Everett was going to miss her, he was very happy she was gone. He needed time to think about the things he and the Pastor talked about. He needed to think about whether the timing was right to propose to Kirsten and whether she would say yes. He needed time to think about a lot of things.

All of a sudden Everett didn't feel well. His palms were sweaty and several sweat beads had started to form on his forehead.

"What is wrong with me?" he asked. "Kirsten is the only woman I want to be with. She's the only person I want to wake up to; why am I getting so nervous about marrying her?"

Everett felt very hot. He didn't know what was going on with him so he got a bath towel, wet it, wrapped it up with ice, and put it on his forehead.

The responsibility of being a husband and eventually a father was nearly giving him an anxiety attack. Everett wasn't afraid to marry Kirsten, but he was definitely nervous about everything that came with marriage.

"I'll just lie down on the couch for a minute and see if that helps," he said. Everett looked up at the ceiling and took a few deep breaths. He looked over at a picture of his parents. He noticed how happy they looked, then he looked at a picture of him and Kirsten.

Hmmm, we look very happy, too.

Everett smiled at how much he enjoyed being around Kirsten.

That woman truly makes me happy; I'd be crazy not to marry her.

Just then Everett got a call from Kirsten.

"Hey, Honey," Kirsten said, excitedly.

"Hey, baby! How's Seattle?" Everett asked.

"Oh, you should have come with me. The mountains are breathtaking. I climbed Mount St. Helens this morning."

"You lie like a rug, girl. There's no way you climbed a mountain."

Kirsten snickered, "You know me far too well, but I did look at the mountains and pictured myself climbing them; that should count for something."

"No, actually it doesn't," Everett replied, with a smile.

"You're just jealous because you have no imagination."

Everett chuckled, "I imagine lots of things, but you climbing Mount St. Helens isn't one of them. Sorry, babe. You'll be back Friday, right?"

"Yeah, probably Friday morning," Kirsten responded.

"Do you need me to pick you up from the airport?"

"Awww, you're so sweet, but no, I have to go into work for a little while, so Mr. Wayne is sending the new girl to pick me up."

"Oh, the girl that took Lena's place?"

"Yeah, do you know her?"

"Nah, not really, but she was the one who gave me Michelle's phone number off of your caller ID."

"Oh, really? Hmmmm," said Kirsten, in a suspicious tone.

"What is that supposed to mean?"

"Did she flirt with you? Of course she did, you don't even have to answer. So did she?"

"I thought you said I didn't have to answer."

"You don't, but I'll just give you the silent treatment until you do."

Everett laughed, "You act like I flirted back with her."

"So she did flirt with you?"

"My head hurts Kirsten, and what's with you acting so jealous lately?"

"Have I really? I've been acting jealous?"

"Yes, and I don't like it. Your last boyfriend must have cheated on you or something?"

Kirsten became deathly silent. She knew she was over Jason and she wanted nothing else to do with him, so she didn't understand why hearing those words stung so bad.

"Kirsten, are we going to have trust issues?" Everett asked in a concerned toned, "Because I—"

"No, don't be silly," she said, cutting him off. "Of course I trust you; there are no issues, Everett," Kirsten responded, reassuringly.

"Hmmm, ok. Well, I'm really not feeling well. I'm going to lie down, but you and I will talk more about this later. Kirsten, you have to be able to trust me. If you don't, then we have nothing worth investing in."

"I do trust you, Everett. I don't know why I get a little jealous sometimes. Do you trust me?"

"You've never given me any reason not to, have you?"

"No, I haven't and I never will."

"That's good to know! Kirsten, I don't expect us to be perfect, but if you have concerns about something, you've got to talk to me about it. Don't just sit and ponder on them and please don't go to your friends. Talk to me, alright?

"Okay baby, that's a deal."

"Well, I'm going to take a shower and go to bed."

"Okay, good night and I hope you feel better," Kirsten said, before hanging up.

When Friday came, the receptionist picked Kirsten up from the airport, just as Mr. Wayne had instructed.

"Hi, Ms. Jabard, your taxi is here," she said, all bubbly and chipper.

Kirsten looked down at the short skirt and low cut blouse the receptionist had on. She threw her bags in the back seat, mumbled something to herself, hopped into the passenger seat, and tried her best to avoid any conversation. Since the girl was extra chipper that day, Kirsten knew avoiding her would not be easy, but she was determined to give it a try.

Kirsten was the one who hired her, so if she didn't like what she saw, Kirsten knew she had no one to blame but herself. On the day of the interview, the girl wore a nice pants suit, but as soon as she got the job, she went straight to tight mini skirts and blouses that showed at least forty percent of her boobs. If the truth be told, Kirsten felt somewhat betrayed.

I would have never hired her if I knew she lacked good taste in dress code etiquette, but the company's dress code is an unspoken rule and unspoken rules can't be enforced. Besides, I don't want to fire her, I just want her to—"

"Ms. Jabard," the receptionist interjected, while Kirsten was deep in thought.

"Yes," Kirsten responded, in an aggravated tone.

"You don't like me, do you?"

"No, I can't say that I do." Kirsten said, without hesitation. "I'm hoping you wanted an honest answer, correct?"

"But, why? Why don't people like me when they don't even know me?"

Kirsten rolled her eyes. She was not in the mood. "Why do people come to an interview with an elegant pants suit on and once they get hired they start wearing short skirts and low-cut tops to work? We hire a whole, complete person. Dressing professionally is a part of that whole, complete package. I'm sorry if that hurts your feelings but anyone who represents a company should always maintain professionalism. This is your job, not your back yard barbecue, so if we're asking questions here, then I have a few to ask myself."

Kirsten realized that she was a bit harsh. She looked over at the girl, whose name she could barely

remember. Kirsten took a deep breath.
What is this girl's name? Oh yeah!

"Menda, listen, I'm a
straightforward person, so please
excuse my bluntness, but if you ever
expect to get promoted and move on to
bigger and better things, you're going
to have to stop dressing like you want
to get laid." Kirsten paused, "and
you're going to have to stop flirting
with other people's boyfriends."

The girl looked like she had just
seen a ghost. The car went completely
silent, so Kirsten reached for her
phone, put in her earbuds, and listened
to some music, in hopes that the
receptionist would not want to continue
the conversation.

"I'm sorry, Ms. Jabard. I didn't
mean to flirt with your boyfriend. I
don't mean to flirt with anybody's
boyfriend, but I'm a friendly person.
Sometimes I just take it too far."

Kirsten took out her earbuds and
gave her a cold, blank stare.

"I won't do it again," she said,
shamefully, "But Ms. Jabard, my name is
Mandy, not Menda, and I would like us
to start over. I would like you to be
my mentor," she said in a soft,

innocent tone. "Do you think that's possible?"

This time, Kirsten gave her the frown of death. Kirsten couldn't help but think that this was another "Lance" project that would surely have the same ending.

"I'm not much of a mentor, Mandy. I just come to work and do my job like everybody else. I don't think I—"

"Ms. Jabard, you're a great mentor. Please give me a chance."

"Mandy, you don't work for me. Yes, I hired you, but you work directly for Mr. Wayne. As far as I'm concerned, we are equals."

"Ms. Jabard, we are far from equals. Mr. Wayne thinks the world of you. He trusted you when you told him to hire me and he will trust you if you tell him to fire me. You have influence in this company, I'm not crazy. All I'm asking for is a fresh start and for you to teach me the ropes a little. Someone had to teach you, right?"

"Do you always talk this much?" Kirsten asked, intentionally not answering Mandy's question.

"Yes, I do," Mandy said, with a smile, as if she thought Kirsten had just given her a compliment.

"Okay, fine! If you will forgive me for judging you by your outer appearance, which is something I thought I had stopped doing, then I will mentor you."

"AWWWWWWWESOME!!!!!" Mandy screamed, almost running off the road.

"Hey, please get me back to work safely."

"I will take good care of you, Ms. Jabard. No worries," Mandy said, sounding like she just found a new best friend.

When they arrived at the office, Mr. Wayne was just getting ready to leave for a meeting.

"Oh, look what we have here," he said. "I take it that you two bonded on your way back from the airport?"

"Yes, we sure did," Mandy said, enthusiastically.

Mr. Wayne's eyes were fixed on Kirsten's sour expression. He grinned. "Well, Mandy, Kirsten is the best employee in this company. I trust her with my life and my money. She knows just about everything I know, so it will serve you well to find out all you can from her. She can be a sourpuss at times, but I can't think of anyone else I'd rather have on my team."

Mr. Wayne tipped his hat at Kirsten and Mandy. "You ladies enjoy your day. I won't be back until Monday."

"Bye, Mr. Wayne and thank you. I'll do just as you said," Mandy responded.

Kirsten said nothing at all, which made Mr. Wayne laugh even harder. Kirsten had never heard Mr. Wayne say such nice things about her. Up until that point, she thought he only tolerated her, but that still wasn't going to get him out of the dog house for the stunt he just pulled with Mandy.

I don't like her, why would he ask me to mentor her? Kirsten let out a sigh. *Okay, Kirsten, that is not what Jesus would do. You are a Christian, and you need to show kindness to others.* Kirsten let out another big sigh and hurried into her office to see all the work that had piled up on her desk. She returned a few phone calls, then tried to make some kind of dent in the pile.

After a few hours, she decided she was done and was going home for the day.

"Mandy, you're in charge of yourself for the rest of today. I'll see you on Monday," she said, as she walked by Mandy's desk.

"Oh, you're leaving, too? Gee whiz!" Mandy said, as if Kirsten was trying to play hooky from work.

"Yes, Mandy, I just came from Seattle, remember? I woke up at 4:00 this morning, so I could catch a 5:30 flight. I'm tired. Yes, I'm going home."

Kirsten headed for the door and Mandy yelled, "Okay, well please tell that cute guy with the dimples I said hello." Mandy slapped her hand on her desk as if she just told a "rolling on the floor laughing" joke. "I'm kidding, I'm kidding," she said, still laughing.

Kirsten stopped abruptly. She turned around and went back to Mandy's desk.

"The first thing you need to learn is that I keep my personal life separate from my professional life. I will mentor you because I know Mr. Wayne told you to ask me, but not for

one minute should you think that we're
friends. I don't talk about my
boyfriend to you and you don't talk
about my boyfriend to me, understood?"

Mandy frowned. "It was a joke.
I'm sorry. You don't have to bite my
head off."

Kirsten walked away, not offering
Mandy any reassurance that she believed
she was joking. The look in Kirsten's
eyes told Mandy that she and Kirsten
were no closer to bonding now than they
were before they ever knew each other
existed.

"Ms. Jabard, it was just a joke,"
Mandy yelled, remorsefully as she
watched Kirsten walk out the door
unfazed by her apology.

Kirsten left work, ran a few
errands, then went home and crashed on
the couch.

The next day, she woke up to
Everett mowing her lawn. She rubbed
the crumbs out of her eyes and looked
at the clock. It was 6:55 am. She
took another look to make sure she was
seeing the right time. It was barely
even light outside. *What is Everett doing
here?* Kirsten thought as she got up and
washed her face.

She stepped out on the porch. "What are you doing here so early, man?" she asked, with a huge smile on her face.

She knew Everett couldn't hear her, but he stopped the lawn mower and said, "Because this is a special day and you need to get out of bed. We have somewhere to be. If I called you, you would've gone back to sleep as soon as we hung up, but no one can sleep with this lawn mower making all this noise at 7:00 in the morning," Everett said, jokingly.

She laughed, "Yeah, and I'm sure the neighbors are just as happy about the noise as I am, and how did you even know what I said?"

"Because I know how you think," he responded.

Kirsten always did enjoy Everett's sense of humor and she loved how in tune he was with her. They could communicate without even talking. It was like they were born to be together.

"I missed you so much," she said. "I'm sorry I didn't return your call last night, I fell asleep."

"Good, then you should be well rested, now go on and get dressed so we can go," Everett shouted.

"Where are we going?" Kirsten asked.

"To the Land of Oz, but we won't get there in time to get you any courage if you don't hurry up and get dressed."

"Hush up!" Kirsten shouted, as she went back inside to get dressed, as Everett requested.

Kirsten had no clue what Everett was up to. She took a shower and got dressed while Everett finished the yard. He brought a change of clothes with him so he could shower at her place, and they could leave from there.

Since Kirsten didn't know where they were going, she wasn't sure how she should dress for the occasion; she just threw on a white sundress with white sandals.

When Everett came in the house and saw her, he grinned and said, "Perfect!"

She smiled and looked in her makeup bag for her lip gloss.

"I beat you getting dressed," she bragged.

"Of course you beat me, you had a two-hour head start, woman!"

She liked when Everett called her "woman." She always pictured him as a cave man ready to throw her over his shoulder and carry her off into the woods.

"So what did you do when you got back in town yesterday?" Everett asked.

"Well, for one, I had to tell Mandy off! My head was hurting so bad when I left the office. I will do anything for Mr. Wayne, but I'm tired of him giving me all of his problem children and asking me to perform miracles on them. He thinks it's hilarious! He called me a sourpuss! I'm not a sourpuss, am I, Everett?"

"You? A sourpuss? No Way!" Everett said, with a smile.

Kirsten paid no attention to his sarcasm. "I'm trying to be a Christian, Everett. I'm trying to do the right thing, but I think this girl wants to get under my skin. I think she does it on purpose."

"What did she do?"

"She told me to tell you 'Hi.'"

Everett looked at her like he was waiting for the rest of the story.

"She's got some nerve. Can you believe she said that to me?" Kirsten asked, angrily.

"Who cares, Kirsten? Why are you so upset about that? She doesn't even know me."

"Exactly, and that's all the more reason why she doesn't need to be speaking to you."

Everett laughed. "I thought you said you weren't jealous."

"No, I never said that I wasn't jealous. I said that I trusted you, that's what I said, Everett. There's a difference," Kirsten explained, with a frustrated look on her face.

Everett grabbed her hand, "Then that's all that matters. Just trust that God will lead and guide me and help me to see when women have bad intentions. You have to trust me to make the right decision. Kirsten, you and I have something that people only dream of. You can't spend your time telling off every woman who flirts with me. You are a classy lady, a woman of God. Your time is too precious to waste it on someone you know is trying to push your buttons. You can't let those types of people consume any of your time or drain your thoughts and energy. Just pray for them and go on."

Kirsten took a deep breath. "How did you learn how to handle women so well?"

Everett laughed. "A woman just needs a man to hear what she's saying and try to understand what she's feeling. When a woman gets emotional, most men shut down because they don't know how to make it better, then the woman feels like she's being ignored. Having five sisters and a mom, I learned very early on that ignoring a woman will never, ever make things better."

Kirsten let out a big scream, "You are sure right about that! I don't know how I ended up with such an awesome man, but I'm very thankful that I have you in my life."

"God put us together, I have no doubt in my mind about that," he responded, then he asked, "Babe, do you mind if I take a shower, so we can just leave from here?"

"Sure, go ahead," Kirsten said, as she started back applying her lip gloss in the bathroom mirror, then grabbed a comb and started fluffing up her hair.

Everett stood there with a puzzled look on his face. "Kirsten, would you like me to get undressed in front of you or are you planning to leave the bathroom any time soon?"

Kirsten thought about how she and Everett hadn't seen each other all week. She didn't want to have another episode of what happened at the beach and in the car, but the thought of Everett getting undressed in front of her made all of her body parts yearn for him.

She knew there wouldn't be anything to stop them this time. She knew what the right thing to do was, but she wanted so badly to tell him to go ahead and get undressed. She let out a sigh, "I should probably go," she said, sorrowfully.

Everett wondered what took Kirsten so long to come to that conclusion. He responded with a smirk, "Yeah, that would be best for both of us."

While Everett showered, Kirsten tried hard not to imagine him naked and when that didn't work, she tried hard to talk herself out of going in the bathroom and attacking him.

431

"Cut it out, Kirsten. You've finally met a man who doesn't see you as a sex machine, so don't mess it up."

"Gosh, he's so darn cute though; look at those pretty dimples. Lord, I love dimples."

"Kirsten, pull yourself together and stop acting like you're on fire."

"I am on fire! I just want to be with him this one time. One time won't hurt, will it."

"No, Kirsten, he made a vow to God and so did you. You know he's the one for you, so just wait it out."

"I know, I know. God help me! Lord help me!"

This conversation went on between Kirsten and herself the entire time Everett was in the shower. When he came out of the bathroom, Kirsten was still somewhat pacing the floor.

"Who were you talking to?" Everett asked.

Kirsten laughed, "Ummm, no one, other than myself."

Everett shook his head, "You know that's crazy, right?"

"Yeah, I know, but we had a small dilemma and it needed to be rectified," she said, snickering.

"Well, did y'all rectify it?"
Everett asked.

Kirsten looked at Everett who was
now showered up and fully dressed, with
the exception of his shoes.

"Yes, I think we're okay now."

They both laughed as Everett
reached for his shoes. He said.
"Please, let's hit the road before you
ask me to talk to y'all too."

Kirsten chuckled and said, "That
sounds like a great plan," so he and
Kirsten jumped in the car and drove
off.

~TWENTY-SIX~

"Where are we going, Everett? Please tell me where we're going," she begged.

"Why do women feel the need to know everything that's going on?" he asked.

"Because, there's nothing going on that we shouldn't know about," she responded with a giggle, then she twisted her mouth.

Everett gave her a big sigh.

Kirsten loved how manly Everett was. He wasn't a male-chauvinist by any means, but he definitely believed that men and women had distinct roles. A man should always take care of his woman and a woman should trust her man to make good decisions.

Everett was only about 180 pounds, but to Kirsten he seemed so big and strong; she felt safe with him. She knew he wouldn't let anyone or anything hurt her and she loved that about him. However, regardless of how awesome Everett was, behind all of his awesomeness, was a lot of stubbornness, and there was no way Everett was going to tell Kirsten where they were going.

She looked over at Everett and said, "Well, can I please stop by the mall before we go? There's this dress on sale and I have to have it."

Kirsten was messing up Everett's plans and he was not happy about it. Just as they were approaching the mall, Kirsten started whining even more about this dress that she just couldn't do without. Everett looked over at her and shook his head. He figured it couldn't hurt to stop for a few minutes, if indeed that was all it was going to be.

Women plus shopping never equals a few minutes, he thought. He just hoped this "few minutes" didn't set them back too far on their trip, but he also knew that if they stopped, it would make Kirsten very happy and he definitely wanted this day to be a happy one.

Everett learned from his dad and his Pastor that it was the little

things a man does for a woman that
makes a big difference in their
relationship.

*Besides, I will have her for the rest of my life, so I
might as well get used to being set back on time.*
Everett did an inward laugh, then
quickly got off at the next exit and
pulled into the mall parking lot.

Kirsten was so excited. She gave
him a big kiss and started running
towards the mall door.

Everett yelled, sarcastically,
"No, thank you. I don't want to go in
with you. I'll just sit here and wait
in the hot sun, thanks for asking."

She looked back, blew him a kiss
and said, "I knew you didn't want to
go, that's why I didn't ask. I'll be
right back, babe."

"I won't be holding my breath on
that," he yelled. Everett decided this
would be a good time to catch up on a
nap. He slept for a while, then a loud
noise woke him up. He looked at his
watch and saw that Kirsten had been
gone for forty-five minutes.

"Women!" he said, "They simply do
not know how to tell time. A few
minutes should always be less than ten,
but what a few minutes should never be,

is forty-five minutes. That's not a few," he said, as he grabbed his iPad and decided he'd finish waiting inside the mall.

Everett complained as he walked in the mall, "This is why I don't like to go shopping with her."

"'Everett, why won't you shop with me?' she asks."

"Well, Kirsten, I would shop with you, but you don't know how to leave the stores, and I'd much rather be at home watching sports."

Everett chuckled because he was talking to himself just like Kirsten. *Oh gosh, she's rubbing off on me.*

Everett smiled. He thought about the first day he saw Kirsten, when he came to her house to give her a quote on how much his company would charge to cut her yards. He had no intentions of cutting her yards himself, but when he saw her, he knew that was the only way he could get to know her.

I knew I would marry her the first day I met her. He smiled, then he thought about the perfect night he had planned at the beach. *If we ever make it to the beach!*

Everett sighed, then found himself a comfortable spot on a bench and started playing games on his iPad.

He texted Kirsten to tell her he was in the mall, but she had obviously gotten very distracted and no longer had her eye on just one dress, or her phone, for that matter. She saw several dresses and she wanted them all. She gathered them in her arms and was about to head to the dressing room when she heard a voice say, "They will all look good on you, Kirsten."

Her heart stopped. Only one man had the ability to make Kirsten's heart stop and she was too afraid to turn around to see if it was who she thought it was. She stood there frozen, just like she did the first day she met him over four years ago in the conference room at work. She took a deep breath, then mustered up enough strength to turn around.

"Hi, Jason," she said, trying not to show any emotion.

"You look very beautiful," he said, staring into her eyes.

This was just about the time when Everett got tired of waiting outside the store and decided he had had enough

and was going in to get Kirsten. He
walked towards the ladies' section and
that's when he saw Kirsten talking to a
man. Everett knew this wasn't just any
ole man; he could tell there was
something different by the expression
on Kirsten's face.

Everett didn't remember seeing
Jason before, but he did look somewhat
familiar. Everett started to walk up
and introduce himself, but their
conversation seemed intense and Everett
was interested to know what they were
talking about. He ducked behind the
pole, so Kirsten wouldn't see him. He
tried to position himself close enough
so he could hear what Kirsten and Jason
were saying.

As he pretended to be looking at
dresses for his wife or mother, he saw
a sales lady heading in his direction.
Everett gave her a dirty look, then
fanned his hands at her so she would go
away. At first, the sales lady looked
shocked, then she looked offended, but
she dared not go over to where Everett
was.

Everett kneeled on the floor like
he was tying his shoelace, except he
had on sandals. He didn't care,

though. He needed to know who this man
was that had his soon-to-be wife so
captivated.

He eased over a little more so he
wouldn't miss anything. Jason
complimented Kirsten again, but this
time he rubbed his finger across her
arm. Kirsten politely moved his
finger, but her body language told
Everett that this guy meant something
to her and that bothered him.

"Thank you, Jason," Kirsten
responded.

*Jason, Jason, Jason. Who is Jason and why is
he rubbing on my wife, and why is she over here acting
like she's got the goo-goo eyes for him? Where do I
know this man from?*

Everett wasn't in Corporate
America so the name Jason B. Glaznyte
never rang a bell for him, but then he
suddenly remembered that one day
Kirsten had mail on her cabinet
addressed to a Jason somebody. He knew
Kirsten wasn't home a lot, but he never
noticed a man living there, so he just
assumed it was work related or either
the mailman put the letter in the wrong
box.

*Wait a minute! This is the guy that came by
Kirsten's house when she was out of town one weekend. I*

remember him now. **It was all coming together for Everett.** *This is the guy Kirsten used to date.*

Everett knew in his heart that this was a defining moment for his relationship with Kirsten.

"How are you?" Jason said to Kirsten, while staring at her with his piercing light brown eyes.

"I'm great, how's Ryan?" she asked. Jason noticed that she didn't bother asking how he was doing; Everett noticed it, too.

"Ryan is good, he's with his mom."

Before, those words always brought a sick feeling to the pit of Kirsten's stomach, but this time, Kirsten didn't seem to care.

"How's Lacey?" Kirsten asked, sarcastically.

Jason laughed, "Lacey is Lacey. Ryan always asks about you, Kirsten. He really misses you."

"He does?" Kirsten asked, as the cold, hateful look left her face. Jason knew he had found Kirsten's soft spot.

"Yes, he talks about you all the time."

Kirsten felt her heart ache a little, "Please give him a kiss for me," she said.

Everett felt that this conversation was getting way too friendly. He was very tempted to interrupt, but he didn't. Something told him to just wait it out and hear the conversation.

"Well, I have to go," Kirsten said, as she started walking off.

Jason gently grabbed her arm. "I miss you too, Kirsten," he said, licking his lips, hoping to get a reaction out of her. It didn't work, though. Kirsten just gave him a blank stare. It was kind of like the same response she gave Mr. Wayne when he tried to tell jokes.

Everett was very angry that any of this was taking place. He wasn't sure what to make of it or what his reaction should be.

Periodically, people would pass by and look at him on the floor tying his pretend shoe laces, but they didn't seem to be too bothered by it. Everett was too busy looking at Kirsten and Jason to even notice what anyone else was doing behind him.

Everett asked God for help because
he knew he was going to need some
supernatural power to not hurt Jason
for all that touching he was doing.
Everett's entire face was hot; he felt
like he was on fire. It took
everything in him to stand there and do
nothing, but deep down inside he knew
he needed to know how Kirsten felt
about this guy, especially if he was
planning to marry her.

"I miss you so much, Kirsten. Why
are you trying to fight the love we
have for each other?" Jason asked.

"I don't know what your definition
of love is, Jason, but that's not what
we had."

"Come'on, baby, you know what we
had was special. You were the best
thing that ever happened to me; I need
you in my life, Kirsten. I know I
didn't appreciate you when I had you
and I'm so sorry, but I've changed.
Just give me another chance and I'll
prove it to you."

"There are no more chances to
give, Jason. We dated for three years.
I did whatever you wanted to do, when
and how you wanted to do it. I was a
mother to Ryan and a wife to you, but

you never deemed me worthy of the title. You didn't even have the decency to remember my birthday."

Everett's eyes got big. *Wow, I didn't know all that was going on.*

Jason grabbed Kirsten's arm again. "Marry me now, Kirsten. I still have your ring right here," he said, showing Kirsten the ring he had on a necklace tucked in his shirt. "I wear it around my neck. I wasn't ready then, but I'm more than ready to be your husband now. We can leave from here and go straight to the courthouse if you want."

"It's Saturday, Jason, the courthouse isn't even open, and no thank you," Kirsten said, sounding aggravated.

"Just let me know what I need to do so we can be together," Jason said, as he lifted the ring up on his thumb. "It's still yours if you want it, baby," he said, smiling.

Kirsten looked at the ring and gave a faint smile back.

God that sure is beautiful!

Everett didn't know what to think. He wondered if Kirsten was really the girl he thought she was. He didn't know her relationship with Jason was so

horrible and he definitely didn't know
it ended in some kind of proposal. He
decided to listen some more to see what
else he could find out.

Kirsten thought of all the
memories that lead up to her getting
that ring and how happy she thought she
and Jason were. If she would have been
honest with herself, she would've
realized that she wasn't happy at all.
Jason was happy because he was having
his cake and eating it too, but she was
never truly happy. She never felt good
about Jason not inviting her on his
trips when he went to see Ryan, and she
never felt good about all the business
functions he went to and never bothered
to ask her to come as his date.

*He assumed I didn't want to go on his trips with
him and he assumed that I didn't want to spend my
birthdays with him, but he didn't assume I didn't want to
cook his dinner for him and he definitely didn't assume
that I didn't want to be his sex-slave. He never assumed
that, now did he?*

Kirsten realized that she didn't
feel good about a lot of things when
she was with Jason. She looked up at
him, then she looked down at his thick,
strong, sexy, chocolate hand still
resting on her arm. She looked at his

beautiful brown eyes that always made her insides scream.

"Jason, I loved you so much, but you made a complete fool out of me. Now I know that what I want and need, you can never give me."

"Kirsten, I can give you what you want and need. Let me prove it to you. I never intended to make you look like a fool. I always loved you, I was just so torn between having you and keeping my family together, but now I realize that my son and I could still be a family with you Kirsten; we need you so bad. Please forgive me and come back to us."

Kirsten's eyes filled with water; she missed Ryan so much, but Jason could never be to her what Everett is. Everett made her feel like a lady; he made her feel secure and confident in what they had. Everett had self-discipline (something Jason couldn't even spell if you gave him all the letters). Everett cherished her and she knew that anywhere Everett went, she was always welcome to go. Kirsten knew that Everett was all she needed.

She looked up at Jason again, as he was still begging for forgiveness.

"Jason, I forgave you a long time ago,"
she said, then walked away.

"What does that mean, Kirsten?
Does that mean we have a chance?" Jason
asked, as Kirsten kept walking. "Will
you at least think about it, Kirsten?"
Jason yelled as Kirsten left the store.

Jason wasn't sure if he had gotten
through to Kirsten. He started to
chase after her, but he didn't. Jason
turned to walk in the other way, but
instead he looked right in Everett's
face, which by this time was red as
scarlet. Jason could clearly see that
Everett was angry. He didn't know what
to make of Everett's stare. It
reminded him of the old cowboy days
when they did the stare down right
before they started shooting. Everett
walked closer to Jason.

"You had your chance, you screwed
it up, and now I have mine. I assure
you I won't need a second chance. I'm
advising you that you'd better stay
away from my wife."

Jason was very confused, then he
looked closer at Everett. "You're the
lawn guy!" he said, with a smirk on his
face. Everett looked at Jason, unmoved
by his sly remark. "I'm way more than

a lawn guy and I'm way more of a husband than you could ever be. Stay away from her!" Everett said, pointing his finger at Jason and walking off in the direction that Kirsten went.

It took Jason a minute to compose himself. Then he realized that Everett must have eavesdropped on his and Kirsten's conversation. He also realized that Everett knew what a wonderful jewel Kirsten was. Jason knew that Everett was not going to give her up without a fight.

"Well, neither am I," Jason said, as he walked off.

He noticed that folks were looking and waiting for his response, but Jason's battle wasn't with Everett. He respected him as a man for standing up for his woman, but Jason was still confident that he had something Everett would never have, he had Kirsten's heart. He was sure that she still loved him by the way she responded when he touched her, and since he didn't see a ring on her finger, he figured there was still hope to win her back.

~ TWENTY-
SEVEN ~

When Everett got to the car,
Kirsten was standing there waiting for
him. It had started to rain. Kirsten
was dripping wet but she was standing
there like she didn't even care. Her
beautiful dress was soaked and water
was all over her face. When Everett
looked in Kirsten's eyes, he could tell
that the water wasn't all from the
rain; some of it was tears. He popped
the trunk and gave her a towel and a
bottle of water that he had in a
cooler.

Kirsten had no idea that Everett
knew what just happened between her and
Jason. When he started the car,
Kirsten was still wiping the "rain"
from her eyes. Everett didn't say a
word. He tried not to look at Kirsten,
because it only made him angry. *I can't
believe she's crying over that loser,* he thought, as

he turned on music, trying to change the mood, but the truth was neither of them was in the mood for a get-a-way trip anymore.

"You wanna just call it a day and go home?" he asked, trying not to sound aggravated.

Kirsten could not hide her flow of tears. "Can we just go back to your place if you don't mind? I really don't want to be alone."

Everett took a deep breath, turned the car around and headed to his house. The ride to Everett's house was totally silent. He didn't know why she wanted to go back to his place; her mind was obviously with someone other than him.

And what's with that "I don't want to be alone" hoopla? Is the princess too torn to pieces over her prince that got away?

Everett was trying hard not to be angry, but there were a lot of things he was not happy about. For one, the mall was a good 15-20 minute drive to his house, and Kirsten was too busy wetting up his towel with her crocodile tears to tell him what just happened with Jason. He was also angry that Kirsten allowed Jason to touch all over her, and that Jason had the nerve to

ask Kirsten to marry him on the same
day he was planning his special evening
for them. If that wasn't enough, now
she was over there crying on his
freshly polished Camaro seats.

*I just bought this car two months ago and here she
is, dropping tears all over everything; TEARS OVER
ANOTHER MAN,* he screamed, with his
inside voice.

Everett questioned if he even
wanted to be with someone who was
obviously still in love with her ex.
He wondered if she thought of Jason
when they were together. He wondered
if given the chance, would she cheat on
him with Jason. All of these
tormenting thoughts ran through
Everett's mind, and looking over at
Kirsten, who was doing all that
ridiculous sobbing, didn't help ease
any of his concerns.

Everett wasn't sure what had
happened between Kirsten and Jason. He
could only assume that it was a bad
breakup, which he thought Kirsten would
be over by now. He loved Kirsten, but
he was not about to entertain drama,
and her sitting there crying over
another dude was definitely drama.

Everett decided to try and calm himself down. Although he wasn't feeling the best about things, he tried to focus on what his true feelings were. He still believed that God put him and Kirsten together, and down inside, Everett knew he could trust her. Well, at least he hoped he could trust her. She had never given him any reason to not trust her before and he honestly believed she would break up with him before she would cheat on him. She was more than just his girlfriend; she was his friend. He looked over a Kirsten.

I waited for her for five years and there's no way I'm going to let some punk, who mistreated her, take her from me.

Everett tapped his hand on the steering wheel. Instead of blowing up at Kirsten, which is what he was very tempted to do, he decided to pray.

God, I'm not sure what just happened, but I need a woman who loves only me, a woman whose tears are not from unhealed wounds from her past. Despite what it looks like right now, I do believe in my heart that you gave this woman to me and I'm going to trust you to show me how to respond to her the way she needs me to respond and the way you want me to respond. I want to throw my hands up right now and walk away, but I know no relationship is perfect. There are going to be some bumps in the road; I don't expect there not to be, but God, I'd be lying if I didn't say I'm having second thoughts about this whole situation, so please show me what I should do.

When they got to Everett's house, Kirsten went straight to his bed, flopped down and continued to cry. Everett just looked at her and shook his head.

She's soaked with rain and tears and she has the nerve to lay on my bed, and then she's still crying over that pea brain. At least she wrapped herself in the blanket, he thought, sarcastically.

Everett pulled out a t-shirt and some shorts. "Here! You can put these on so you won't have to stay in those wet clothes."

"Thank you so much, you're so good to me," she said.

Everett rolled his eyes. *If I was so good to you, we'd be on our trip right now, but we're not.*

Everett had a lot of inward thoughts but he was trying his best not to say much to Kirsten. He knew that whatever he said was going to come out really harsh. He knew the best thing for him to do was just to wait and see if Kirsten was going to try to explain.

Surely she doesn't think I haven't noticed all the crying.

Kirsten changed into Everett's t-shirt and shorts, then laid back down. Within seconds his entire pillow was soaked. Everett just shook his head; he was very agitated with Kirsten's behavior. After a few minutes he decided he'd interrupt her sob-fest.

"Kirsten, I heard the whole thing. I heard Jason propose to you and I heard what you said to him. I saw him touching all over you while you just stood there like you were helpless. You're laying here crying your eyes out on my bed over a dude who obviously didn't treat you right. If you love the man, just go be with him. I don't want anyone who's attached to someone else. I don't need or want the drama."

Everett threw up his hands like he was done with the relationship. Everett knew that he was a good man and he knew he deserved a woman who could give him the same level of commitment he was willing to give her.

Kirsten's heart was aching too bad to be surprised by Everett overhearing her conversation with Jason. She was surprised that he told her to go be

with him though; she knew he didn't
mean it. She had never seen Everett so
upset, but there was something so
genuine about him expressing how he
felt. It was strangely attractive.
She could see the fire in his eyes and
how his dimples curved in as he talked
so sternly. Everett stood there
staring at her, waiting for a response,
but Kirsten didn't have one. She
thought about how good Everett was and
how happy he made her. He had
something Jason would never have;
realness. Everett was true and
genuine. Although she knew he was
angry with her, she was very happy to
have him in her life and there was no
way she was going to let him go.

Kirsten finally stopped sobbing
long enough to look in Everett's eyes;
she could see the hurt in them.
Hurting Everett was something she never
wanted to do. Parts of Kirsten's face
had black smudges on it from where her
tears made her mascara run.

This is not attractive! Everett thought.

Kirsten stared at Everett without
blinking once. It almost scared him to
even look at her. He'd never seen
Kirsten look like this before, but if

there was another side to her, he'd prefer to see it now. *When it rains, it pours, so bring it on,* he thought.

"Everett, I loved him, PAST TENSE! I love you, PRESENT TENSE! I'm staying in the present with you. I hope you'll keep me because there is no other place I'd rather be," then she laid her head back down on his pillow and continued to sob.

Everett didn't know what to think. He heard the words that came from Kirsten's mouth but they clearly didn't match her actions.

"Well, if you want to be with me, why are you crying over this dude?"

"I'm not crying over him, Everett. I'm crying over what I had to go through with him to get me to this point; to get me to the point where I could appreciate having a good man. I'm crying because of how I allowed him to rip out my self-esteem and make me feel like I wasn't worthy of being loved or committed to. I'm not crying over him; he's unworthy of my tears. I'm hurt because I should have followed my intuition a long time ago when I knew something wasn't right. I'm crying over my regrets, Everett, not

over him. I could have been here five
years ago, but I was too stupid to see
what was right in front of me. I
wasted three years of my life being
somebody's fool. That time should have
been yours and I wasted it on an
unworthy jerk. You are all I want
Everett; you are all I need. I would
have saved myself a lot of heartache if
I had seen it sooner."

Everett leaned over to kiss
Kirsten's forehead, but when he leaned
over her, a ring box fell out of his
pocket and onto the bed.

"What is that?" she asked, with a
strange look on her face.

"It's nothing," Everett said,
quickly grabbing the box.

"Can I please see it?"

Everett rubbed his hands across
his mouth. "Sure Kirsten, go ahead."

Kirsten opened the box and her
mouth fell open. The ring was so
gorgeous. She looked up at Everett.

"Is this a wedding ring, Everett?"

"Yes, it is."

"Was this the surprise you had for
me?"

"Yeah, it was."

"You were going to ask me to marry
you?"

"Yes, I was."

"Do you still love me?"

"Of course I still love you."

"Do you still want to marry me?

Everett took a deep breath, which
made Kirsten nervous. Everett looked
down at the floor, then back up at
Kirsten.

"More than anything baby," he
said, rubbing the wet hair out of her
face.

When Kirsten was out of town for
the week, Everett called her parents to
get their blessings and thoughts on him
and Kirsten getting married. Everett
was a hardworking, manual-labor type of
man just like Mr. Jabard, which
immediately gave Mr. Jabard a liking
towards Everett. Mr. Jabard told him
he would be very happy to have him as
his son-in-law whenever he and Kirsten
decided the time was right. Mrs. Jan,
on the other hand, wasn't so sure that
Kirsten was ready to marry Everett.
She knew Everett was perfect for
Kirsten, but she also knew how in love
Kirsten had been with Jason. She
wasn't sure if Kirsten would allow

another man to get that close to her heart again. She just hoped Kirsten would make the right decision for herself, whatever that was.

"Yes! Yes! Yes," Kirsten screamed. "I'll marry you, Everett. I'll marry you right now."

Kirsten grabbed Everett and pulled him on the bed with her. "Make love to me, Everett! Make love to me right here, right now."

Kirsten kissed Everett and he could feel himself getting weak in the knees. He was sure that he wanted to make love to Kirsten way more than she wanted to make love to him and she seemed pretty sure.

Think with your big head, Everett. Think with your big head, he repeated to himself, trying to remember the Pastor's advice, but then he looked at her wearing his t-shirt with no bra and his shorts. He couldn't help but think about what was underneath them. Everett didn't remember how he got there, but the next thing he knew, he was on top of Kirsten. He pulled off her shirt and started kissing parts of her body that he hadn't yet had the opportunity to explore. He and Kirsten were both ready to throw their vows away and do what they had wanted to do for eight months. Things were so intense, that both of them felt totally out of control, but all of a sudden Everett stopped, leaving Kirsten panting like a dog in heat. He pressed his face against her neck, and made some grunting noise.

"DANG IT!!!!" he yelled, getting up and hitting the side of the bed like someone had punched him and he was ready for a good fight. He stood up, rubbed his hands up and down his face, really fast, then started pacing back and forth with his arms over his head as he kicked the air.

Kirsten wasn't sure what to make of his abrupt stop in the middle of what was surely about to be a wonderful experience. She had finally gotten a peek of Everett's package and it was quite delightful, but now Everett was pacing the floor like a mad man, so she was certain that all the action was over.

So close, yet so far, she thought. She looked over at Everett as he paced some more. He glanced over at Kirsten, "Baby, you look so horrible right now with all that mascara running down your face, but I swear I have never been so turned on in my life." He paced some more, then he screamed. "AAAAHHHHHHH!"

Kirsten smiled. "Everett, it's okay, baby. You're doing the right thing and I love you for it."

He kept pacing as if he didn't hear Kirsten; she didn't mean to make him suffer.

Everett kicked the air some more, rubbed his hands across his face again, and made some other strange noise, then he finally turned and kneeled beside Kirsten.

"Give me one week, baby. Just one week! We will get our marriage license on Monday. We will call the pastor, my parents, your parents and our friends and whoever else you want to invite. If they can come, fine; if they can't, fine, but by next Saturday night, you will be Mrs. Everett Larson and if you keep wearing those shorts and t-shirt, we might have to move it up to Friday."

Kirsten smiled, "Okay, baby. I can't wait to be Mrs. Larson."

Everett did not return the smile; he looked like he was in a lot of pain. He kissed her forehead, turned the lights off, went back into the living room and flopped down on couch. Kirsten could hear him hitting the couch repeatedly.

At that moment, Kirsten realized just how much she loved Everett. She realized just how much Everett loved her and how much more he loved God and how committed he was at keeping his promise.

She fell backwards onto the bed, with her arms spread out and looked up at the ceiling.

Lord, thank you!

There was no doubt in Kirsten's mind that she had made the right decision.

~The End~

Would you like to know more? Do you want to know how things turned out between Kirsten and Everett, do you want to know if anything else happened between Kirsten and Jason, or better yet, between Everett and Jason? Would you like to know if Jason gave up or if he's determined to win Kirsten back?

Well, you can find out, because the story continues in my next book, titled, *Why Keep Us Divided?* If you've enjoyed this book, then *Why Keep Us Divided* will be a delightful read as well.

It gets into the real struggles people face when they decide to date outside their race. It also shows how cruel and vindictive some people can become when they encounter interracial couples.

The couple in this book, Daniel and Melah ultimately has to decide if their relationship is worth the obstacles, confrontations, and missed opportunities they will surely undergo if they decide to stay together.

As a token of my appreciation to you for being a loyal Orr Novels reader, I have placed a sneak peak for you on the next few pages.

463

Why Keep Us Divided?
Sneak Preview

CHAPTER

"I've had it with this place! It's nothing but a bunch of fake, racist, bigots here, Mel! If I'm ever going to get promoted, I have to move away from here!" Daniel said, angrily to his girlfriend, Melah.

"I don't understand why you didn't get that promotion, baby. They pretty much promised it to you. They trained you for it and everything," Melah said, sorrowfully.

"Baby, I could do that job with my eyes closed. I was the most qualified person in the organization, but they gave it to some kid down the hall, then he had the nerve to ask me if I would train him. I said, 'Nope, sure won't. You can learn it on your own just like I did.' Mel, I don't know if I can keep working for this company. I've got to move baby, that's all there is to it!"

"Well, what about—"

Just then, Daniel's phone rang; it was his mother.

"Hold on, babe. My mom is calling."

"Tell Mrs. Sarah I said hello," Melah responded, but Daniel was so glad to hear from his mom, he didn't hear Melah.

"Hey, ma," Daniel said, answering the phone as if a call from his mother was all it took to make everything better."

"Hey, baby son, you were on my mind and I decided to give you a call. How are you doing?"

"I'm okay, ma. I'm making it."

"You don't sound okay. What's wrong, Daniel?"

Daniel paused. He decided to go into to the other room so Melah couldn't hear him, but it didn't matter, because Melah put her ear to the door and listened anyway.

"Ma, I didn't get the promotion. That job was supposed to be mine, but the minute they found out about Melah, everything changed. Of course I can't talk to her about it because it's only going to cause problems between us; she'll get offended and start acting all funny! It's just better to keep it to myself!"

"Awe, baby! I'm so sorry to hear that, but I can't say that I'm surprised."

"Well, I am. Ma, I think I need to move somewhere else. I don't think I can stay here much longer."

"Yeah, maybe so. You know Kirsten is doing very well in Atlanta. Maybe she can help you find a job up there!"

"Hmmm, Atlanta may be just the change I need. Do you have Kirsten's number?"

"Nah, I have her mom's number, though. You can give her a call; she'll be glad to give you Kirsten's number."

"I haven't talked to Mrs. Jan or Kirsten in years. Ma, you and Mrs. Jan have been friends a long time, huh?"

"Yeah, we sure have and it wasn't always easy with all the racial tension going on back in the early 60s, but our friendship prevailed and if you care enough about Melah, then your relationship will prevail too.

"Yeah, I guess you're right."

"Just hang in there, son. It'll work out for ya. You know Kirsten just got married? Oh, it was a lovely wedding, Daniel. They seemed really happy together."

"Oh yeah? Ma, you went? Why didn't you tell me? I would have loved to see everybody."

"Sorry, son. I didn't even think about it, but if you come home to see your momma more often, you'll know what's going on."

"Okay, ma. I hear you. I'll do better with that. "

"Good! I look forward to seeing how well you do," she said, giggling. "Now here's Jan's number." Go on and give them a call. Call me later and tell me how it goes."

"Okay, I will. Thanks, ma."

Daniel walked back into the room where Melah was. "Where do you want to go eat, baby?" Melah asked, as if she didn't hear any of Daniel's conversation with his mom. "It's my treat."

"You're treating me to dinner?" he asked, surprisingly.

"Yes, anywhere you wanna go. It doesn't matter whether you got the promotion or not; we both know you deserved it. I think we should celebrate."

Daniel smiled, "And that's why you've managed to steal my heart in this small amount of time," he responded.

Melah gave Daniel a big smile. They had only been dating four months, but Daniel loved how Melah treated him. She made him feel like he could rule the world. Melah didn't make much money, but she was very thrifty and always spent her money wisely. Everything was an investment. Even taking Daniel to dinner was an investment to Melah. She needed to know what happened at work that day and the only way to find out was through his stomach.

A full stomach and a glass of wine will get anyone talking, she thought.

Another thing Daniel loved about Melah was that she never raised her voice, even when she was upset. Being around Melah was always very peaceful to Daniel, who'd been in quite a few rocky relationships in his lifetime.

Daniel grabbed his jacket, while Melah locked up her apartment. They jumped in the car and headed downtown for dinner. The restaurant they went to was nice and quant, chosen by Daniel for his "not getting his dream job/promotion" celebration.

Since Melah was being so thoughtful, Daniel tried not to ruin it with his bad mood. They sat there chatting, while they waited for their food to come. Daniel did everything he could to avoid talking about what happened at work, while Melah did everything she could to try and coax it out of him.

"Daniel, do you trust me?" she asked, abruptly.

Daniel looked at her like she had grown a horn in the middle of her forehead. "Yeah, of course I do. Why would you ask that?"

"Well, then tell me why I was the reason you didn't get that promotion."

He let out a huge sigh. "Baby, they are stupid, don't worry about them. I'll get another promotion."

"Where, Daniel, Atlanta?"

"Wherever I can get a job, baby; wherever that takes me."

"Us?" Melah asked.

"Huh, what do you mean?"

"You mean wherever that takes us, right?"

"You would go with me?"

"Would you want me to?"

"Well, yeah, but we've only been dating four months, Mel. I don't think we're at the point of picking up and moving together, do you?"

"So, how long does it take to get to that point?"

Daniel laughed, "I think it takes more than four months and surprisingly enough, I just learned today that my wonderful, sweet girlfriend is an eavesdropper, so I don't quite know how that factors into the picture either.

Melah huffed. "Well, if it was something you were planning to tell me, you wouldn't have gone into the other room to talk on the phone."

"My point exactly, Mel. My point exactly!"

WHY KEEP US DIVIDED?
~COMING SOON~

Meet The Author

Hi, I'm Colette Orr, the creator of Orr Novels. I discovered my love for writing in high school when my English teacher, Ms. Smith made us write in our journals while listening to classical music. Not only did I discover a passion for writing in this class, I also developed a love for classical music; Beethoven's *Moonlight Sonata* being my favorite. Ms. Smith, wherever you are today, thank you for making a difference!!!!

Orr Novels is a name I pray everyone will come to love. My goal is to write about everyday situations that anyone can relate to; I hope you enjoy reading my novels as much as I enjoy writing them. I have several book projects in the works, so please check back with me to see what's coming next.

Thank you for all your love and support. I'm looking forward to our journey together!

Love,

Colette D. Orr